Show Sold Separately

Show Sold Separately

*Promos, Spoilers, and
Other Media Paratexts*

Jonathan Gray

NEW YORK UNIVERSITY PRESS

New York and London

NEW YORK UNIVERSITY PRESS
New York and London
www.nyupress.org

Library of Congress Cataloging-in-Publication Data

Gray, Jonathan (Jonathan Alan)
Show sold separately : promos, spoilers, and other media paratexts /
Jonathan Gray.
p. cm.
Includes bibliographical references and index.
ISBN-13: 978-0-8147-3194-9 (cl : alk. paper)
ISBN-10: 0-8147-3194-5 (cl : alk. paper)
ISBN-13: 978-0-8147-3195-6 (pb : alk. paper)
ISBN-10: 0-8147-3195-3 (pb : alk. paper)
1. Advertising—Television programs—Social aspects. 2. Advertising—
Motion pictures—Social aspects. 3. Television programs—
Marketing—Social aspects. 4. Motion pictures—Marketing—Social
aspects. 5. Paratext. 6. Intertextuality. 7. Mass media and culture. I.
Title.
PN1992.8..A32G73   2009
659.1'9302234—dc22   2009029212

New York University Press books are printed on acid-free paper,
and their binding materials are chosen for strength and durability.
We strive to use environmentally responsible suppliers and materials
to the greatest extent possible in publishing our books.

Manufactured in the United States of America
c 10 9 8 7 6 5 4 3 2 1
p 10 9 8 7 6 5 4 3 2 1

This book is about where value and meaning come from. Therefore, I dedicate it to my wife, Monica Jane Grant, for constantly giving my life so much of both.

Contents

Acknowledgments

This book examines how meaning and value are constructed outside of what we have often considered to be the text itself. Thus, in its writing, I have constantly been aware of how often my own arguments, and the meaning and value of this text, have come from colleagues and friends whose sage counsel, astute criticism, and warm offers of assistance have considerably refined and advanced my thinking about paratexts. With this in mind, I offer thanks to a small band of friends who never seem to tire of discussing texts and paratexts with me, and who have shared their own thoughts on the topic so readily and generously: Ivan Askwith, Will Brooker, Kristina Busse, Derek Johnson, Derek Kompare, Amanda Lotz, Jason Mittell, Cornel Sandvoss, and Avi Santo. Will's comments on the manuscript were particularly invaluable and warrant especially profuse thanks.

Many others have also helped significantly with thoughts, criticism, or encouragement here, an article, book, or blog post there. Thanks, then, to Robin Andersen, Miranda Banks, Martin Barker, Geoffrey Baym, Nancy Baym, James Bennett, Bertha Chin, Mike Chopra-Gant, Lynn Clark, Paul Cobley, Nick Couldry, Max Dawson, Ana Domb, Sam Ford, Joshua Green, C. Lee Harrington, John Hartley, Timothy Havens, Heather Hendershot, Matt Hills, Jennifer Holt, Nina Huntemann, Henry Jenkins, Victoria Johnson, Jeffrey Jones, Michael Kackman, Beth Knobel, Elana Levine, Ernest Mathijs, Matthew McAllister, Tom McCourt, John McMurria, Lothar Mikos, David Morley, Susan Murray, Michael Newman, Laurie Ouellette, Roberta Pearson, Martyn Pedler, Allison Perlman, Aswin Punathambekar, Bob Rehak, Jean Retzinger, Brian Rose, Sharon Ross, Kevin Sandler, Louisa Stein, Ethan Thompson, Serra Tinic, Chuck Tryon, and Michael Tueth. To this roster must also be added many of my excellent students, full of excellent ideas.

For discussing their (para)textual creations with me, I am indebted to Jesse Alexander and Mark Warshaw, formerly of the NBC series *Heroes*; Stephen Andrade at NBC-Universal; Ivan Askwith at Big Spaceship; Patrick Crowe at Xenophile Media; Matt Wolf of D20 Productions; and the vidders "GK," here's luck, Luminosity, and obsessive24. Thanks too to the International Radio and Television Society Foundation and Disney for making my attendance at their 2008 Digital Media Summit possible; to Brian Leake, David Jessen, and Damon Lindelof for their openness at that event; and to the National Association of Television Production Executives for making my attendance at their 2008 convention possible. And many thanks to all those who participated in the *Lost* spoiler survey I conducted with Jason Mittell in 2006.

Parts of this book have appeared in other forms elsewhere. Profuse thanks go to Bertha Chin for allowing me to reprint parts of our article, "'One Ring to Rule Them All': Pre-Viewers and Pre-Texts of the *Lord of the Rings* Films" (*Intensities: The Journal of Cult Media* 2) in chapter 4, and to Jason Mittell for letting me reprint some of our article, "Speculation on Spoilers: *Lost* Fandom, Narrative Consumption, and Rethinking Textuality" (*Particip@tions: The International Journal of Audience Research* 4.1) in chapter 5. I also extend thanks and acknowledgment to Matt Hills and Martin Barker, editors of *Intensities* and *Particip@tions*, respectively, for allowing me to reprint those pieces, and to Sage for allowing me to reprint parts of my article "Television Pre-Views and the Meaning of Hype" (*International Journal of Cultural Studies* 11.1) in the Introduction and chapters 1 and 2; to Wallflower Press for allowing me to reprint parts of my chapter "Bonus Material: The DVD Layering of *The Lord of the Rings*" (in *The Lord of the Rings: Popular Culture in Global Context*, ed. Ernest Mathijs [New York, 2006]) in chapter 3; and to Routledge for allowing me to reprint a section of my chapter "The Reviews Are In: TV Critics and the (Pre)Creation of Meaning" (in *Flow TV: Essays on a Convergent Medium*, ed. Michael Kackman et al. [New York, 2009]) in chapter 5. Thanks too to Gary Wines for so kindly providing the art for figure 6.1. At New York University Press and beyond, thanks to Eric Zinner, Emily Park, Ciara McLaughlin, Despina Papazoglou Gimbel, and the rest of the team.

And of course, no acknowledgments section could be complete without once more paying due homage and respect to the fantastic foursome that are my brother Matthew Gray, my mother and father, Anne and Ian Gray, and my wife, Monica Grant. I've moved thirteen times in my life so far, nine of those across national borders, and through all the packing and unpacking, meeting new friends and leaving old ones, passport renewals, and learning new accents and television schedules, my family members have remained my constants, as has Monica for these last eight years. My love and eternal gratitude to all four.

Introduction

Film, Television, and Off-Screen Studies

A common first line for books on contemporary media, and for many a student essay on the subject, notes the saturation of everyday life with media. Certainly, my list of available cable channels seems to grow every month, while the list of movies in cinemas, on television, for rent, or available for purchase similarly proliferates at a precipitous rate. However, media growth and saturation can only be measured in small part by the number of films or television shows—or books, games, blogs, magazines, or songs for that matter—as each and every media text is accompanied by textual proliferation at the level of hype, synergy, promos, and peripherals. As film and television viewers, we are all part-time residents of the highly populated cities of Time Warner, DirecTV, AMC, Sky, Comcast, ABC, Odeon, and so forth, and yet not all of these cities' architecture is televisual or cinematic by nature. Rather, these cities are also made up of all manner of ads, previews, trailers, interviews with creative personnel, Internet discussion, entertainment news, reviews, merchandising, guerrilla marketing campaigns, fan creations, posters, games, DVDs, CDs, and spinoffs. Hype and synergy abound, forming the streets, bridges, and trading routes of the media world, but also many of its parks, beaches, and leisure sites. They tell us about the media world around us, prepare us for that world, and guide us between its structures, but they also fill it with meaning, take up much of our viewing and thinking time, and give us the resources with which we will both interpret and discuss that world.

On any given day, as we wait for a bus, for example, we are likely to see ads for movies and television shows at the bus stop, on the side of the bus, and/or in a magazine that we read to pass the time. If instead we take a car, we will see such ads on roadside billboards and hear them on the radio. At home with the television on, we may watch entertainment news that hypes shows, interviews creative personnel, and offers "sneak peaks" of the making of this or that show. Ad breaks will bring us yet more ads and trailers, as will pop-ups or visits to YouTube online. Official webpages often offer us information about a show, wallpaper for our computer desktops, and yet more space for fan discussion, thereby supplementing the thousands of discussion sites run by fans or anti-fans. The online space also offers the occasional alternate reality game or particularly creative marketing campaign. Stores online and offline sell merchandise related to these films and shows, ranging from collectible *Lord of the Rings* (2001, 2002, 2003) "replica" swords or rings, to Dunder Mifflin t-shirts for *The Office* (2005–), to a talking Homer Simpson bottle opener. They sell licensed toy lines, linens, breakfast cereals, vitamins, and clothing to children. Bookstores and comic book shops sell spinoff novelizations and graphic novels. Game stores sell licensed videogames and board games. Fast food stores sell the Happy Meal or Value Meal. Music and video stores sell soundtracks, CDs of music "inspired by" certain films or shows, and DVDs and Blu-Ray discs rich with bonus materials, cast and crew commentaries, and extra scenes. Tour companies offer official *Sex and the City* (1998–2004) or *Sopranos* (1999–2007) tours of the New York area, while *Lord of the Rings*–themed tours of New Zealand are possible, and some fans lead themselves on their own tours of filming sites. Fans also write stories and songs and make films or vids about or set in film and television's storyworlds. Film and television shows, in other words, are only a small part of the massive, extended presence of filmic and televisual texts across our lived environments.

Given their extended presence, any filmic or televisual text and its cultural impact, value, and meaning cannot be adequately analyzed without taking into account the film or program's many proliferations. Each proliferation, after all, holds the potential to change the meaning of the text, even if only slightly. Trailers and reports from the set, for instance, may construct early frames through which would-be viewers might think of the text's genre, tone, and themes. Discussion sites might then reinforce such frames or otherwise challenge them, while videogames, comics, and other narrative extensions render the storyworld a more immersive environment. In the process, such entities change the nature of the text's address, each proliferation either amplifying an aspect of the text through its mass circulation or adding something new and different to the text. While purists may stomp their feet and insist that the game, bonus materials, or promos, for instance, "aren't the real thing," for many viewers and non-viewers alike the title of the film or program will signify the entire package. Individuals or communities will construct different ideas of what that package entails, based on their own interactions with its varying proliferations, and on their own sense of its textual hierarchy. But rarely if ever can a film or program serve as the only source of information about the text. And rather than simply serve as *extensions* of a text, many of these items are filters through which we must pass on our way to the film or program, our first and formative encounters with the text.

While many consumers deride the presence of hype and licensed merchandise as a nuisance, we also rely upon it, at least in part, to help us get through an evening's viewing or a trip to the multiplex. Decisions on what to watch, what not to watch, and *how* to watch are often made while consuming hype, synergy, and promos, so that by the time we actually encounter "the show itself," we have already begun to decode it and to preview its meanings and effects.

We are all familiar with the vernacular imperative to not "judge a book by its cover." But we all do so nonetheless. Our world is heavily populated by promos and surrounding textuality, and these form the substance of first impressions. Today's version of "Don't judge a book by its cover" is "Don't believe the hype," but hype and surrounding texts do more than just ask us to believe them or not; rather, they establish frames and filters through which we look at, listen to, and interpret the texts that they hype. As media scholars have long noted, much of the media's powers come not necessarily from being able to tell us what to think, but what to think about, and how to think about it.[1] Mediated information and narratives are frames par excellence, trimming and editing the object of their attention for us with significant power and skill. Advertisers especially are charged with the task of creating frames for many of the items that surround us, harnessing semiotics and cultural scripts to frame everything from soft drinks to vacuum cleaners to back-pain medicine. They do so not simply by telling us to buy such products or services, but by creating a life, character, and *meaning* for all manner of products and services. Hype, in short, creates meaning. And by doing so, it regularly implores us to judge books by their glossy covers.

This book is about the machinations of those glossy "covers," about how hype, synergy, promos, narrative extensions, and various forms of related textuality position, define, and create meaning for film and television. Promotion is vitally important in economic terms, of course, as a proper understanding of media multinational corporations' strategies of synergy and multi-platforming tells us much about the political economy of the mass media. But for synergy to work, meaning must first be established; otherwise, *why* would one buy a Disney toy, get excited about a movie sequel or television spinoff, eagerly anticipate the release of a DVD or podcast, or trawl through the Internet for spoilers or vids? Why, too, might one spend significantly *more* time with such spinoff- or promo-related items than with the film or television show itself? Synergy works because hype creates meaning. Thus, this book represents an attempt to study how this meaning is created, and how it both relates to and in part constructs our understanding of and relationship with the film or television show. It is a look at how much of the media world is formed by "book covers" and their many colleagues—opening credit sequences, trailers, toys, spinoff videogames, prequels and sequels, podcasts, bonus materials, interviews, reviews, alternate reality games, spoilers, audience discussion, vids, posters or billboards, and promotional campaigns.

Consequently, the book argues for a relatively new type of media analysis. While engaging in close reading, audience research, and structural/political economic analysis of films and television programs, we must also use such techniques to study hype, synergy, promos, and peripherals. Charles Acland writes that "the problem with film studies has been *film*, that is, the use of a medium in order to designate the boundaries of the discipline. Such a designation assumes a certain stability in what is actually a mutable technological apparatus. A problem ensues when it is apparent that film is not film anymore."[2] This is also a problem with television studies, for, I would quibble with Acland, film has never been (just) film, nor has television ever been (just) television. Thus, while "screen studies" exists as a discipline encompassing both film and television studies, we need an "off-screen studies" to make sense of the wealth of other entities that saturate the media, and that construct film and television.

Of Texts, Paratexts, and Peripherals: A Word on Terminology

We might begin by finding a single term to describe these various entities. *Promos* and *promotion* involve the selling of another entity. Or, stepping beyond "normal" levels of advertising is *hype*. The *Oxford English Dictionary* (*OED*) defines "hype" as "extravagant or intensive publicity or promotion." Hype is etymologically derived from "hyper-," meaning "over, beyond, above" or "excessively, above normal," which is in turn from the Greek "*huper*," meaning "over, beyond." The term alludes to advertisements and public relations, referring to the puffing up, mass circulation, and frenetic selling of something. Hype is advertising that goes "over" and "beyond" an accepted norm, establishing heightened presence, often for a brief, unsustainable period of time: like the hyperventilating individual or the spaceship in hyperdrive, the hyped product will need to slow down at some point. Its heightened presence is made all the more possible with film and television due to those industries' placement—at least in their Hollywood varieties—within networks of *synergy*. Deriving from the Greek "*sunergos*," meaning "working together," synergy refers, says the *OED*, to "the interaction or cooperation of two or more organizations, substances, or other agents to produce a combined effect greater than the sum of their separate effects." Within the entertainment industry, it refers to a strategy of multimedia platforming, linking a media product to related media on other "platforms," such as toys, DVDs, and/or videogames, so that each product advertises and enriches the experience of the other. And whereas hype is often regarded solely as advertising and as PR, synergistic merchandise, products, and games—also called *peripherals*—are often intended as other platforms for profit-generation.

All of these terms have their virtues. Promotion suggests not only the commercial act of selling, but also of advancing and developing a text. Hype's evocation of images of puffing up, proliferation, and speeding up suggest the degree to which such activities increase the size of the media product or text, even if fleetingly. Synergy implies a streamlining and bringing together of two products or texts. Peripherals, meanwhile, suggest a core entity with outliers that might not prove "central" and that might not even be doing the same thing as that entity, but that are somehow related.

Although each of these terms has its utility in given instances, all have inherent problems. Hype is often regarded in pejorative terms, as excessive. In addition to its listing of "hype" as "extravagant," for instance, the *OED* provides a second definition, as "a deception carried out for the sake of publicity," while the verb form means "to promote or publicize (a product or idea) intensively, *often exaggerating its benefits*" (emphasis added). The term thereby evokes the image of an entity whose existence is illegitimate, inauthentic, and abnormal, when I will be arguing that hype is often mundane and business as usual. Hype, promotion, promos, and synergy are also all terms situated in the realm of profits, business models, and accounting, which may prove a barrier for us to conceive of them as creating meaning, and as being situated in the realms of enjoyment, interpretive work and play, and the social function of media narratives. To call such elements "peripherals," meanwhile, is to posit them as divorced and removed from an actual text, discardable and relatively powerless, when they are, in truth, anything but peripheral. Moreover, hype, promotion, and promos usually refer only to advertising rhetoric, and synergy and peripherals only to officially sanctioned textual iterations. Thus, while fan and viewer creations may work *textually* in similar ways to hype, promotion, promos, synergy, and peripherals, they are nearly always unauthorized elements that are thus not covered by such terminology.

Throughout this book, then, while I will occasionally use the above terms as context deems appropriate, I will more frequently refer to *paratexts* and to *paratextuality*. I take these terms from Gerard Genette, who first used them to discuss the variety of materials that surround a literary text.[3] A fuller definition of these terms will be offered in chapter 1, but my attraction to them stems from the meaning of the prefix "para-," defined by the *OED* both as "beside, adjacent to," and "beyond or distinct from, but analogous to." A "paratext" is both "distinct from" and alike—or, I will argue, intrinsically part of—the text. The book's thesis is that paratexts are not simply add-ons, spinoffs, and also-rans: they create texts, they manage them, and they fill them with many of the meanings that we associate with them. Just as we ask *para*medics to save lives rather than leave the job to others, and just as a *para*site feeds off, lives in, and can affect the running of its host's body, a paratext constructs, lives in, and can affect the running of the text.

Paratexts often take a tangible form, as with posters, videogames, podcasts, reviews, or merchandise, for example, and it is the tangible paratext on which I focus predominantly. However, I will also argue that other, intangible entities can at times work in paratextual fashion. Thus, for instance, while a genre is not a paratext it can work paratextually to frame a text, as can talk about a text (though, of course, once such talk is written or typed, it becomes a tangible paratext), and so occasionally I will examine these and other intangible entities within the rubric of paratextuality too.

I must also be clear from the outset that throughout this book, I use the word *text* in a particular fashion. I elaborate upon and justify this use in chapter 1, but early warning should be provided to those readers who are accustomed to calling the film or television program "the text" or, in relation to paratexts, "the source text." To use the word "text" in such a manner suggests that the film or program *is* the entire text, and/or that it completes the text. I argue, though, that a film or program is but one part of the text, the text always being a contingent entity, either in the process of forming and transforming or vulnerable to further formation or transformation. The text, as Julia Kristeva notes, is not a finished production, but a continuous "productivity."[4] It is a larger unit than any film or show that may be part of it; it is the entire storyworld as we know it. Our attitudes toward, responses to, and evaluations of this world will always rely upon paratexts too. Hence, since my book argues that a film or program is never the entire sum of the text, I will not conflate "film" or "program" with "text." When I call for an "off-screen studies," I call for a screen studies that focuses on paratexts' constitutive role in creating textuality, rather than simply consigning paratexts to the also-ran category or considering their importance only in promotional and monetary terms.

Nevertheless, the money trail might guide our initial foray into an off-screen studies, as an invigorated study of paratexts could address an odd paradox of media and cultural studies: while the industry pumps millions of dollars and labor hours into carefully crafting its paratexts and then saturates our lived environments with them, media and cultural studies often deal with them only in passing. How important are they? By late 2008, major studios were spending, on average, $36 million per film on marketing—a full third of the average film budget—while blockbusters could require considerably more. Smaller companies such as Lionsgate habitually spend up to two-thirds of their budget on marketing. [5] Meanwhile, DVD sales and rentals handily eclipse Hollywood's box office revenues, with, for instance, 2004 seeing $7.4 billion in rentals to theaters, yet $21 billion from home video.[6] Even blockbusters and box office giants are seeing vigorous "competition" from DVDs; New Line's $305.4 million of revenue for DVD sales of *The Lord of the Rings: The Two Towers* (2002) in 2003, for example, fell just shy of the film's huge yield at the box office.[7] And cineplexes are also being rivaled by the videogame industry—some of whose biggest hits are film and/or television spinoffs.[8] In the world of television, as Amanda Lotz records, American networks and cable channels devote substantial advertising space to hyping their own programs. Network television alone, for instance, foregoes an estimated $4 billion worth of ad time in order to advertise its programs, airing over 30,000 promos a year. In 2002, the old WB network accepted more ads from parent company AOL Time Warner than from any other advertiser, suggesting how one of the great economic benefits of conglomeration has been the ability to advertise on commonly owned channels.[9] Add to this the potentially colossal sums that media corporations can earn from merchandising, licensing, and franchising (in addition to *Lord of the Rings*, think Disney, *Star Wars* [1977], or *The Simpsons* [1989–]), and paratextuality is not only big business, but often much bigger than film or television themselves. Janet Wasko cites estimates that the licensed children's products market is valued at $132 billion, that licensed products in general generate more than $73 billion a year, and that movie-based games earned the major studios as much as $1.4 billion in 2001.[10]

And yet media, film, television, and cultural studies frequently stick solely to the films and television programs with a loyalty born out of habit. John Caldwell notes the film and television industries' widespread devaluation of "below the line" workers as lesser than the "above the line" directors, producers, writers, and actors.[11] Media studies, too, often risk a similar devaluation of those whose labor and creativity can be just as constitutive of the text as that of the above-the-liners. While this move is evident in the relative dearth of materials studying or even theorizing "below the line" work on films and television shows, it is similarly evident in the relative lack of attention paid to the semiotic and aesthetic value of the "below the line" paratext, or to its creators. Synergy is seen in terms of profits, but too rarely in terms of *textuality*, as something that creates sense and meaning, that is engaged with and interpreted as is the filmic or televisual referent, and that can ultimately create meaning for and *on behalf of* this referent. A key starting point for this book, then, is that if the film and television industries invest so heavily in previews, bonus materials, merchandise, and their ilk, so should we as analysts. It is time to examine the paratexts.

The Movie of the Trailer

Illustrating the power of paratexts with a playfully parodic nod was a brief video released in spring 2008 by the online satirical news outlet *The Onion*. "Iron Man," the Onion News Network's faux anchor announced, "was one of the most popular trailers of last summer, but controversy is sweeping the fan community today, following the announcement that Paramount Pictures is planning to adapt the beloved trailer into a feature-length motion picture" (fig. 1.1). He then cut to a supposed entertainment reporter, who noted mixed reaction to the controversial plan to make a movie of the trailer:

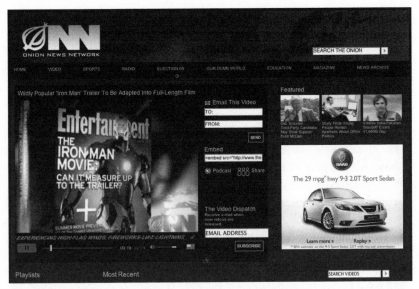

Fig. 1.1. The Onion News Network speculates on whether fans will accept the film adaptation of the *Iron Man* trailer.

The *Iron Man* trailer is near and dear to a lot of fans' hearts, so you can imagine how worried people are about this news. Apparently, the plan is to expand that fast montage of very short shots seen in the trailer into full-length, distinct scenes, and in between those scenes, they plan to add *additional* scenes that weren't in the trailer.

She also speculated on the prospects of the studio taking the fan favorite Gwyneth Paltrow, whose "notable" appearance in the trailer they clocked at three-quarters of a second, and placing her at the center of a "tedious romantic subplot that [is] twenty or thirty minutes long." Both "reporters" react with mock incredulity at the notion that Paramount would jeopardize "the integrity of the trailer" and risk "alienating the trailer's core fan base" with such a move, but the entertainment reporter reassures viewers that at least Paramount has announced that they will keep everything that audiences loved, "right down to actual lines from the trailer," and have even brought Robert Downey, Jr., back to "reprise" his role from the trailer, and that they will release the film with eight "entirely new entertainment-packed trailers. So, even if the movie is no good, hopefully the trip to the theater will be worth it anyway."

The item plays with many anxieties of consuming media in a hype-, synergy-, and franchise-filled era, in particular the concern that the ads can prove better than the product itself, and that adaptations risk killing the core elements of the original. In doing so, it points to how complex our interactions with media are, and to how contingent they are on anticipation and expectation, on networks of paratexts, and on previous relationships to a story, character, actor, or genre. The parodic clip suggests the degree to which many if not all people going to watch the *Iron Man* film (2008) will already have started the process of making sense of it. Those who have read *Iron Man* comics, or perhaps played Marvel videogames, will have a sense of what lies ahead, as will (in different ways) those with a past knowledge of Downey's, Paltrow's, or director Jon Favreau's work. And many will have seen the trailer, which was indeed spectacular, thereby creating the groundwork for the Onion News Network's parodic story. Others will have seen posters, visited the website, read reviews, and heard or read interviews with Downey, Paltrow, or Favreau. Some viewers will have had expectations created simply due to the cinema in which the movie was playing, or due to the friends who invited them to come see it. Meanwhile, of course, thousands will have avoided the film, whether due to its genre, cast, or any of the above-mentioned instances of hype and synergy. In short, then, if we really wanted to make sense of the "moment" of interaction between film and audience, we would need to explore all those things that preceded the film, set the frames through which audience members would make sense of it, and set the stage for the kind of movie-going experience they would have. As categorically absurd as *The Onion*'s suggestion that the trailer has "integrity" to uphold might seem, the trailer would play a key role in determining how audiences came to the cinema, and what they came expecting. The film would have begun in earnest, then, with the trailer, or with the comics, the videogames, the interviews, the reviews, the ads, and so forth. The text, the essence, of *Iron Man* began long before the film hit theaters, so that when the film finally arrived, yes, it could radically revise that text, but it would not be working with a blank slate; rather, it would need to work through, with, and/or in spite of the multiple meanings that had already begun to form in audiences' minds.

However, this book is not simply arguing that paratexts *start* texts, for they also create them and continue them. Thus, this book is also about the paratexts that we find after a text has officially begun, and that continue to give us information, ways of looking at the film or show, and frames for understanding it or engaging with it. Their work is never over, and their effects on what the film or show *is*—on what it means to its audiences—are continual.

The Onion News Network's short clip plays with the notion of continuing paratexts, too, for in its suggestion that the integrity of the trailer might be jeopardized by the movie, the clip reflects on how each new iteration of a text—wherever it may be, and of whatever length (ninety seconds or ninety minutes)—can affect the public understanding of, appreciation of, and identification with that text. Quite simply, a "bad" adaptation will inevitably affect the public standing of a text, just as would a "good" one. But to be able to call an adaptation "good" or "bad" requires an audience member or community to have developed a notion of the ideal and proper text, and in this book I will argue that paratexts play as much of a role as does the film or television program itself in constructing how different audience members will construct this ideal text.

Where Is Springfield? Placing The Simpsons

Another illustrative example lies in the army of merchandise and spinoff products that surround *The Simpsons*. *The Simpsons* is, of course, one of the world's most successful television programs worldwide, having produced more than four hundred episodes by the time of writing. But surely few if any know *The Simpsons* solely as a television program, for it is also a brand, a world, and a set of characters that exist across clothing, toys, videogames, a film, ads, books, comics, DVDs, CDs, and many other media platforms. For the purposes of my argument here, though, I wish to focus on one particular platform: a set of online ads for *The Simpsons Game* (2007). Since this videogame followed in the wake of *The Simpsons Movie* (2007), in effect we have a third-level paratext: an ad for the game that followed the movie of the television program. As such, if we were to examine this as media studies has more traditionally examined such products, we would focus on it wholly as a hypercommercialized money-grab, as a synergistic attempt to squeeze as much as possible from a successful media product. Ads for games of a movie of a television show rate low on most traditional scales of artistic value.

However, upon closer examination of these ads, we can see a viable source of *The Simpsons* as text. Upon navigating to the webpage for *The Simpsons Game*, a visitor was met with a series of links to parodic trailers for supposed stand-alone videogames, each of which used *The Simpsons* to parody established and popular games or game genres (and each a level in the actual game). Thus, for instance, *Medal of Homer* deftly parodies both the *Medal of Honor* games specifically (1999–) and war games and war films more generally. With a somber yet sweeping orchestral and choral soundtrack worthy of *Saving Private Ryan* (1998), the ad opens with a series of zoom-and-pan scratchy black-and-white war "photos" (yet drawn in *Simpsons* style), playing with the visual style of Ken Burns documentaries, and of *Medal of Honor*'s cut sequences (fig. 1.2). Title cards interlace such photos, reading "In the Last Great Invasion" "Of the Last Great War" "They Gave Each Other the Strength" "To Make History." This reverent spectacle is interrupted following the third title card, though, as we cut to a shot of Homer and Bart in which Homer is scratching his butt. The irreverence then bubbles up further following the last title card, as a prancing Homer interrupts, "Oooh, I'm France, I'm a little girl. I don't want to be bombed and attacked." The ad continues to its conclusion, cutting between shots of, for instance, Homer belching flame, or rolling around as a huge human blob, and shots framed to mimic war movie trailers.

In short, many of the key ingredients of *The Simpsons* are in the ad. We see significant irreverence and bodily humor, especially from Homer. We see *The Simpsons*' signature brand of attractive animation. We see and hear a smart, brilliantly executed media parody that lampoons the seriousness with which both war games and war films take themselves. And we see the snark for which the show is famous. All of this takes place in a brief, eighty-second clip, again replicating the television show's style of offering short bursts of media parody. And while the *Medal of Homer* ad is executed with great skill, a deeply funny piece of work, so too is the *Mob Rules* ad, which parodies the *Grand Theft Auto* series' (1997–) trailers and camerawork to a tee. The *Mob Rules* ad also parodies *GTA*'s signature use of violence and male bravado, parodically recontextualizing the line "we're gonna clean up this town," for example, as Marge's appeal to Lisa to help her rid Springfield of the violent videogame. Two other ads parody *Everquest* (1999) and other role-playing games, and odd Japanese puzzle games, respectively. After watching these ads, one has gained an experience similar to that of watching the television show. As ads, the clips may be seen by some as less authentic, as simply hawking their wares, and as purely secondary to the primary text that is *The Simpsons* television show. But the clips produce and continue the text of *The Simpsons* with considerable skill. These third-level paratexts, in other words, are part of the text, becoming sites not only of the production of the text but also of engagement with it.

Fig. 1.2. An online ad for *The Simpsons Game* parodies the *Medal of Honor* franchise, complete with its nostalgic documentary-style cut sequences.

Nor are they alone in this regard, as *The Simpsons'* history, and many of its public meanings, has often relied heavily upon its paratexts. While above I suggest that the paratexts were viable parts of the text, at times the show's paratexts have done *more* to create the text as it is known than has the show itself. In particular, we might look at the furor that surrounded the show in its early years, directed primarily at Bart as irreverent youth, but one that centered on—and was in many ways ignited by—the mass popularity of t-shirts labeling Bart an "Underachiever," while he responds, "And Proud of It, Man." Many parents, teachers, principals, and pundits around the United States worried about children learning a slacker attitude from the t-shirt's sentiment, and as a result, many schools banned the t-shirts, and conservative rhetoric and complaints swarmed around the show.[12] This rhetoric completely failed to realize the sly message in the t-shirt: as Laurie Schulze notes, "Bart has managed to turn the tables on the system that's devalued him and say, 'In your face. I'm not worthless, insignificant, or stupid. If you want to label me an underachiever, I'll turn that into a badge of courage and say I'm proud of it.'"[13] Nevertheless, as paratext, the t-shirt created an image for many Americans of *The Simpsons* as a show of little to no values, intent on corrupting children's minds.

Then, in 1992, at the Republican National Convention, another paratext further sealed this image of the show, when President George H. W. Bush insisted that the United States needed more families like the Waltons and less like the Simpsons. Just as Bush's vice-president, Dan Quayle, had brought *Murphy Brown* (1988–98) into the culture wars between conservative and liberal America, Bush made *The Simpsons* a front in that war (as did First Lady Barbara Bush, who also shared her hatred for *The Simpsons* with the press). While *The Simpsons* was already infused with Matt Groening's anti-establishment beliefs, sly satiric edge, and irreverence, the t-shirt controversy and the Bush speech suddenly amplified these qualities. Now, to watch *The Simpsons* and/or to wear the t-shirt was to posit oneself proudly against Bush's neo-conservatism, while to dislike the show and/or to ban one's children from seeing it was to publicly declare one's allegiance to those ideals. The paratexts made the show considerably more controversial, edgy, and anti-establishment than many of its episodes made it; certainly, in England, where the t-shirt controversy never bubbled up to the same degree, and where Bush's comments received considerably less attention, the show was often seen as endearingly *pro*–family values, to the point that Archbishop of Canterbury Rowan Williams has often proudly and unflinchingly sided with Bart over Bush, claiming that *The Simpsons* is "on the side of the angels."[14]

We must also turn to *The Simpsons*' paratexts if we wish to understand its relationship to advertising and consumerism. As I have examined elsewhere, *The Simpsons* is one of the only commercial television programs in the United States to have consistently attacked American consumerism and capitalism.[15] It regularly savages advertising's ethics and style, and rarely involves product placement while doing so (thus avoiding the *Wayne's World* [1992] mock-yet-show strategy of parodying product placement), and many of its key figures serve allegorical functions with relation to consumerist capitalism—see, for example, Homer, the anti-hero who mindlessly buys anything he is told to; Krusty the Klown, the Ronald McDonald sell-out children's entertainer; Mr. Burns, the evil corporate overlord; and Lisa, the hero whose environmentalism and anti-consumerist ethos is all too rare on American television. So, were we to evaluate the show's relationship to and messages regarding advertising based solely on the television program, we would likely judge it as resolutely leftist in sentiment. However, to do so would be to overlook the apparent hypocrisy that while it criticizes Krusty's lust to put his brand on everything, so too does *The Simpsons* brand at times appear to be on everything, and while it criticizes advertising, from the early use of Bart to advertise Butterfinger candy bars to countless other appearances in ads, *The Simpsons* has been complicit with more advertising than have most other shows on television.[16] Yet some of its other paratexts also criticize ads, as with *The Simpsons Hit and Run Game* (2003, discussed further in chapter 6), in which destroying ads rewards one with money and quicker travel time, and whose story is based around advertising run amok. Matthew McAllister notes *Simpsons* creator Matt Groening's commitment to privileging licenses that are self-conscious and mocking of their commercialism.[17] Thus, at the paratextual level, or, rather, between the level of the show and the level of the paratext, the text is deeply conflicted, complex, and contradictory when it comes to advertising, consumerism, and capitalism. Individual audience members will see it as either anti-consumerist, rampantly consumerist, or somewhere in between, based in large part on their own interaction with not only the television program, but also the paratexts. Once again, a central popular understanding, or understandings, of *The Simpsons* come to us in part through the meanings created by the paratexts, not just the show.

To understand why paratexts might be so powerful, we might reframe the issue as being one of time and place. In the United States, at the time of writing, *The Simpsons* plays on the FOX network, on Sundays at 8 p.m. when in season. Thus, the show itself is strictly contained by time and place, even if we factor in its syndication, and VHS, DVD, and DVR recordings and replayings. However, *The Simpsons'* paratexts allow Springfield to exist well beyond those boundaries. Echoes of Springfield are in most shopping malls, throughout cyberspace, in countless souvenir stores worldwide (as Russian nesting dolls in the Czech Republic, as porcelain Homers in the night markets of Tijuana, and as soapstone carvings in Kenya, to list a few), in games and electronics stores, on newsstands, in comic stores and bookstores, in TV specials, lying on the floor of many a child's room, on many an adult collector's shelf, on people's chests and heads, and in countless other venues. Such is FOX's strategy of synergy: that people will not be able to escape Springfield. But when Springfield is seemingly everywhere, many people will only experience Springfield outside of the television show, and even many of those who regularly watch the show at its scheduled time and place will also experience Springfield in countless other locales. In a very real sense, then, *The Simpsons* often exists in the paratexts, and those paratexts are fostering many of its meanings and its fans', non-fans', and anti-fans' reactions.

My task in this book, then, is to engage in a textual cartography of sorts, mapping texts and making sense of the complex social geography not only of Springfield, but of multiple other storyworlds. I will be examining the types of meanings created by paratexts, how they variously dovetail or clash with meanings from their related texts, and how paratexts give value and/or identity to texts. I will move through various types of paratexts, and various entertainment properties from film and television, offering both a theory of paratextuality and numerous illustrations of how it creates textual meaning.

An Overview of the Book

Paratexts, this book argues, are a central part of media production and consumption processes. But precisely because of their centrality, no single book can do more than scratch the surface of their overall importance to a better understanding of media and culture. The present book focuses on paratexts as textual entities, emphasizing the relationship between paratexts, films, and television programs and audiences. But given their textual properties, and their prominent placement in consumption cultures, greater attention should also be paid to how paratexts are created and regulated. Taking the eye off the paratext, as media studies has often done, impoverishes our understanding of production and regulation cultures, and hence our ability to intervene meaningfully in these cultures. The present project, however, limits itself primarily to consideration of the paratext's impact on texts and on audiences, as a way of establishing why paratexts matter in the first place.

The book also focuses exclusively on television and film paratexts, though of course the music, videogame, online, and print industries have their own thriving examples. And while theater layout and branding, channel identification sequences, and the like may work as paratexts, and are thus worthy of attention,[18] they do so for multiple texts, whereas here I have chosen to stick to paratexts that "belong" to a particular show. The book's focus is also restricted mostly to popular and recent Hollywood film and television, in part because Hollywood produces so much paratextuality that it offers an embarrassment of riches for study, and thus rich soil in which to plant a theory of paratexts that I hope can grow elsewhere too, and in part because many of these examples are more accessible than older, independent, or non-American products. I deliberately return to some texts (such as *Lost* [2004–] and *Lord of the Rings*) with different paratexts, so that readers can see various facets of their paratextual entourage, but I would like my readers to be able to fill in a fuller picture themselves, hence my choice to restrict most analysis to more prominent shows. By doing so, I do not mean to imply that paratexts are either a recent or an American phenomenon: Hollywood's current fondness for a franchise-based economy perhaps makes paratexts more voluminous today, but they have always existed and thrived, as they do outside Hollywood and America.

From the outset, it should also be noted that many of my examples are of paratexts attached to niche or fan properties, but the book is not about fan cultures per se. Rather, I argue that paratexts often construct some of the wider audience's scant encounters with the text, and thus while the *show* might be a niche or fan property, many of its paratexts (such as trailers, movie posters, hype, reviews, and audience commentary) are not only quintessentially mainstream, but also the mediators of niche and fan entities to both fans *and* the wider audience. Admittedly, not all will work this way. Paratexts are the greeters, gatekeepers, and cheerleaders for and of the media, filters through which we must pass on our way to "the text itself," but some will only greet certain audiences. Many fan-made paratexts, in particular, address only those within the fandom. Other paratexts will scare away potential audiences, as the semblance of being a "fan text" is often enough to detract some. In such cases, though, the paratexts create the text for the fleeing would-be audience, suggesting a "geek factor" or an undesired depth that may turn them away. In other instances, paratexts will insist that a text is more mainstream, less niche or fannish. However, regardless of whether the paratexts greet or turn audiences away, they often prove to be vital mediators of the niche or fan property to a wider audience: just as Bart Simpson t-shirts and Butterfinger ads constructed an idea of what *The Simpsons* was about, for non-fans arguably more than for fans, so too do paratexts regularly address the non-fan, even when attached to fan properties. As such, this book is neither about fan cultures nor not about them; it instead aims to make sense of the textual residue that often flows between all "audiences," fans, non-fans, and anti-fans.

Chapter 1 begins by defining the phrase "paratext" more precisely and situating it within other existing theories of what texts are, what work they do, and how they do this work. The chapter establishes the textual importance of paratexts, examining the constitutive role they play in creating public understandings of the text. It also distinguishes between "entryway" and "in medias res" paratexts, the first being those that we encounter before watching a film or television program, the latter those that come to us in the process of watching or at least interpreting the film or program. All successive chapters examine a few central case studies, so that the depths of paratexts' meanings, and of audiences' interactions with them, can be examined up close. However, throughout chapter 1, in order to set up exactly why paratextual study might be necessary in the first place, I offer a wide variety of examples from film and television and from existing scholarship that further excavates the importance of paratexts.

Chapter 2 offers several examples of how paratexts work as gateways into the text, establishing meanings and frames for decoding before the audience member has even encountered the film or television program. The iconic examples here are movie posters, trailers, and advertising campaigns that surround films and television programs, not only encouraging us to watch the shows, but also establishing the frames through which we "should" interpret and enjoy the shows. Through examining first several movie posters, and then the promotional campaign in New York City for ABC's *Six Degrees* (2006–7) and its official website, I argue that hype can determine genre, gender, theme, style, and relevant intertexts, thereby in part creating the show as a meaningful entity for "viewers" even before they become viewers, or even if they never become viewers. I then turn to trailers, examining the starkly different trailers for Atom Egoyan's film *The Sweet Hereafter* (1997)—one American, one Canadian—and arguing that the difference resulted in the sale of, effectively, two different films. Finally, I maintain an interest in paratexts' abilities to create "proper interpretations" that audience members are encouraged to adopt, by discussing television opening credit sequences and their roles as both mini-trailers for new viewers and ritualistic anthems for returning viewers. Ultimately, chapter 2 takes several examples of producer-created paratexts to study the degree to which producers can proffer interpretations and readings of their texts even before they begin.

If chapter 2 is about how paratexts create meaning for texts, chapter 3 is about how they create scripts of value for them. In particular, the chapter examines how author, aura, and artistry—all qualities often said to be lacking in the age of big-budget blockbusters and for-profit art—are hailed and awarded to texts by their paratexts. I begin by examining how reality makeover shows' promise to serve society is given weight by their webpages' attempts to code them as philanthropic, community-generating programs with considerable civic value. Much of the rest of the chapter examines the particularly important role that DVDs play in giving value to fictional texts through their bonus materials such as commentary tracks, making-of documentaries, special effects galleries, and alternate scenes. I turn to the prominent example of the Platinum Series Special Extended Edition DVDs of *The Lord of the Rings: The Two Towers*, a four-disc set replete with various bonus materials. I argue that these materials richly layer the text, paralleling the cast and crew's travails in making the film to the epic campaign against the ultimate evil depicted in the tale. As a result of these materials, the DVDs posit the film as above the mundane products of a commercial industry, and as a crowning aesthetic achieve-ment that represents an "older," nobler form of art. Part and parcel of this process, too, is the lionization of Peter Jackson, the film's director. Thus, I will also examine the role of DVDs, both *The Two Towers* and numerous DVDs for television shows, and of podcasts and other sources of authorial interviews, in attempting to resurrect the figure of the author that literary and cultural studies theory has long thought dead. My argument is not that television or film have improved with DVDs and podcasts, but rather that the DVDs and podcasts repeatedly insist that their shows are better, becoming a key site for the construction of discourses of value.

Chapter 4 focuses both on how paratexts manage a broader system of intertextuality and on how grouped, sequenced, or otherwise related films and television programs can become paratexts themselves, their decod-ing processes so intricately intertwined with those of their related films or television programs that we might regard them as occurring under the long shadow of former texts. My first case study draws on work con-ducted with Bertha Chin into online would-be audiences' reactions to the *Lord of the Rings* films before they had even been made. Chin and I found not only enthusiastic discussion of the films, but actual early interpreta-tion and evaluation of them, and thus this case study examines the degree to which their proposed frames for making sense of the films had been inherited from the *Lord of the Rings* books by J. R. R. Tolkien, and how audience discussion managed this system. Continuing the story, I then look at how the *Lord of the Rings* films, after release, became their own paratexts for would-be viewers of Peter Jackson's next outing, *King Kong* (2005), and for the adaptation of C. S. Lewis's *Chronicles of Narnia: The Lion, the Witch, and the Wardrobe* (2005). Next I turn to *Batman Begins*

(2005) to see how the film's plot and casting seem to have been guided in large part by an awareness of the dark shadow cast over the Batman franchise by the previous Batman film and cinematic atrocity, *Batman and Robin* (1997). Finally, I turn from films as paratexts to the author as paratext, examining online postings from the early days of television producer J. J. Abrams's *Lost* and *Six Degrees* that suggested fans were using Abrams's previous work and their constructions of him as artist to make sense of and predict plot threads in his new work. Through these various examples, chapter 4 aims to analyze how dependent all interpretation is on various other films and television programs, on audiences' varying levels of familiarity with those films and programs, and on how the paratext of audience discussion circulates and coordinates intertexts.

Chapters 2, 3, and 4 all take products of the entertainment industry as their topic. Given Hollywood's huge coffers, its intense need to make each of its films and programs stand out in a media-saturated environment, and its success in turning many paratexts into revenue-generators, a large proportion of the paratextual world is commissioned into existence by Hollywood. However, it would be a grave mistake to consider audience-created paratexts as lesser in potential importance or complexity. Thus chapter 5 studies numerous examples of audience-created paratexts. Much has been written elsewhere on how fan fiction and mash-ups can be used to contest the "official" meanings proffered by Hollywood, but the chapter's first two case studies instead examine how paratexts can be used to intensify certain textual experiences, less working against the industry's version of the text than cutting a personalized path through it. First, I draw on work conducted with Jason Mittell into *Lost* fans' consumption of spoilers (advance information of what will happen in the plot) to study how this consumption shows a move away from the strict plot-based mode of engaging with *Lost* and toward a more puzzle-, character-, and/or experiential-based mode. Second, I examine "vids," fan-made videos that splice and edit together multiple scenes from a film or television program with a piece of music. While, again, vids have been studied within the framework of fan rebellion and critique, this section instead concentrates on how character-study and relationship vids can be used to examine a particular character's or theme's path through an otherwise busy film or program, thereby allowing time for the viewer to pause and reflect. Finally, I turn to press reviews as audience-made paratexts that do battle with Hollywood's own paratexts, usually before the film or television program has even aired, and I focus particularly on reviews of NBC's *Friday*

Night Lights (2006–) as an example of a show whose reviewers engaged in a concerted effort to reframe NBC's own publicity for the show. This final example grows from a discussion of the ways in which various audiences have differing levels of power and privilege to frame or reframe films or programs.

Many of the book's examples are of paratexts that have been appended to a text, either before or after the fact, but in chapter 6 my interests turn to paratexts that more directly challenge the binary of paratext and film or program, forcing us to wonder exactly what is "primary" or "the original" and what is "secondary" or "peripheral." *Star Wars* action figures feature first, as I examine their significant imprint and impact on the films, and on both public and fan understandings of them. Whereas cultural critics have long seen licensed toys as a particularly egregious instance of mindless and manipulative consumerism, I argue that the toys became a viable source of the text, framing and intensifying many of the film's themes, while also allowing the *Star Wars* universe to be inhabitable. This concern with making storyworlds accessible and inhabitable then extends into a discussion of various forms of film- or television show–related games that allow players into a text to explore, sample, and/or create parts of the storyworld interactively. In particular, I explore licensed videogames that place the player in control of an avatar situated in the storyworld, enabling a limited set of interactions with characters and places within the broader text. I also examine an increasingly popular form of game, the alternate reality game (ARG), focusing on the *What Happened in Piedmont?* ARG that preceded the broadcast of A&E's *Andromeda Strain* (2008), and that opened up significant room for audiences to learn about, engage with, and "taste" the storyworld independent of the mini-series.

Finally, since the book argues that paratexts create texts, in the Conclusion I discuss examples of the entertainment industry ignoring this logic and producing facile paratexts of little to no value or intelligence, or, alternately, embracing this logic and surrendering parts of their texts to their paratexts, often producing fascinating and significant results. Drawing from numerous interviews with paratext creators, conducted by myself and others, I briefly address the practical issue of how film and television creators can more meaningfully integrate paratexts into the storytelling and production process. To be of value or impact, and to be worthy of close study, paratexts need not be integrated, but by ending with a discussion of integration, I hope to highlight several key issues involved in the production and study of paratexts and their worlds.

Ultimately, through the book's multiple examples and through its theoretical wrestling with concepts of paratextuality and textuality, I hope to illustrate how vibrant and vital a contribution to meaning-making and the development of storyworlds paratexts offer us. While paratexts can at times be seen as annoyances, as "mere" advertising, and/or as only so much hype, they are often as complex and intricate, and as generative of meanings and engagement, as are the films and television shows that they orbit and establish. To limit our understanding of film and television to films and television shows themselves risks drafting an insufficient picture not only of any given text, but also of the processes of production and reception attached to that text. Paratextual study, by contrast, promises a more richly contextualized and nuanced image of how texts work, how and why they are made, and how and why they are watched, interpreted, and enjoyed.

1

From Spoilers to Spinoffs

A Theory of Paratexts

Paratexts surround texts, audiences, and industry, as organic and naturally occurring a part of our mediated environment as are movies and television themselves. If we imagine the triumvirate of Text, Audience, and Industry as the Big Three of media practice, then paratexts fill the space between them, conditioning passages and trajectories that criss-cross the mediascape, and variously negotiating or determining interactions among the three. Industry and audiences create vast amounts of paratexts. Audiences also consume vast amounts of paratexts. Thus, paratexts' relationship to industry and audience is most obvious. However, the secret to understanding paratexts lies in working out their relationship to textuality: What is the paratext in relationship to the text? How does it contribute to the process of making meaning? And how does it energize, contextualize, or otherwise modify textuality? This chapter attempts to answer these questions by presenting a theory of paratextuality. To do so, first we must examine the nature of this relationship. I will then offer a definition of textuality that accounts for the paratextual, examining multiple instances of paratexts at work in the interpretive trenches. In particular, I will distinguish between paratexts that grab the viewer before he or she reaches the text and try to control the viewer's entrance to the text ("entryway paratexts"), and paratexts that flow between the gaps of textual exhibition, or that come to us "during" or "after" viewing, working to police certain reading strategies in medias res ("in medias res paratexts").

Watching on a Hope and a Prayer

Let us begin by asking how one makes sense of a text. A simple question, this has nevertheless challenged artists, scholars, politicians, and everyday readers for centuries and has yet to yield anything close to a simple answer.

Throughout humankind's long history of debates over what and how texts mean, and hence what they "do" to us and what we can "do" to them, the most common method of analyzing a text has been close reading. The intuitive purchase behind such a method is obvious: if you want to understand a finely crafted machine, you look at it and take it apart; so it would seem that if you want to understand a book, a film, or a television program, you could similarly look at it and take it apart. However, especially if we care about social meanings and uses—what place a text has in society—close reading does not suffice. Whether of machines or texts, close reading fails to reveal vital aspects of the object under analysis. In particular, just as taking apart a machine would not necessarily explain why a given person chose that machine over another tool or machine, close reading may tell us little about how a viewer *arrived at* a text. Why view *this* program, or *this* film, as opposed to the many thousands of other options?

Sometimes our consumption choices are motivated by previous consumption: "I loved it the first time, so let's watch it again." Thus, in such cases, the issue of context may seem rather trivial. But a great deal of our textual consumption instead involves new texts. When faced with a multiplex full of unwatched movies, or an extended cable television package full of unwatched shows, one must engage in *speculative consumption*, creating an idea of what pleasures any one text will provide, what information it will offer, what "effect" it will have on us, and so forth. As such, with all the hype that surrounds us, announcing texts from subway cars, website margins, or highway roadsides, we can spend a surprisingly large portion of our everyday life speculatively consuming new texts. Especially with film, as Thomas Elsaesser notes, buying a movie ticket is an "act of faith," in which we pay for "not the product itself and not even for the commodified experience that it represents, but simply for the possibility that such a transubstantiation of experience into commodity might 'take place.'"[1] If we do not like the film, we cannot get our money back, since we paid for the *chance* of entertainment, not necessarily for actual entertainment. Even watching television, though sometimes less deliberative an experience than going out to the movies, still requires an investment of time, and amidst channel-surfing, many of our decisions to watch are still based on prior speculative consumption, and hence on the hope, the possibility, of transubstantiation. Or, as Roger Silverstone notes, "We are drawn to these otherwise mundane and trivial texts and performances by a transcendent hope, a hope and a desire that something will touch us."[2] Much of the business of media, in both economic and hermeneutic terms, then, is conducted before watching, when hopes, expectations, worries, concerns, and desires coalesce to offer us images and scripts of what a text might be.

Synergy, paratexts, and intertexts are responsible for much of this faith in transubstantiation—the high priests of and for much of the textuality that allows speculative consumption. To choose to watch a movie, for instance, we may factor in any of the following: the actors, the production personnel, the quality of the previews, reviews, interviews, the poster, a marketing campaign, word of mouth, what cinema it is playing at (or what channel it is on), or the material on which it is based (whether prequel, sequel, or adaptation). All of these are texts in their own right, often meticulously constructed by their producers in order to offer certain meanings and interpretations. Thus, in effect, it is these texts that create and manage our faith, and we consume them on our way to consuming the "film itself."

Gerard Genette entitled such texts "paratexts," texts that prepare us for other texts. They form, he notes, the "threshold" between the inside and the outside of the text, and while paratexts can exist without a source—as when we read commentary on films or television shows that have been lost to time, for instance—a text cannot exist without paratexts.[3] Writing of books, Genette offered a long list of paratexts, including covers, title pages, typesetting, paper, name of author, dedications, prefaces, and introductions as examples of "peritexts"—paratexts within the book—and interviews, reviews, public responses, and magazine ads as "epitexts"— paratexts outside the book.[4] He also allowed for paratexts of fact, so that, for instance, knowing an author's gender could serve its own paratextual function. Genette argued that we can only approach texts *through* paratexts, so that before we start reading a book, we have consumed many of its paratexts. Far from being tangentially related to the text, paratexts provide "an airlock that helps the reader pass without too much difficulty from one world to the other, a sometimes delicate operation, especially when the second world is a fictional one."[5] In other words, paratexts condition our entrance to texts, telling us what to expect, and setting the terms of our "faith" in subsequent transubstantiation. Hence, for instance, an ad telling us of a film's success at Cannes and Sundance would prepare us for a markedly different film than would, say, an ad that boasts endorsement from Britney Spears (even if both ads refer to the same film). Each paratext acts like an airlock to acclimatize us to a certain text, and it demands or suggests certain reading strategies. We rely upon such paratexts to help us choose how to spend our leisure time: they tell us which movies and television programs to watch, which are priorities, which to avoid, which to watch alone and which to watch with friends, which to watch on a big screen, which to save for times when we need a pick-me-up, and so on. Thus, paratexts tell us what to expect, and in doing so, they shape the reading strategies that we will take with us "into" the text, and they provide the all-important early frames through which we will examine, react to, and evaluate textual consumption.

As such, the study of paratexts is the study of how meaning is created, and of how texts begin. Moreover, precisely because paratexts help us decide which texts to consume, we often know many texts only at the paratextual level. Everyone consumes many more paratexts than films or programs. When we move onward to the film or program, those paratexts help frame our consumption; but when we do not move onward, all we are left with is the paratext. Hence, for instance, when at a multiplex we choose to watch one of the ten films on offer, we not only create an interpretive construction of the film that we saw; we have often also speculatively consumed many of the other nine. Paratexts, then, become the very stuff upon which much popular interpretation is based. As analysts of media, making sense of the film or program itself remains a vitally important step, but such a step will only tell us what it means to those who have watched it. From *Star Wars* to *The Passion of the Christ* (2004), *American Idol* (2002–) to *The Jerry Springer Show* (1991–), many shows have meaning for an "audience" that extends well beyond those who actually watched the show. To understand what texts mean to popular culture as a whole, we must examine paratexts too. If media audiences have for too long been seen as unthinking, purely reactive monads, this is in large part because the analysis of media has consistently underplayed the importance of worries, hopes, and expectations in preparing us for texts. As full as the world is of films and television programs, it is more full of worries, hopes, and expectations concerning them. Ultimately, therefore, paratextual study not only promises to tell us how a text creates meaning for its consumers; it also promises to tell us how a text creates meaning in popular culture and society more generally.

"Only Hype": From Soda to Soderbergh

In creating worries, hopes, and expectations, paratexts work in a remarkably similar manner to advertisements. Ads, of course, are the pariah of the media world, and thus just as paratexts are too often discounted as "only hype," so too do ads often provoke more scorn than study. It is beyond the scope of this book to heap yet more scorn on ads. However, if we look beyond a moral evaluation of ads to see how they function semiotically, we find the same skeletal form that lies behind most paratextuality.

An ad's purpose appears simple—to sell and brand a product. As Celia Lury and Alan Warde note, ads exist in such numbers because of "a permanent source of insecurity, uncertainty and anxiety for any producer: for they cannot *force* people to buy their products and can never be sure that people who already do use them will continue to want to do so."[6] Ads must continue the ministry of consumerism, making us want to buy their products, and giving us faith in the transubstantiation that they in turn promise. However, as many critics of advertising have noted, most ads have long since graduated from the form's early days of merely listing what a product can do, and many have graduated from selling a specific product. Nike ads do not tell us that a particular line of Nike shoes pad our feet while playing sports, then let us decide whether to purchase them or not. They do not even *excitedly* tell us what their shoe is. Rather, as Sut Jhally observes, a key function of ads is often to *erase* much information of what a product is and where it came from, so that the entire history of how it came to be is a mystery: Nike's labor practices in developing countries, for instance, are neatly left out of the picture, as is even a simple description of the product. Rather, ads aim to create new, metaphysical meanings for a product, so that "once the real meaning has been systematically *emptied* out of commodities [. . .] advertising then *refills* this void with its own symbols."[7] Much advertising aims to sell products by creating brand identity and by promising value-added—product *and* metaphysics.

Nike, for instance, is famous for its ads featuring basketball stars, a hip urban drum beat in the background, and stark, edgy black backgrounds and high-quality cinematography that highlight the stars' remarkable displays of athletic prowess. As Judith Williamson explains, everything in an ad works as a gestalt and condensation of the product,[8] so that here, by being hip, edgy, and urban cool, the ad hopes to create an image of Nike shoes as hip, edgy, and urban cool. By blacking out the background, the ads suggest that sports alone matter. By frequently featuring prominent African American athletes, the company hopes to suggest that it is "all about equality"; and since public mythology holds that many such athletes began playing in housing projects in inner cities, the ads subtly celebrate these athletes' success and (Nike being the Greek goddess of victory) their victorious navigation of the American Dream. The ads also rely on a racial stereotype of blacks as being more in touch with their bodies, perhaps offering the non-black consumer the opportunity to achieve parity. Thus, the ads aim to create a brand identity, a semiotic entity called Nike that represents victory, the American Dream, equality, urban hip, sporting excellence, raw masculinity, and looking cool while winning. In doing so, they imply that by buying Nike shoes, you are stating publicly your allegiance and dedication to this image. Meanwhile, of course, Nike aims to attach itself to the public images of the stars it uses, hoping that their aura and meaning will rub off on the shoes.

As Gillian Dyer observes in her close study of the semiotics of advertising, in ads, "the meaning of one *thing* is transferred to or made interchangeable with another *quality*, whose value attaches itself to the *product*."[9] For instance, the black background (one thing) is made interchangeable with hipness and edginess (a quality), which attaches itself to the Nike shoes (the product). Effectively, then, ads create elaborate semiotic chains, which might seem to be logical in the moment of watching, but which offer no necessary correlation upon examination. To take another example, many ads for snack foods offer an image of a family in a beautiful, tidy home, yet with a hungry teenage son; usually the mother rescues the day by offering the supposedly ideal snack food, restoring perfection to the family. In such a script, the semiotic chain, "snack food brings happiness to son, which makes son happy with mother, and mother a good provider," shortens itself to "snack food equals family bliss." With such stunning sleight of hand, ads frequently add a rich layer of symbolism to any product, literally giving it meaning, rather than simply explaining the product. As such, ads are constitutive of a product's meaning. Sometimes the proposed meaning and the product's actual function are related, with the former growing organically from the latter, but this is never a necessity. When Che Guevara or Gandhi can be used to sell computers, advertisers prove themselves capable of creating a whole new slate of meanings for any product. These meanings not only work for those of us new to a product, but they also aim to continue providing meaning and value-added for longtime or return customers, so that one's already-made purchases either maintain their added meanings or gain new ones. Not all consumers will follow all ads' semiotic chains (hence the need for ever more ads), but in intent if not always in actuality, ads aim to create meaning. Or to rephrase, we could say that ads aim to make products into texts and into popular culture.

Toward this end, moreover, contemporary branding practices require much more than just ads. Just as the use of stars in ads proves especially helpful, because ads can thereby attach their product's brand identity to an already established unit of meaning, so too have advertisers long since realized the utility of attaching their brand identity to other established texts, whether individuals, events, or shows. Hence, for instance, for many years, du Maurier cigarettes sponsored the annual Montreal Jazz Festival in an attempt to "borrow" the festival's meanings. Sears prominently sponsors the "miracle work" of ABC's *Extreme Makeover: Home Edition* (2004–), in an attempt to become synonymous with good deeds, family values, great and selfless service, and a strong presence in local communities. Or, as Victoria Johnson notes of Dodge's longtime sponsorship of *The Lawrence Welk Show* (1955–71), the goal was to associate the automaker with "simple," "Heartland" values of family, community, and conservatism; as Johnson playfully notes:

> Welk's "citizen" stature as a man of tradition, community, and character was essentially defined by his denial of conspicuous personal gain in favor of a rigorous code of moral and behavioral standards. If Welk refused to play Las Vegas because it might offend some of his staunchly religious fans, must it not be the moral thing to do to drive a Dodge?[10]

In each case, the advertiser attempts to create meaning for a product or brand not at the site of the product or brand itself (i.e., not by simply making a funky cigarette, or a moral store or car, whatever they might look like), but at the site of the ad or promotional venue.

Much of the world of media hype and synergy is pure advertising and branding: posters on subways and at bus-stops and construction sites; roadside billboards; ads in newspapers or magazines; usually one ad spot out of every television commercial break; trailers and previews; "next week on . . ." snippets following television shows; appearances by stars on talk shows or entertainment news programs; interviews in industry or fan magazines; a toy promotion at a fast food chain; a new ride at an amusement park. Even revenue-generating synergy, such as a toy or clothing line, a CD or DVD, or a videogame, act as advertisements in their own right. The product in question, though, is a show, and hence a text, with or without the ad/synergy/hype. This allows advertisers to draw more deeply from the show when constructing an image of that text, as with trailers that lace together multiple scenes from a film or program, or interviews that draw on a star's already well-manicured public image. Film and television shows therefore often weigh down their paratexts more heavily than in the tabula rasa world of product advertising (where Hummer ads insist that the car is at one with the natural environment that we all know it's killing). Nevertheless, the advertiser is still faced with the same fundamental need to create a desire, hope, and expectation for the show that will convince a consumer to "purchase"/watch it. As such, hype, synergy, and promos are just as much about *creating* textuality, and about promising value-added as are ads for Nike or snack foods. As with other ads, too, they create this meaning away from the "product"/show itself. And just as the images and qualities attached to the "text" of Nike shoes by the company's ads often remain attached, so too then do the images and qualities assigned and attached to shows by their paratexts stick to them, becoming an inseparable part of "the text itself." In this way, paratexts help to make texts.

What Is a Text?

If paratexts fashion and/or act as "airlocks" to texts, what does the text itself look like? The strange merging of synergistic text with "actual" text and the resulting confusion in vocabulary of textuality demand a reappraisal of what a text is and how it works. Roland Barthes famously insisted that the text is always on the move and hence impossible to grasp or to study as a set object. Barthes drew a distinction in this respect between the *text* and the *work*. The work, he explains, "can be held in the hand," whereas "the text is held in language, only exists in the movement of a discourse," and is "*experienced only in an activity of production.*"[11] One can hold a roll of film or a tape of a television program, but that is the work alone—the *text* is only experienced in the act of consumption. However, Barthes defines this act of consumption as one of production because no text can be experienced free of the individual reader. In effect, all of us bring to bear an entire reading and life history to any act of textual consumption, so that each one of us will find different resonances in the same text. To offer an exaggerated example, when watching a war film, a person with a family member at war will likely experience a different text than will a second viewer in the middle of a fraternity's action film marathon. Thus, while the work consists of letters on a page or images on a screen, the text comes alive in the interaction between these letters or images and the reader. The text, as Barthes notes, "decants" the work and "gathers it up as play, activity, production, practice," thereby asking of its reader "a practical collaboration."[12] The magic and majesty of art rely upon the individual spark that occurs between work and reader as the reader participates in the birth of the text.

Texts make sense because of our past textual experiences, literacy, and knowledge. At a basic level, for instance, if we are new to a language, we can only decode small parts of anything that we read or hear. But fluency extends beyond mere vocabulary and grammar, to visual, imagistic, and artistic literacy and experience. As such, intertextuality—the inescapable links between texts—creates added meaning. Stories that begin with "Once Upon a Time" immediately signal their fairytale roots for those of us who have heard such stories before. Should we hear a character in a television show demand "a room of my own," if we have read Virginia Woolf's famous feminist treatise "A Room of Her Own," the demand may have added resonance. Or, should we be watching a film in which a hand-held camera is following a character by peering through foliage, a history of watching horror films will likely suggest that the character is being stalked, and that the camera's "eyes" are those of the predator. Language, images, and texts never come to us in a vacuum; instead, as Valentin Volosinov notes, "*The utterance is a social phenomenon,*" for each shard of textuality or meaning comes to us in a given context. "Any utterance—the finished, written utterance not excepted—makes response to something and is calculated to be responded to in turn. It is but one link in a continuous chain of speech performances. Each monument carries on the work of its predecessors, polemicizing with them, expecting active, responsive understanding, and anticipating such understanding in return."[13] This means not only that texts talk back to and revise other texts, either implicitly or explicitly calling for us to connect their meanings to previous texts, but also that we will always make sense of texts partly through the frames offered by other texts.

Much intertextuality is random, entailing links that an artist could never have predicted. Indeed, much communication is chaotic: change channels from a news item about a rise in local crime to a channel that is advertising home security systems, and the former text may handily intensify the effect of the latter. Or turn from the cannibal-serial-killer film *Silence of the Lambs* (1991) to a hamburger ad and one may be repulsed. But much intertextuality is intentional too. Michael Riffaterre in particular writes of intertextuality as a means by which writers "guarantee" that readers will come to the same meaning. He argues that all texts rely upon other texts for their meaning and value, so that "the most important component of a literary work of art, and indeed the key to the interpretation of its significance, should be found outside that work, beyond its margins, in the intertext," the recovery of which "is an imperative and inevitable process."[14] Riffaterre's faith in intertextuality as conditioning and guaranteeing the "proper interpretation"[15] is unrealistic, holding out for a world of perfectly informed readers. Similarly, his inability to recognize the disruptive force of invasive or corruptive intertextuality underplays the multiple roles that intertextuality plays in the reading process, as I will discuss shortly. Nevertheless, he is correct to point out the degree to which intertextuality can act both as a constraint upon reading and as a guide for interpretation. Character names, in particular, often offer intertextual "guides" on how to read a text, as do ways of filming, mise-en-scène, generic codes, and the like. Surfing through television channels, then, many of us need only a few seconds, if that, to determine a text's genre, as many subtle and overt clues—film stock, mode of acting, use of color, rhythm of dialogue, and so on—immediately make sense to us based on our past viewing.

As Michael Iampolski spells out, to understand and to recognize "is to place what you see alongside what you know, alongside what has already been."[16] Thus our reading of any text is illuminated by potentially thousands of texts that have "already been," each intertext serving as a different energy source, and the shape and nature of the resulting text for any given individual will depend upon from where the energy comes. If, then, "any text is constructed as a mosaic of quotations,"[17] Iampolski (echoing Barthes) notes, "only the viewer or reader can unite the text, using his [sic] cultural memory to make it one."[18] The text is the consequence of the meeting of work and reader, but each work and each reader will bring multiple intertexts that energize and animate the text.

Such a process risks sounding wholly individual, as indeed all interpretation is open to personal nuances, quirks, and redirections. Within the field of textual studies, Stanley Fish is most notorious for espousing his belief in personalized texts, as his reader response theory allows for readers *in theory* to imprint any meaning upon a text that they desire. However, Fish argues that *in practice*, reading and interpretation are limited by context and by "interpretive communities." "I want to argue for, not against, the normal, the ordinary, the literal, the straightforward [interpretation], and so on," he notes, "but I want to argue for them as the products of contextual or interpretive circumstances and not as the property of an acontextual language," so that "the category 'in the text,' like 'the ordinary' [interpretation], is always full [. . .], but what fills it is not always the same."[19] To Fish, context determines interpretation, so that, for instance, he recalls the radically different interpretations that two of his classes—one an early English religious poetry class, the other a literary theory class—made of the same string of names on the blackboard. Fish sees interpretation as constrained; the constraints, though, "do not inhere in language but in situations, and because they inhere in situations, the constraints we are always under are not always the same ones."[20] In effect, he crowns context as king, and precisely because context of interpretation will often be shared by others, readings will tend not to be random and wholly individualistic. Rather, Fish proposes the "interpretive community" as the prime filter for reading, a group of similarly minded (or contextualized) individuals whose strategies for interpretation "exist prior to the act of reading and therefore determine the shape of what is read rather than, as is usually assumed, the other way around."[21] When a text seemingly has one meaning, to Fish this only means that one interpretive community is dominant, effectively controlling the context of reception, setting the terms by which any reader will approach the text.

Fish's siren rhetoric is wonderfully seductive, but he is guilty of overstatement. In particular, one is left wondering how interpretive communities form, or how one moves from one to another, if not through language, and if not, therefore, through textuality. His reading schematic is also considerably more acceptable when contemplating a single text; when a singular interpretive community is met with a second text, producing a different meaning, the schematic proves unsuccessful in attributing all meaning to the act of reading alone. Surely texts contribute to their meaning in some way. Nevertheless, having slipped out of Fish's trap, we could still take away a better appreciation of the utter importance of context, and of how interpretive communities with set reading strategies exert considerable pressure upon the reading process. For all the problems with Fish's theorization of textuality, therefore, his work still insists that we regard readers as often ready for texts before they encounter them and, not only as individuals but as groups, as predisposed to find or create certain interpretations.

Moreover, if we reintegrate Fish's interest in context and interpretive communities with a belief in texts as having something to say in and of themselves, we can examine the role that texts and paratexts play in constructing the contexts and interpretive communities that will be activated when interpreting other texts. As such, intertextuality can be directed. Here, Laurent Jenny offers that if, following Ferdinand de Saussure's linguistics, *langue* is the system and rules of a language and *parole* is the given utterance, through intertextuality other texts can create a "super-parole" as the meanings and context-setting apparatus of other texts encircle the text at hand.[22] Jenny writes of arguably the most obvious instance of such directed intertextuality: parody. As I have examined elsewhere, parody works as a form of "critical intertextuality" that aims precisely to bump a text or genre's meaning-making process off its self-declared trajectory.[23] Works such as *The Simpsons* or *South Park* (1997–) thus gouge at all manner of traditional family sitcom rules, so that subsequent viewings of *Full House* (1987–95) or other similar happy-happy sitcoms renders them all the more obviously artificial and saccharine. *The Daily Show with Jon Stewart* (1999–) and *The Colbert Report* (2005–) teach a form of news literacy that sets itself up on the perimeter of news discourse, so that subsequent exposure to the news may be recontextualized. In Jenny's words, the author of such parody works in order "to encircle [the parodic target], to enclose [it] within another discourse, thus rendered more powerful. He [*sic*] speaks in order to obliterate, to cancel. Or else, patiently, he gainsays in order to go beyond."[24] More than simply speaking to individual viewers, successful parody has also proven remarkably adept at networking and encouraging interpretive communities to build around it.[25]

Parody is certainly the most overt and flashy instance of directed intertextuality, yet it is a small subset of a much larger universe of texts and paratexts that refer to other texts and, in so doing, set up reading filters and create interpretive communities. For an example of a particularly successful para-/inter-textual network, Tony Bennett and Janet Woollacott offer the case of James Bond, a figure who exists across films, books, merchandise, and ads. Each of these sites of Bond, they note, work as "textual meteorites, highly condensed and materialised chunks of meaning."[26] These meteorites orbit any interaction we might have with another Bond text, so that we approach the text with a sense of who and what Bond is; via the pre-existing para-/inter-textual network of Bond, we will always arrive at any new Bond text with a sense of what to expect, and with the interpretation process already well under way. Bennett and Woollacott see no need to reduce text to context, as does Fish, but they do argue that when texts such as any new Bond film are made sense of by first moving through the dense collection of intertexts and paratexts, we must therefore "rethink the concept of context such that, ultimately, neither text nor context are conceivable as entities separable from one another."[27] In other words, as much as we may still use terms such as "text," "intertext," and "paratext" for analytical purposes, in fact intertext and paratext are always constitutive parts of the text itself.

Getting into a Program: Entryway Paratexts

James Bond presents an especially rich example of para-/inter-textuality, given his appearance in multiple movies, books, and ads over the last fifty years. However, every text has paratexts. As Bennett and Woollacott also show, the para-/inter-textual network surrounding Bond works in two key ways: (1) not only will our history of Bond serve as an airlock into the world of any new Bond text, but in turn, (2) Bond is always open for re-decoding, for any new text or paratext can re-inflect our notion of who and what Bond in general is. Therefore, as noted earlier, we can divide paratexts crudely, and for analytical purposes alone, into those that control and determine our *entrance* to a text—*entryway paratexts*—and those that inflect or redirect the text following initial interaction—*in medias res paratexts*. I will now turn to instances of the former, so that we might see paratexts in action; later in the chapter, I will return to instances of the latter, thereby developing a notion of textual phenomenology.

One of the more detailed accounts of paratextuality—though not using that term—can be found in Jason Mittell's *Genre and Television*. Mittell seeks to illustrate how genre is created as much outside of generic texts as within them, arguing that "we need to look outside of texts to locate the range of sites in which genres operate, change, proliferate, and die out."[28] Mittell therefore charts how advertising, policy, patterns of exhibition, public talk, and so forth all position a genre, as do "trade press coverage, popular press coverage, critical reviews, promotional material, other cultural representations and commodities (like merchandise, media tie-ins, and parodies), corporate and personal documents, production manuals, legal and government materials, audience remnants, and oral histories."[29] For instance, he notes that cartoons began their televisual life as texts that appealed to adults too; however, over time, public discourse surrounding cartoons penned them into a kids-only category that, although challenged by texts such as *The Simpsons*, still inflects how many people react to and consume cartoons. Elsewhere in his book, he charts how audience talk about talk shows delimits their boundaries in popular culture, especially since much of this talk originates from those who do not watch talk shows, or who watch small amounts, and is therefore not simply reactive to "the show itself." Genre serves an important duty in the interpretive process, of course, because it acts much as I have said paratexts do, by providing an initial context and reading strategy for the text—so that, for instance, if we see cartoons as a children's genre, we will be more startled by crude adult humor in a cartoon than in a Judd Apatow comedy. But Mittell shows that paratexts play a considerable role in establishing genre, and hence that they control our interactions with and interpretations of texts. If genres are, as Stephen Neale notes, "systems of orientations, expectations and conventions that circulate between industry, text and subject,"[30] paratexts form much of this realm of the "between," a realm through which we must travel in order to consume and make sense of a text.

Paratexts can also be seen to establish themselves around the interpretive perimeter of an entire medium. Highly illustrative here is Lynn Spigel's examination of the role that women's magazines played in establishing attitudes toward television in its early days. Spigel shows how ads and columns in magazines such as *Better Homes and Gardens, American Home*, and *House Beautiful* acted as arbiters of taste with regards to television's place in the home.[31] Not only would they dictate where one should place one's television, but what one should be careful of and how one should use it. Manufacturers proposed that the television was a new member of the family, and these magazine paratexts offered instruction on how we should treat this relative. Certainly such lessons and moral guidelines remain prevalent today, as all media are surrounded by cautionary tales, "Best of" lists, enthusiastic ads, published effects studies, and a whole host of other paratexts that aim to delineate how we should or should not use such media. Whether these take the form of ads for home entertainment systems that encourage us to create a home fortress based around our televisions,[32] or whether they take the form of conservative commentary on the liberal, immoral, anti–family values narratives that supposedly pervade film and television, paratexts draw many of the battle lines that surround media consumption. Beyond instruction on how to consume a given text or genre, they at least attempt to create entire interpretive communities and hermeneutic recipes for daily living in a media-saturated world.

As in the case of parody, some paratexts work as critical intertexts, actively trying either to deflect readers from certain texts or to infect their reading when it occurs. Reviews from journalists and/or religious or political figures are often obvious examples of critical paratexts. Martin Barker, Jane Arthurs, and Ramaswami Harindranth, for instance, chart the effect that British moral panic regarding David Cronenberg's *Crash* (1996) had on viewers.[33] Cronenberg's film focuses on a group of individuals who become sexually aroused by car crashes, and when news of the film broke in England, several prominent politicians and newspaper columnists campaigned for it to be banned, thinking it perverse and dangerous. Interestingly, many of those who fought for a ban never watched the film; rather, they allowed the paratext of a small plot summary and/or descriptions of individual scenes to stand in for the text as a whole. But as Barker, Arthurs, and Harindranath show through careful qualitative audience research, the media circus that surrounded the text worked as its own critical paratextuality, inflecting the reading of the text for those who did watch it. Many of the research participants found it hard to look beyond the critical paratextuality, or to find alternative frames for viewing, to the point that the media circus and paratextuality virtually took over the text for many viewers. Even those who refused to precode the film as depraved often wanted to watch the film just to see what all the fuss was about, and hence still with a firm, controlled interest in the violent, sexual content. As the authors write of such a viewing position, "to go to see *Crash* to check if it is 'violent' or 'sensationalist' is not like looking to see if there is water in the kettle. It importantly *prefigures* how [viewers] prepare to watch it."[34] Similarly, we might observe that following the controversy regarding *Passion of the Christ* in the United States, few viewers could watch it without particular attention drawn to whether it was anti-Semitic or not, or a devotional text or not, following the critical paratextuality that, respectively, the Anti-Defamation League and prominent church figures threw around the text. Or, as Janet Staiger observes, given reviews and commentary on D. W. Griffith's *Birth of a Nation* (1915), few viewers can approach it expecting anything other than racist propaganda;[35] due to critical paratextuality, its racism has almost subsumed the text before one can even watch it.

Paratexts can also inflect certain parts of a media text or certain characters. David Buckingham notes, for instance, how the knowledge of an *East Enders* (1985–) cast member's past criminal record hit the press in England. The actor played a villain on the show, but knowledge of his life behind bars contributed to the tabloid press naming him "Dirty Den" and to their construction of him as a folk devil. For any viewer aware of the press commentary, Den's villainy was potentially amplified and made to seem all the more realistic and authentic.[36] As C. Lee Harrington and Denise Bielby insist, the daytime press has long played an important role for soap operas. Soap opera magazines and news frequently announce storylines before they occur, sometimes testing the waters for fan reactions, or allowing viewers to "catch up" on what they missed. Moreover, "by rendering the subculture [of soap fandom] visible and accessible both to itself and to outsiders, the daytime press contributes in important ways to defining the boundaries of the subculture and to managing those boundaries,"[37] hence playing a key role in the construction of interpretive communities for soap viewing. In such instances, paratexts can amplify and/ or clarify many of a text's meanings and uses, establishing the role that a text and its characters play outside the boundaries of the show, in the everyday realities of viewers' and non-viewers' lives.

Soap magazines may direct criticism toward texts, but they also provide an example of what we could call *supportive intertextuality*. As innovative and as semiotically active as parody and criticism may be, many paratexts reinforce a text's meaning or otherwise set up a welcoming perimeter. Here we reach the realm proper of hype and synergy. To take the average animated Disney film, for instance, before release, the film has usually been preceded by an army of plush toys, coloring books, watches, bedspreads, and action figures. It will likely have been advertised during a hit Saturday-morning kids' show, and McDonalds or some other fast food company will have released a specially themed "Happy Meal." Thus, the movie suggests fun and good things to children—it is associated with cuddly toys, playtime, good television shows, and sugary food. Meanwhile, of course, the average Disney marketing campaign so heavily populates the kid universe with film-related merchandise that any given child could understandably feel as though "everyone" is watching the film. Ultimately, then, when it works, Disney paratextuality creates a well-fashioned image of all that the film represents, and it exhorts the child to watch the film. Writing of such instances, Robert Allen states that "a film is no longer reducible to the actual experience of seeing it"—as if it ever was!—as this paratextuality not only precedes the act of watching, but feeds into, conditions, and becomes part of that act. The toys, burgers, and so on are now *part of the text*. Allen even suggests that in such a paratextual/synergistic marketplace, films are often no longer the text in the first place, but rather "the inedible part of a Happy Meal" and the "movie on the lunchbox."[38] When Disney might make several hundred dollars' worth of product sales off a single young consumer, compared to the child's paltry five dollars at the box office, we might be foolish to see the film as ipso facto the "primary text." Allen is hyperbolically fatalistic in declaring that cinema has died and that "it is now time to write the last chapter of the history of Hollywood cinema and its audience,"[39] but the Disney hype and synergy machine nevertheless illustrates the increasingly hazy boundaries between primary and secondary textuality, or between text and paratext, boundaries that we will return to in chapter 6.

Disney is quite exceptional in the degree to which its paratexts fill stores and lives, but many other companies have followed its lead, resulting in the heavy population of the world with paratexts. Quite simply, in a cluttered media environment, all texts need paratexts, if only to announce the text's presence. Thus, media corporations are investing ever more time, energy, and capital into producing previews and spinoff merchandise, into public relations tours that get their cast and crew on anything from *Entertainment Tonight* (1981–) to *The Late Show with David Letterman* (1993–) to guest appearances on reality shows, into creative marketing campaigns (such as when *Lost* announced its forthcoming arrival on television by covering a beach with ads in bottles), into inviting the press to preview screenings, into plugging their texts for Oscars, Golden Globes, or Emmys, and into various other traditional and non-traditional forms of hype and synergy. Paratextuality is a vital part of the media business, precisely because paratexts play the key role in determining if a text will sink or swim. The public, the press, and the industry regularly evaluate movies based on opening weekend box office draw alone, for, as Tad Friend notes, "If a film doesn't find its audience the first weekend, exhibitors pull it from their best theatres, and eventual television-licensing fees and DVD sales fall correspondingly."[40] Many network heads, too, will cancel a new television show after only two episodes. As such, the industry desperately needs its paratexts to work, since both industry and audiences habitually count on paratexts' relative success or failure as an index to the success or failure of the text as a whole. Moreover, while paratexts have surrounded all media throughout history, as Hollywood grows fonder of franchises and multi-platform brands or characters, yet more paratexts are being produced. Simultaneously, though, with all sorts of random paratextual or intertextual collisions threatening the encoded meanings of texts, and with devious and critical paratexts or intertexts working to hijack their meaning-making processes, the industry requires a strong frontline of paratexts. A continuing question for this book, therefore, will be the degree to which paratexts overtake and subsume their texts, and the conditions under which they do so.

"We Interrupt This Broadcast": Paratexts In Medias Res

Paratexts do not merely control our entrance to texts, and thus as much as Genette's metaphor of paratexts as airlocks is evocative of some of their functions, its utility is limited. After all, many paratexts are encountered after "entering" the text. For instance, using the term and metaphor of "overflow," Will Brooker writes of how numerous contemporary television series are accompanied by clothing lines, websites, CDs, and fan discussion forums. Speaking of his own interaction with one such series, the short-lived BBC program *Attachments* (2000–2002), he writes:

> After watching the episode where Soph is punished by her boss for her article "Hell is Other People Shagging," I went to the seethru.co.uk website, which treats Soph and her colleagues as "real" people, with no mention of BBC2 or *Attachments*. On the front page I was able to read the full article, which could only be glimpsed in the actual episode. I then took part in a quiz compiled by Reece, the series' womanizing programmer, and sent a semi-ironic mail to the character pointing out that he'd misspelled a *Star Wars* reference.[41]

He goes on to ask: "At what point, then, did the show 'end' for me? Technically, I stopped watching television at 9.45 pm, but I was engaging with the characters and narrative of the show for at least an hour afterwards, even to the point of sending a mail to a non-existent programmer."[42] As such, Brooker proposes the notion of "overflow," evoking an image of a text that is too full, too large for its own body, necessitating the spillover of textuality into paratexts. As much as synergy attempts to capture audiences' attention and bring them to the show, much modern synergy is best understood as offering value-added, rather than simply announcing the show's presence. Brooker points to the notable example of *Dawson's Creek* (1998–2003), which while in active production had an elaborate official website via which viewers could navigate to the title character's computer desktop (even reading his email) and that linked to a website for the show's fictional university. American Eagle and J. Crew sold clothes worn by the cast. Each episode ended with information on how to buy the music played throughout the episode. And fan discussion forums ran 24/7, allowing critical, laudatory, or other talk by viewers.

Dawson's Creek led the way at the time but has since been eclipsed by shows such as *Lost* with alternate reality games, podcasts, spinoff novels written by characters from the show, and "mobisode" mini-episodes filmed for mobile phone or Internet distribution, for instance, by *Heroes* (2006–), with a supplementary online comic book and other transmedia initiatives (see chapter 6), and by countless other shows' variously innovative or derivative "overflow" techniques. And while Brooker's metaphor of "overflow" might suggest a movement *away from* "the show itself," Henry Jenkins refers to such multi-platformed media texts as "convergence," suggesting a grand *confluence* of media texts and platforms under the broad heading of the single text. Jenkins's recent book, *Convergence Culture: Where Old and New Media Collide*, charts the proliferation of many such franchised, convergent texts. For instance, he examines how *The Matrix* (1999) gave birth not only to two sequels, but to anime spinoffs (collected in the DVD *The Animatrix* [2003]), comic books, and a videogame that were authored either in part by or in coordination with the Wachowskis, so that the *Matrix* narrative weaved through various platforms. Meanwhile, fans create their own paratexts, writing fan fiction, making fan songs and films, and, as Jenkins notes, even staging fully costumed re-enactments of scenes from *The Matrix* and other media texts in certain Japanese parks.[43]

Rather than choose between metaphors of "overflow" or "convergence," I find the ebb and flow suggested by employing both terms indicative of the multiple ways in which many media texts are now both moving outward yet incorporating other texts inward, being authored across media. Between the outward overflow and inward convergence of paratextuality, we see the beating heart of the text.

What, though, are we to make of such paratexts presented in medias res, and what control do they have over the text? To answer this, we must move away from questions of textual ontology—what *is* the text?—to questions of textual phenomenology—how does the text *happen*? In particular, we can turn to the textual theory of Wolfgang Iser and to Stanley Fish's "Affective Stylistics" period that preceded his above-mentioned theoretical excesses. Both writers insisted on the importance of studying a text as it happens, from sentence to sentence, page to page. Fish argued that we as analysts too often interpret the text as a whole, hence forgetting how it developed and took form in the act of reading.[44] He wrote of literature as "kinetic," in that it moves, and "does not lend itself to a static interpretation because it refuses to stay still and doesn't let you stay still either." He further reasoned that readers respond not only to a finished utterance, but rather to the "temporal flow" of a text: "That is, in an utterance of any length, there is a point at which the reader has taken in only the first word, and then the second, and then the third, and so on, and the report of what happens to the reader is always a report of what has happened *to that point*" (emphasis added).[45] Iser too was interested in how sequent sentences act upon one another, and in how texts leave "gaps" between sentences and ideas that readers must fill in, producing an ebb and flow (a beating heart?) of anticipation, retrospection, and accumulation, an "experience [that] comes about through a process of continual modification."[46] "Every moment of reading," he notes, "is a dialectic of protension and retention, conveying a future horizon yet to be occupied, along with a past (and continually fading) horizon already filled; the wandering viewpoint carves its passage through both at the same time and leaves them to merge together in its wake." Meaning arises, he argues, out of the process of "actualization,"[47] in the act of reading, and both he and Fish point to the active nature of texts—they are experiences, not just monuments, and so our interpretation of a text must occur as itself an experience, not in a lightning-strike moment of sense-making.

For television series in particular, the ramifications of a phenomenological approach to interpretation are profound.[48] Many shows take years to play out from supposed start to finish, and thus the televisual equivalent of the moment between pages in a book may be a week between episodes, or a summer hiatus. However, it would be ludicrous to think that we simply tuck away our interpretive efforts into small corners of our brains, waiting until after the series finale to make sense of a text. Rather, we constantly interpret as we go along. Furthermore, television shows give us significant time between episodes to interpret them, and so we will often make sense of them away from the work itself, in the moments between exhibition. As we have seen, though, these moments, or what Iser would call "gaps," are often filled with paratexts: as Brooker's narrative above illustrates, we might go online and read others' opinions of a show, we might consume tie-in merchandise, or we might consume any number of other paratexts.[49] Consequently, just as paratexts can inflect our interpretations of texts as we enter them, so too can they inflect our *re-entry* to television texts. For texts that destabilize any one media platform as central, each platform serves as a paratext for the others. Since our process of textual "actualization" remains open with most television series, paratexts are free to invade the meaning-making process. Especially, too, since many serial programs leave us wondering what will happen next, frustrating the narrative delivery system by dragging it out over multiple years, many viewers will actively look for clues in producers' paratexts regarding what will happen next. Of course, a similar process occurs in serial films, so that, for instance, Brooker charts the debates and discussions among *Star Wars* fans about the films' many paratexts (games, novels, comics, etc.) as to what entails the "canon," or the accepted *Star Wars* universe.[50]

With an increasing number of television and film serial texts opening up what Matt Hills dubs "endlessly deferred hyperdiegesis"[51]—huge, seemingly never-ending plotlines—and set in elaborate textual universes, we might expect both the frustrations of wanting to know what will happen, and the experience of a text as comprising much more than just the show, to increase markedly. Such cult texts invite their viewers in and give their imaginations acres of space in which to roam, and it is this openness that often proves most attractive to many viewers. Thus, these texts seemingly welcome in all manner of other texts and paratexts to delineate small portions of the universe, plotline, thematics, and characterization.

Arguably the most clear-cut example of an in medias res paratext at work is the "last week on . . . " or "previously on . . . " segments that precede many television serials. Such segments usually consist of a carefully edited fifteen- to thirty-second sequence of images and plot-points from previous episodes, designed to give audiences necessary backstory. For new viewers, these segments clearly serve as entryway paratexts, but they also act as reminders for returning viewers, designed to focus attention on specific actions, themes, or issues. Thus, for instance, if two characters are best friends, and yet five weeks ago we learned that one has betrayed the other, the "previously on . . . " segment will likely replay the moment of revelation only if this information is seen as pertinent to the current episode. Should the betrayed friend return the betrayal in this episode, the absence of a "previously on . . . " tip-off may result in us judging him negatively, whereas with the tip-off, we are more likely to understand or even forgive his actions. Beyond "previously on . . . " segments, though, *all* in medias res paratexts work in a similar way, offering frames through which we can interpret the text at hand, and subtly or radically inflecting our reading accordingly. In effect, they build themselves into the text, becoming inseparable from it, buoys floating in the overflow of a serial text that direct our passage through that text.

Serial television programs and films are not unique in being vulnerable to paratextual influence. Rather, all films and television programs can be jostled by paratexts, whether we have "finished" reading them or not. As is especially evident in the case of serial television texts, each of us carries with us thousands of open texts that can be re-decoded and re-inflected at any point in their progression, whether this be one episode into a three-hundred-episode run or fifty years following the watching of a film. Of the latter instance, Annette Kuhn's work with "enduring fans" of 1930s films is illustrative. Kuhn interviewed numerous women in their seventies who still enjoyed watching and talking about the films and stars of their twenties, and who still found new meanings in them. She argues, "For the enduring fan, the cinema-going past is no foreign country but something continuously reproduced as a vital aspect of daily life in the present." As these women grew older, watched different films, and gained new experiences, they were able to return to their beloved texts with new interpretive strategies or nuances, hence keeping the texts alive and active for decades. "As the text is appropriated and used by enduring fans, further layers of inter-textual and extra-textual memory-meaning continuously accrue."[52]

Since intertextuality works by placing the text at hand into a conversation with previously viewed texts, not only will earlier-viewed texts be able to talk to a current text—the current text will also be able to talk *back to* earlier texts. We may well find, then, that many years, months, days, or minutes after we thought we had finished with a text, it is once more active, and we are once more consuming, decoding, and making sense of it. Such is the case with, for instance, many texts that we watched as children rather naïvely, only to learn of deeper nuances later in life, and such is potentially the case with any text that we find reason to think about, rewatch, or reference "after" consumption. As Mikhail Bakhtin ended his last-known article, in words poetically befitting the close of the great intertextual theorist's career:

> There is neither a first word nor a last word. The contents of dialogue are without limit. They extend into the deepest past and into the most distant future. Even meanings born in dialogues of the remotest past will never finally be grasped once and for all, for they will always be renewed in later dialogue. At any present moment of the dialogue there are great masses of forgotten meanings, but these will be recalled again at a given moment in the dialogue's later course when it will be given new life. For nothing is absolutely dead: every meaning will someday have its homecoming festival.[53] The intertextual dialogue and life of texts remains perpetually open.

If the notion of a paratext changing our understanding of a text "after the fact" sounds odd, we might think again of the analogy of product branding. Throughout their lifespan, many prominent brands have engaged in rebranding attempts, so that, for instance, McDonalds' move from their "You Deserve a Break Today" campaign to their current "I'm Lovin' It" campaign toggles the brand's semiotics without any discernible change in the product whatsoever: the paratext of the campaign has aimed to change the text of McDonalds. Or, for another analogy, we might think of the construction and telling of history, wherein despite the seeming immutability of a past event, each retelling of the story can ascribe different symbolic value to it. Even the day after an event, one will often find stark differences in how that event is reported and framed from, say, CNN to Fox News to *Daily Kos* to a non-American source. "Anniversary journalism" will later, in all likelihood, assign new meaning to the event,[54] and with the benefit of hindsight, history books in years to come may reframe the event yet again: "every meaning will someday have its homecoming festival." In other words, each invocation of a moment in history can paratextually rewrite the text of the event, since, at the moment of the telling, the "text" is only accessible through the "paratext." *The Onion* humorously illustrates this process of the infinite reassigning of value in a parodic article about the sinking of the Titanic, entitled "World's Largest Metaphor Sinks,"[55] tipping its hat to the endless narrativizations of exactly what the ship and its sinking (the "text") represented that have proliferated since the fateful event.

With texts alive interminably, forever open to toggling, paratexts may always work in medias res. Especially thoughtful reviews may cause us to reflect once more upon an already-seen film or television program; academic articles and close readings may open up whole new realms of texts for us; toys or games might place a text in a whole new setting, bit by bit shifting our understanding of it; and so forth. In other words, there is never a point in time at which a text frees itself from the contextualizing powers of paratextuality.

Wear the T-Shirt, Skip the Film: Paratextual Superiority

Nevertheless, paratexts sometimes take over their texts. A child can, for instance, eat the Disney movie Happy Meal, buy the toys and the coloring books, and play the game with his or her friends without actually watching the film. Similarly, some fans recount the experience of falling more heavily for a text's fan discussion site than for the text itself. If today's television and film paratextuality extends the horizons of the narrative universe well beyond what "the text itself" offers, surely some audience members will find that the universe is more interesting at its horizons. In such cases, these audience members may still consider themselves fans or at least viewers of the text, but here rather than simply modify or inflect the text, the paratexts may in time *become* the text, as the audience members take their cues regarding what a text means from the paratext's images, signs, symbols, and words, rather than from the film or program's. As analysts, we might be tempted to think of the paratexts here as mere residue, or a long shadow, of the show, but individual audience members may not care to make the distinction between paratext and show. Precisely because the language of "paratextuality" is absent from everyday talk of film and television, and because the desire to delineate exactly what is and is not "the text" is often an analyst's alone, not an average audience member's, frequently we may find that audience talk of and reaction to a text may have originated with the paratext, yet been integrated into the individual audience member's conception of "the text itself."

Shunning the text in favor of the paratext may appear a somewhat anomalous practice, but as we have said, any given individual speculatively consumes thousands of texts over the course of his or her life. We cannot watch every show in order to choose what we would prefer to watch, and thus, by force of necessity, we all regularly allow paratexts to stand in for texts. As I have written elsewhere, non-fan and anti-fan texts in particular are often only partially consumed, therefore shifting the burden of textuality to the paratext.[56] *If* all paratexts were accurate depictions of their related texts, and *if* no paratexts introduced any meaning other than those meanings which are in the related shows, paratexts would be unremarkable. However, since paratexts have, as I have argued and as the remaining chapters will show, considerable power to amplify, reduce, erase, or add meaning, much of the textuality that exists in the world is paratext-driven.

2

Coming Soon!

Hype, Intros, and Textual Beginnings

Academic and popular accounts of film and television are frequently suffused with discussion of what happens *after* watching, following such questions as "What did you think of such-and-such a show?", "What effects might it have?", and "What does it mean?" The social science tradition of studying media has also produced considerable work examining what happens *before* watching, with, for instance, a strand of "uses and gratifications" research that studies the motivating factors behind one's choice to watch, and another strand of production studies and political economy that explores the creative and economic processes that go into creating media. But comparatively little work exists from within a humanistic tradition examining how meaning begins and where *texts* come from, suggesting by its absence that texts begin when the first scene of a film or program begins. A refreshing exception is Charles Acland's reading of multiplex geographies, construction, and contexts.[1] Exploring similar terrain for television (and for films on television), Barbara Klinger has also examined the geography of the home theater.[2] As important as such work is, and as much as it reminds us of the paratexts of geography and technology, in this chapter I argue that films and television programs often begin long before we actively seek them out, and that their textual histories are every bit as complex and requiring of study as are their audience, creative, or economic histories. This chapter is thus about the true beginnings of texts as coherent clusters of meaning, expectation, and engagement, and about the text's first initial outposts, in particular trailers, posters, previews, and hype.

As was discussed in the Introduction, Hollywood invests large amounts of money, time, and labor into hyping its products. Therefore, just as one would not expect Nike to construct its ads half-heartedly, there should in theory be nothing random or accidental about the meanings on offer in

Hollywood's trailers, posters, previews, and ad campaigns. Clint Culpep-
per, president of Sony Screen Gems, warns, "You can have the most ter-
rific movie in the world, and if you can't convey that fact in fifteen- and
thirty-second TV ads it's like having bad speakers on a great stereo."[3] As a
result, DreamWorks' head of creative advertising David Sameth has said
of trailers, "We'll spend five months to a year obsessing about them, every
single cut and every single moment we use,"[4] showing how carefully man-
icured many texts' ads are. In a rare academic account of trailers, meanwhile, John Ellis writes of them as offering a "narrative image" in which
everything can be assumed to be there for a reason, and "can be assumed
to be calculated. Hence everything tends to be pulled into the process
of meaning."[5] Rather than regard trailers, previews, and ads as textually
removed from the shows they announce, therefore, Ellis suggests, albeit
briefly, that they are *part of* the show's narrative, and that they are concentrates of the show's meaning. Precisely because trailers, previews, and
ads introduce us to a text and its many proposed and supposed meanings,
the promotional material that we consume sets up, begins, and *frames*
many of the interactions that we have with texts. More than merely point
us to the text at hand, these promos will have already begun the process
of creating textual meaning, serving as the first outpost of interpretation.
Promos often take the first steps in filling a text with meaning. The term
"trailer" is a hold-over from when trailers followed films, but in today's
media environment, movies and television shows are trailing the trailers
and promos in months not minutes, slowly plodding forth while meanings, interpretations, evaluations, and all manner of audience and industry chatter are already on the scene. We may in time resist the meanings
proposed by promotional materials, but they tell us what to expect, direct
our excitement and/or apprehension, and begin to tell us what a text is
all about, calling for our identification with and interpretation of that text
before we have even seemingly arrived at it. This chapter will examine
how texts begin, not in their opening scenes, but in their hype, promos,
trailers, posters, previews, and opening credit sequences, and how these
paratexts may continue to figure into the interpretive process even after
the film or television show has started.

I will begin by discussing the role of promotional campaigns and trailers in initiating textuality, creating a genre, networking star intertexts, and
introducing us to a new storyworld. This discussion leads into examina-
tions of several movie posters and their initiation of their texts, and of
a 2006 promotional campaign for ABC's *Six Degrees*. Looking at a New

York subway poster campaign and at the show's advance teaser website, I will argue that both set up a gender, a genre, a style, and an attitude for the show before it hit the air. This pre-text was not a wholly accurate reflection of the television program that followed, and so too is my next case study one in which the paratext and the show itself failed to work in concert with one another. Close-reading two trailers for Atom Egoyan's film *The Sweet Hereafter*, I examine how one film can "begin" in such starkly different ways depending upon the trailer that precedes it. Then, following this example, I ask what we are to make of the rise of trailers and hype, and of their increasing prominence on television and online in particular, especially given that, as I will argue, they play a constitutive role in establishing a "proper" interpretation for a text. This interest in "proper" interpretations finally leads to a discussion of television opening credit sequences as paratexts that can operate both as entryway and in medias res, telling us how to interpret a text, and then returning to remind us of this official, sanctioned interpretation, and serving a ritual purpose of transporting us once more into that storyworld. Throughout the chapter, my interests lie in where texts come from and how we return to them.

Hype, Promos, and Trailers: "A Cinema of (Coming) Attractions"

Trailers and previews have rarely warranted much attention from media studies critics, except as yet more advertising. But Hollywood takes them very seriously, and so it should. If we consider that most films make over a third of their box office in their opening week,[6] and since high opening-week box office figures have a compounding effect, giving rise to further hype to bring in audiences for the rest of a film's run, we cannot underestimate the importance of a good trailer to the film industry. If a film triumphs in its opening week, good promos will have played a significant role in this victory. Thus, on average, movie studios will budget $10 million per film for producing the marketing, even before adding triple that figure on ad buys.[7] Some even hire multiple agencies to compete with each other for the best trailer.[8] Meanwhile, the television industry similarly dedicates large amounts of money, time, and labor to hyping its shows. Especially in late summer, before the new television season begins, many cities are covered with various forms of advertising, as entire public transportation systems and roadways seem to be sponsored by the networks, newspapers garner full-page ads for new shows, and stars do the rounds of the talk show circuit. As with film, previews prove remarkably important for a television show's tentative early weeks: many seasons have seen shows canceled after only two or three episodes, when Nielsen ratings are more effectively measuring how many viewers the promos attracted than how interesting the show is in and of itself.

The lone book-length study of film trailers, Lisa Kernan's *Coming Attractions*, opens on the note that trailers are "a unique form of narrative film exhibition, wherein promotional discourse and narrative pleasure are conjoined." Playing with Tom Gunning's famous discussion of a cinema of attractions,[9] Kernan notes that trailers are "a cinema of (coming) attractions."[10] As with all promos, they are ads, but they are also a taste test of films to come, offering some of a film's first pleasures, meanings, and ideas. Film fans have long enjoyed arriving early at the cinema in order to catch a glimpse of what movies to expect a month or season from now. Trailers have thus become an important part of the cinema-going experience and ritual, serving as the transitional, liminal device that navigates us from a loud theater with unruly teens, over-affectionate lovers, and people on their cell phones, to a world of celluloid dreams and spectatorial, narrative pleasures. Trailers announce and introduce the film that follows them by announcing the wonders of the medium in general, and they bring to a head the joys of anticipation, like the opening orchestral hum before a live performance. All the while, they help to reinforce cinema-going as a repetitive event,[11] promising that yet another voyage to the world of dreams awaits, and that though you are watching such-and-such a movie now, *next time* you can watch any one of these movies on offer. Television previews act similarly, encouraging us to keep watching or to return later in the week or month, and creating excitement and anticipation, whether for a new show, or for the next chapter in a continuing narrative.

Moreover, as Kernan argues, trailers circulate discourses of genre and of the star system, often even more so than do films themselves, promising the continued life of a beloved genre or star, extending the joys of cinema-going beyond the presentation at hand. She points out that trailers tend to concentrate their efforts (1) on delineating a film's genre, (2) on celebrating and featuring its star(s), and/or (3) on providing an environmental sampling (as exemplified in the trite opening common to many trailers: "In a world where . . ."). Genre can be established before viewing,[12] outside the realm of the text, and yet since genre is not just a classificatory tool, but also a set of rules for interpreting a text,[13] when trailers or other forms of promotion propose a genre, it may prove hard for an individual viewer to easily shrug off these rules. Barker, Arthurs, and Harindranth's examination of would-be *Crash* viewers' responses to its negative hype, discussed in the previous chapter, gives us a window into how constitutive preliminary paratextual frames can prove for subsequent viewing and interpretation.[14] Genres can work as strong paratexts because they frequently enjoy communal definition and widespread use, and because they are cultural categories used by the industry, reviewers, audience members, politicians, and policy makers alike, often with a relatively shared or at least dominant definition at any given point in time.[15] Thus to say or to imply that a film is an action film, an eco-thriller, a sports biopic, or a romantic comedy is to summon entire systems of distribution, reviewer interest, and audience participation and reaction, ensuring interest, disinterest, and/or specific forms of attention from given studios, theaters, audience members, and would-be censors. Trailers and other advertising play vital roles in announcing a film's genre and in providing initial generic labels. Similarly, a star is his or her own generic signifier and intertext (think of the different filmic meanings and uses of, for instance, Clint Eastwood, Julia Roberts, Neil Patrick Harris, or Miley Cyrus), thus also offering interpretive strategies and expectations. Environmental sampling, too, seeks to outline for potential viewers the sorts of things that might occur "in a world where . . . " As particularly strong paratexts, then, trailers and previews may dictate how to read a text.

The archetypal examples here are trailers for action films, which may introduce us to key characters and/or plotlines, but tend to eschew complexity in favor of multiple fighting scenes, car chases, elaborate stunts, and awe-inspiring pyrotechnics, all accompanied by fast-paced, energetic music. A trailer for an action film that concentrates too heavily on its romantic elements will read as a romance, just as one that concentrates too heavily on a thoughtful plot may risk reading as a drama. That said, well-made trailers can often use scene selection to manicure genre more subtly too. Kernan provides the example of *Return of the Jedi*'s (1983) trailer, which George Lucas used to try to insist that the film was not simply sci-fi, but rather a family adventure film.[16] She also discusses *Men in Black*'s (1997) trailer, which hailed subcultural appeal by steeping itself in Will Smith's urban cool, often bouncing this off Tommy Lee Jones as white straight man. Smith, she notes, "as the *black* man in black, thus adds a cool factor to the film's characterological and star dynamics, and [. . .] serves as a comic aside to African-American audiences, assuming and asserting (through the rhetoric of stardom) that the film holds special appeal for them while also amusing whites."[17] Increasingly, films offer multiple trailers for different presumed audiences, as, for instance, when *Bee Movie* (2007) pegged itself as a kids' film on Cartoon Network and Nickelodeon, but as the return of Jerry Seinfeld and his brand of urban ironic comedy on prime-time network television. Andrew Wernick argues that "a promotional message is a complex of significations which at once represents (moves in place of), advocates (moves on behalf of), and anticipates (moves ahead of) the circulating entities to which it refers,"[18] and a significant part of that representation, advocacy, and anticipation is genred by nature.

Trailers and other forms of promotion serve a vital indexical purpose, too, since the mediascape is simply too large for any one of us to watch everything. Promos allow us to schedule our media consumption patterns, working as something akin to a menu for future consumption, and quickly helping us to consign texts to our personal Must Watch, Might Watch, or Do Not Watch lists. Many of us know and judge much of the media world through promos alone, with every one of us having seen thousands of trailers, posters, and previews for shows that we will never watch. Indeed, while promotional materials are constitutive in terms of hailing an audience for a text, they also create meanings for those who will not be in the audience. For every person who has watched any given film or television program, there are likely more who have watched a trailer, poster, or preview of it and yet not the thing itself. To popular culture, then, and hence to media studies' subsequent analyses of what role a text plays in popular culture, the promo and its editor's or producer's meaning-making may prove more important than the meaning-making going on in the show itself. Even in the many instances in which a trailer results in us resolving to never watch the film, clearly some form of interpretation, judgment, and understanding has occurred *without the show*. As the term "preview" encapsulates, we have a paradoxical situation in which we can apparently view a text before viewing it.

The Poster and Its Prey:
Movie Posters and the Beginning of Meaning

To see advertising's intricate acts of meaning construction at work, we can turn first to movie posters. Though rarely as densely packed with meaning as are their video cousins, trailers, posters can still play a key role in outlining a show's genre, its star intertexts, and the type of world a would-be audience member is entering. Indeed, a browse through an online archive of movie posters, *The Internet Movie Poster Awards* (www. impawards.com), quickly reveals a relatively limited and standardized set of poster styles. Action films regularly feature prominently the lone male (or occasionally female) hero looking steely-eyed and ready for action, with weapons on hand and/or muscles bulging (cf. *Rambo* [2008], *Mission: Impossible* [1996], *Walking Tall* [2004], *Gladiator* [2000], and most Bond films), while star-led comedies regularly offer a close-up of the smiling or goofy star(s) (cf. *Ace Ventura: Pet Detective* [1994], *Bean* [1997], *Big* [1988], *Baby Mama* [2008]). Horror films often feature prominently either an icon of the murderer (cf. Jason's mask in posters for the *Halloween* franchise [1978–] or Freddie's claws in those for the *Nightmare on Elm Street* franchise [1984–]), or a symbol of innocence that has been disturbed (cf. the baby's bottle with a creature in it for *The Kindred* [1987] or the bloodstained Christmas ornament for a teaser poster for *Black Christmas* [2006]). Sex-driven comedies are fond of framing the action with or between women's legs (cf. *Artie Lange's Beer League* [2006], *Bachelor Party* [1984], *Porky's* [1982], *Losin' It* [1983]) or of encouraging leering at half-naked women (cf. *10* [1979], *Hardbodies* [1984], *Spring Break* [1983]). Romances show either the lead couple staring lovingly at each other (cf. *When Harry Met Sally* [1989], *What Women Want* [2000], *Serendipity* [2001]) or simply a close-up of a content-looking woman (cf. *Amelie* [2001], *My Best Friend's Wedding* [1997], *Becoming Jane* [2007]). And many other genres have their set image or style too, so that one glance at the poster in a multiplex or at a bus shelter will immediately tell a viewer what genre to expect. Moreover, since many movie posters prominently feature their star or stars, they hail that star as an intertext of all their past roles and their public performance.

Movie posters can also offer considerably more complex and involved meanings, as is evident in some of the art form's more famous examples. Consider, for instance, the iconic poster for *Home Alone* (1990), in which a young Macaulay Culkin has his hands to his face in (mock?) shock/horror as two clearly ne'er-do-well bad guys (Joe Pesci and Daniel Stern) look on through the window behind him. The top of the poster reads, "When Kevin's family left for vacation, they forgot one minor detail: Kevin" and the tag-line promises "A family comedy without the family," while type just below the center of the poster reassures, "But don't worry . . . He cooks. He cleans. He kicks some butt." Quite simple visually, the poster actually navigates delicate terrain. The set-up is given, namely that Kevin is all alone, having been abandoned by his family, and he's now clearly under threat. This premise could easily be that of a horror film, or of a horrifying drama (as is played with in a parody of the poster available online that replaces Pesci and Stern with Michael Jackson). Yet the poster successfully manages to sell the film as a family comedy, not only because its tagline insists so, but also because Pesci's "evil face" is too comically overdone to be taken seriously, the initial set-up's sarcastic reference to forgetting Kevin as being "a minor detail" elicits humor, and Kevin's face is somewhat playful. The centered text also tries its best to assure us that Kevin is in charge. The poster alludes to a horrifying situation and one of seeming powerlessness, yet promises a flip in those power dynamics. Hence it also promises the child viewer a vicarious experience of power, complete with "I don't need you, mommy" sentiment, the naughtiness of "kicking butt," and the child literally and figuratively at the center of the action. A comic release of tension is hinted at, whereby parents and children can laugh off great fears and enjoy a magic-make-believe scenario in which an otherwise horrifying prospect is stripped of danger. All the while, too, this creates mystery and intrigue: since Kevin seems so obviously in peril, *how* will he reverse the situation and "kick some butt"? The poster speaks quite clearly to parental and kid tensions and concerns, but assuages them, while leaving a narrative hook to bring them to the movie theater.

Another famous poster for another beloved family film, *E.T: The Extra-Terrestrial* (1982), works in a similar way, not only offering genre, but also working through tensions and calming them. The poster depicts Earth from outer space, with a mock-up of the Sistine Chapel's depiction of God touching Adam in the top half of the poster, this time featuring an alien hand touching a child's. Large print at the top of the poster reads "His Adventure on Earth," while smaller print lower down the poster reads, "He is afraid. He is totally alone. He is 3,000,000 light years from home." Aliens often suggest horror films, or at least sci-fi thrillers, and the vast expanse of space seen in this poster has been used in other movie posters (cf. *Alien* [1979]) to suggest isolation and vulnerability, especially when the poster's vantage point—looking down on Earth—would seem to be that of the (invading?) alien. Hence, as with *Home Alone*, this poster could risk scaring off parents and children. However, the text refers to E.T. as a he, not an it, and makes "him" sound like a lost puppy, invoking SPCA ads more than H. G. Wells's *The War of the Worlds*, even while calming these anxieties with the notion of his "adventure." "His Adventure on Earth" reads like the subtitle of an issue of *Boy's Own Journal* or *Tintin*, albeit with a science fiction twist, and thus the invocation of both a lost puppy and a young boy's adventure tale significantly domesticates and tames the film's image.

Furthermore, the Michelangelo mock-up is an arresting image, in part because the calm in the child's hand suggests a reaching to touch the alien, not a retraction from doing so, in part because the alien's bent wrist makes the touch seem less like an aggressive lunge, and perhaps most obviously because of the allusion. Michelangelo's image literally and figuratively connects God and Man, and so this poster suggests that the film will connect extra-terrestrial and human lives, fates, and existence. While Michelangelo depicted God touching an adult, just as *Home Alone* gives kids all the power, this next great step forward will be with child, not adult. Consequently, the poster alludes to Spielberg's Twainian idolicization of adolescence. Instead of threatening nightmares, a fear of the dark, and of the aliens out there, *E.T.*'s poster (as would *Home Alone*'s poster years later) promises a film that will make the child feel more adventurous, more comfortable with the world, and more sure of his or her place in it. An evocative, alluring text, in short, has been created for both child and parent. Once more, too, multiple narrative hooks are offered: *How will they connect? What does this alien look like? Will "he" get home?*

Taking a markedly different approach, the equally famous poster for Spielberg's *Jaws* (1975) actively feeds fears and tensions. A young woman is depicted swimming in the ocean, oblivious to the huge great white shark rocketing toward her, its mouth open and as wide as her body is long, brandishing multiple sharp teeth (fig. 2.1). The text at the top of the poster, reading "The terrifying motion picture from the terrifying No. 1 best seller," hardly needs to repeat "terrifying," as the poster captures the utter helplessness of the woman. The poster may well have *created* a fear of the ocean for many a viewer (myself included!), but it similarly encapsulates this fear, selling little else but the fear. Unlike the posters for *Home Alone* or *E.T.*, the *Jaws* poster offers no plot, and no real characters, other than the shark as predator and the woman as undoubtedly one of many victims. The genre is clearly horror, but rather than simply announce itself as such, it moves toward starting the horror at the poster, thereby seemingly allowing the audience member to sample the emotive feeling of watching the film.

All three posters create their texts, giving vivid ideas of what to expect, and transporting viewers into their storyworlds—as young Kevin ready to kick some butt in his own house, as the lost E.T. in a strange land, as the swimmer waiting to be attacked. Each of the three, in other words, opens its respective film's storyworld before the film has reached the scene.

Fig. 2.1. The *Jaws* poster begins the horror with the image of Jaws' helpless, unaware prey.

Six Degrees of Promotion

Posters are often only one element of a concerted advertising campaign. A classic example here was provided by *The Blair Witch Project* (1999). Its poster art forebodingly sets up the ensuing horror, as well as the faux documentary style of the film, with a forest engulfed by darkness, a close-up of the scared looking Heather Donahue, and text that reads "In October of 1994 three student filmmakers disappeared in the woods near Burkittsville, Maryland while shooting this documentary . . . A year later their footage was found." But the combination of the film's advance website with "Heather's Journal," notes on the Internet Movie Database (IMDb) for all three actors listing them as "missing, presumed dead," and a faux television documentary, *The Curse of the Blair Witch* (1999), worked to compound the sense of real-life horror.[19] Not surprisingly, then, *The Blair Witch Project* has arguably remained as famous (if not more so) for its creative and masterful promotion as for the film itself, since in many ways, the horror *began* online and in front of the television, not simply in the movie theater.

In the wake of *The Blair Witch Project*, Internet advertising has become par for the course with new media products, and innovative campaigns that tread into the spaces of everyday life are all the more common. Such was the case with ABC's *Six Degrees*, which in August of 2006, one month before its television premier, boasted an interesting website and a New York City subway blitz, both of which produced an attitude, a genre, and a gender for the forthcoming program. ABC had purchased all the ad space in numerous subway cars, plastering them with a series of provocative statements: "The man by the door will someday be your boss"; "The girl across the aisle is flirting with you"; "The guy next to you will someday be a good friend"; and "You and the woman in red have a shared secret" (fig. 2.2). Interspersed between these pronunciations were several panels announcing "Everyone is Connected," each of which included the URL www.u-r-connected.com. Clearly, these ads aimed to grab commuters' attention, but more specifically, they encouraged commuters to look around a subway car full of seemingly random faces. Declaring that "Everyone is Connected," they provoked any individual commuter to think about how s/he was connected to fellow commuters, and by extension to the city at large. Moreover, with two of the four statements positing the connection in a future "someday," and a third involving flirtation and hence a *hope* for future connection, they alluded to a notion of serendipity, fate, and destiny.

Fig. 2.2. Ads for *Six Degrees* in a New York subway car pique interest, while giving the show a definite style and character. Photograph by the author.

Meanwhile, the fourth statement posited a shared past, and thus, as did all of the panels, it suggested a common history and link between, if not all passengers in the train, at least a small select few. In doing so, the ads were quite playful, of course, eliciting the occasional shared smile or grimace as two real-life "women in red," for instance, laughed off their momentary allegiance. All of the statements were on the long ad panels above commuters' heads, making them easily visible, while an ad actually linking the slogan "Everyone is Connected" to *Six Degrees*—announcing the premier date, network, and producer J. J. Abrams's involvement—could be found lower down, by the doors. Further adding to the intrigue and mystery, this explanatory ad was therefore obscured from view during peak-hour commutes by commuters' heads for all but those closest to it.

If one followed the URL for clues, a black screen gave way to a series of photos of New York City street life, all time-exposed so that the people in the photos looked like blurs, and so that no faces were clearly visible. Overlaid on these photos, at first text announced, "There is a theory that anyone on the planet is connected to any other person through a chain of six people . . . No one is a stranger for long," before more statements of the subway variety ("One day you'll work with someone you bumped into this morning") followed one by one. After a few seconds of this, the website implored one to "Tell us a little bit about yourself and discover a new connection," before giving way to questions such as "Who Are You? I am my work; I am the sum of my experience; I am my future; or I am my contribution". After six questions, the website would then show six characters, one of whose pictures would be enlarged, as the site announced that you shared a connection with this character. A "character video" would then load, showing character-specific clips from *Six Degrees*. The site also offered one the chance to "Find a New Connection" and start the questions again.

To begin to interpret this elaborate marketing scheme, we might first observe that both sites of advertising clearly evoked dating services. The subway ads were either written in soft purple or printed on a purple background, with phantom pictures of the program's attractive, yet not necessarily recognizable, cast in the lettering. New York subways are frequently home to ads for online dating services, and thus the stereotypically feminine color scheme, pictures of the handsome Jay Hernandez, Campbell Scott, and Dorian Missick (one Latino, one white, one African-American, and hence suitably multi-ethnic—another mainstay of dating ads in New York), and allusions to finding connection in the sea of faces that is New York immediately suggested an online dating service. Within such a framing, the photos of Hope Davis, Bridget Moynihan, and Erika Christensen appear to depict happy customers. Even the URL—u-r-connected.com— sounds like a dating site.

Moreover, the interest in serendipity and fated connection in New York sets up direct links to romantic comedies that have drawn heavily on an ethos of Manhattanite serendipity. Prominent examples of such films include *Sleepless in Seattle* (1993), which famously unites its two lovers atop the Empire State Building; *Serendipity*, which involves many scenes of the hero scouring New York for signs of his would-be lover; *Kate and Leopold* (2001), which sees a character transported through time to meet his lover in modern-day New York; and *When Harry Met Sally*, which sees New Yorkers Harry and Sally bump into each other over a number of years, and gradually come together as a couple. Even when one seeks out the URL, the "Tell us a little bit about yourself" and stylized answers ("I am my future") recall not only the profile forms that dating services would require one to fill out, but also the personality quizzes common to women's magazines such as *Cosmopolitan*. In many ways, the advertising campaign alludes heavily to women's genres of the romance and the magazine personality quiz, to direct its further allusion to dating sites toward women specifically, coding *Six Degrees* as a female-focused text that believes in the fairytale romance qualities of serendipity and fate.

The website's act of "computing" answers to six fairly mundane questions in order to suggest a connection to a specific character also announces a fairly clear pretension to be something akin to the next *Sex and the City*. *Sex and the City* was a hugely popular program during its six-year run, gaining canonic status, particularly in New York City and for a female "post-feminist" audience. The show followed the lives and many loves of four close female friends as they interacted with the city around them, the female equivalents of Baudelaire's "flâneur." In the wake of *Sex and the City*'s popularity, pop culture became suffused with fan declarations that "I am Samantha," "I am Charlotte," "I am Miranda," or "I am Carrie," depending upon which lead character the speaker identified with the most. Such declarations are still common and widely available on t-shirts or mugs. *Six Degrees*' website, without much subtlety, mimics this identification game, by twinning a web-visitor with one of the six characters.[20] Not only does such a strategy declare that *Six Degrees* too will be a show endemic to the city and its ethos of interconnection, but it also suggests something of the sexual politics of the show, given that *Sex and the City* was most (in)famous for its frank discussion of sexuality, and it promises that this show too will offer characters who are "just like you," with whom the viewer can relate, and who represent the various facets of New York life. By referencing *Sex and the City*, too, this promise is once again directed at prospective female viewers in particular, given *Sex and the City*'s huge female fan following.

Such a message and such an intertextual network address a New Yorker with the promise of yet another "insider" show. The *New York Times* reviewer for *Six Degrees* picked up on this most poetically, when she wrote, prior to the network premier, that "the show's forte, for viewers like me who don't mind piety on television, is its ambience of faith, particularly in the ebullient Whitmanian idea of 'contact' in the city," further elaborating that, "there's an amorphous but powerful religion in New York, and just about every newcomer undergoes some kind of conversion to it. [. . .] The shared citywide creed might be called Manhattan paganism: a private, almost secretive belief in coincidence, chance, accident and serendipity."[21] Even by taking its advertising to the subway in such a quirky campaign, the marketing for *Six Degrees* is keen to make it appear a "New York show." Indeed, early television ads played with J. J. Abrams's involvement by observing that Abrams—an executive producer of the castaway-gone-wrong series *Lost*—was turning his attention to "a new island," Manhattan. The island on *Lost* is a complex entity unto itself, and thus such ads similarly suggested Manhattan's own complexity, mystery, and intrigue. However, if all this advertising aimed to flatter New Yorkers and insist that the show "got" the entity that is Manhattan, such an advertising technique also stood to be equally as evocative for potential viewers who visited New York, were alerted to the advertising campaign by media reports, or watched ads and read reviews. The ads seemingly promised to transport viewers from elsewhere to the hard-paved yet magical streets of Manhattan. Just as *Sex and the City* sold a trip to Manhattan for those off the island, *Six Degrees'* advertising and early buzz offered a similar act of teleportation.

Ultimately, then, without watching *Six Degrees*, and based only on seeing its subway ads and its early website, one could already have a quite developed construction of the program: as intended primarily for women; as quintessentially New York, and modern, hip, liberal *Sex*-y New York at that; as romantic in genre and ethos; and as a show about characters "like you and me" and their feelings. If the website's questionnaire aimed to capture an image of its visitors ("I am my future"), it similarly suggested that on a weekly basis it would capture images and moments in the life of New York, reducing the seemingly anonymous, hostile, and gargantuan metropolis to the intimate circle of six people. Also, lest this seem some pretender to the throne, the mere presence of J. J. Abrams's name in marketing (despite later press that questioned the depth of his involvement with the show) gave a firm stamp of quality. Hot on the heels of the ratings giant *Lost*, and of the hip *Alias* (2001–6), Abrams had established himself as one of the medium's premium auteurs (see chapter 4), and through his early involvement with the urban love tale *Felicity* (1998–2002) he had proven his familiarity with New York. Abrams is particularly well-known and -loved for his character-driven writing, and for his ability to handle rich backgrounds and large casts. With *Lost* and *Alias*, too, he had garnered a name for the boldly original and out-of-the-ordinary, and so his name alone seemingly promised a high level of quality, and a text that would develop over time in intriguing and unique ways. Before *Six Degrees* hit the air, ABC's marketing team had therefore already offered many audiences the chance to decode its genre, style, tone, mood, quality, prospects for development, and characterization. At the outskirts of the show, these paratexts had fashioned a text.

Interestingly, looking back on the advertising now, long since the show was first put on a lengthy "hiatus" and later canceled, and after having watched several episodes, I conclude that the paratexts were by no means purely indexical or metonymic. *Six Degrees* focused on relationships, and so in this slight respect may be coded more "feminine" than the overtly masculine run-and-gun worlds of shows such as *24* (2001–); but its world was more gritty and less magical-make-believe than either the romantic comedies to which its advertising alluded, or than its proposed "fore-mother," *Sex and the City*, and it seemed equally open to male viewers. With three interesting male leads in particular, it hardly hailed female viewers alone. For its marketing campaign to label it as an urban romance for women was not entirely inaccurate, but nor was it a label that truly fit. By December 2006, *Six Degrees'* future was in jeopardy, and one might wonder to what degree the advertising had contributed to alienating audiences who may have liked it, and/or to attracting audiences who were doomed not to like it. A show's ultimate failure to stay on air is a product of many things, ranging from the luck of the time slot, to network dedication to the series, to actual quality, and so it is impossible to attribute the program's cancelation to poor advertising alone, especially when the poster campaign described here ran only in New York and Los Angeles. But its ads hardly seemed wholly appropriate for the show, instead creating a different referent text for potential audiences and non-audiences alike. Given the disjuncture between the meanings of the promos and the meanings of the show once it began in earnest, we might speculate as to how many texts fail and get canceled in part because of a poor marketing campaign, and hence because of paratextual dismantling. Many a show's death may be predetermined at birth by its previews and trailers.

However, the television industry does not use previews just to communicate with would-be audiences; previews also play an important commercial role in selling the program, and the entire network, to would-be advertisers. As Amanda Lotz describes, one of the American television industry's more important yearly rituals and events is the Upfront presentations in mid-May, when each network announces a tentative schedule for its fall programming, with much pomp and pageantry in a lavish party in Manhattan.[22] Each network's returning programming is already a known quantity, its Nielsen ratings and audience demographics a matter of public record among advertisers and their designated ad time buyers.

But the Upfronts allow networks a chance to present previews for their newly commissioned shows and to create "buzz" about their schedule. As Lotz describes, the ad buyer's role at the Upfronts is to try to read the buzz, to gauge not only how successful individual shows will be, but how coherent a programming strategy the network has as a whole. A network that appears confident, with a strong slate of programs, can not only set higher ad rates for new programs, but can increase ad rates for all its shows, whereas "a network that reveals itself to be anxious, hesitant, or internally conflicted in its message or programming sends a clear message to advertisers to resist rate increases and buy elsewhere."[23] And since traditionally 75 to 90 percent of a network's advertising time has been sold immediately following the Upfront week,[24] little room exists to make a mistake. Confidence is sold in part by hoopla, with actors in attendance, glitz, and glamour, but good previews that evoke a favorable audience reaction can go a long way toward attracting advertiser money. Ultimately, then, preview production is arguably one of the most important steps in the creation of a new show, with good previews attracting both advertisers and audiences, and bad ones costing a network sorely. Both semiotically and economically, shows and their networks utterly rely upon the strength of their promos.

Trailers and Their Sweet Hereafters

If trailers and promos give birth to a text and promise an audience a mise-en-scène, a genre, and a set of meanings, then different trailers or promos might create wholly different texts. Comically illustrating this point was one of the hottest viral videos making the rounds in 2005, a trailer for *The Shining* (1980).[25] A series of staffers at video production and editing company PS260 had set themselves the task of changing a famous film's genre by weaving together existing footage to create a new trailer. In its new incarnation, *The Shining* became a feel-good father-son bonding film, simply called *Shining*. The newly minted voiceover began by introducing us to Jack Torrance, "a writer looking for inspiration," and Danny, "a kid looking for a dad," before explaining that while "Jack just can't finish his book," he's about to learn that "sometimes, what we need most is just around the corner." At this point, Peter Gabriel's upbeat song "Solsbury Hill" cues, as we are treated to a montage of the film's loving family shots and snippets of dialogue such as "I'm your new foster father" and "I'd do anything for you." While the pleasures and humor involved in watching this trailer depend upon being aware of how inaccurately it advertises Stanley Kubrick's film about a father who goes crazy in an isolated and haunted mountain hotel, and while it was unlikely to have changed an audience member's understanding of *The Shining* as such, it once more illustrates a trailer's ability to play with and radically augment a film's genre. Similarly, another PS260 mock trailer turned the romantic musical and *Romeo and Juliet* retelling *West Side Story* (1961) into a *28 Days Later* (2002) style zombie horror flick, reframing dance sequences as zombie attacks.[26]

Such genre changes are by no means restricted to parody alone, however. Through reruns, the repurposing of television is a daily and pervasive practice, with hype and previews encouraging certain (generic) viewing strategies. Lynn Spigel, for instance, notes how Nick at Nite regularly advertises older sitcoms as camp[27]; parody can be created by viewers as much as by writers or directors,[28] and Nick at Nite encourages audiences to watch its shows as camp, where their original broadcast previews would have presented them as straight. If reruns can be turned into parody, though, as Derek Kompare notes, they can also be turned into classics, parts of our television heritage and national history.[29] Thus, while Nick at Nite is playfully ribbing older shows with its paratextual framing, TV Land in particular presents many of its reruns as the best of television past, steeped in nostalgia and added significance. To rerun a program in the first place is to send a subtle message regarding the show's worthiness of replay, especially for what has often been an ephemeral medium. Beyond simple statements of worth, though, as Kompare notes,[30] cable television in particular has found past television shows invaluable for laying claim to a generic and brand identity. Cable channels will regularly fill their schedule with reruns and films that match the channel's intended tone and identity, but in choosing these programs and films, and in labeling them as such, they further attach certain genres to the apparent surface of the text. For example, if Lifetime were to play *Charlie's Angels* (either the television show [1976–81] or the film [2000]), its advertising and brand identity alone would most likely encourage a "girl power," post-feminist reading, celebrating the three tough and resourceful women, whereas if Spike were to play *Charlie's Angels*, we would now likely be encouraged to see the film as an action romp with women in skimpy costumes.

In this manner, as Jason Mittell states, "Production is an ongoing process in the majority of television, revising notions of genre throughout the run of a series as producers respond to the ongoing cultural circulation of programs,"[31] and each time a show or film is replayed, its surrounding paratextuality "produces" it and its genre anew. Mittell's interests lie in how genre is "a process of categorization that is not found within media texts, but operates across the cultural realms of media industries, audiences, policy, critics, and historical contexts,"[32] and hence in how, over time, various agents and paratexts inflect dominant understandings and uses of a genre. These processes clearly apply to an individual text, too, so that textual meaning will shift across time as its paratexts direct our reading strategies. Of course, any given text will have limits to its uses, but promos and previews can still determine significant variation within a text's broad set of meanings. For instance, we could possibly imagine *Charlie's Angels* receiving play on BET as part of a series on films influenced by blaxploitation, but it is highly unlikely that any preview could convince viewers to see it as a film *about* the African American experience.

Various previews' abilities to inflect texts over time can make for dense and intricate textual histories, but texts can be further complicated within any given moment in time due to differences in promos and previews across space. Just as Mittell notes the varying understandings of cartoons as a genre over time, we should expect genres and texts to change meanings as they travel the planet, according to their different paratextual entourage. Such is the case for the American and Canadian trailers of Canadian director Atom Egoyan's film *The Sweet Hereafter*.[33] Egoyan was well-known in Canada due to his prior films, including *Exotica* (1994), *Calendar* (1993), and *The Adjuster* (1991), but had no popular cachet in America. A "quirky" director whose work rarely conforms to established genres, Egoyan poses a particular challenge to marketers trying to visually summarize his films in two minutes. *The Sweet Hereafter*'s American and Canadian trailers render this difficulty in vivid detail, as the former aimed to peg the film generically, while the latter could rely upon audiences' familiarity with Egoyan as his own genre. As a result, when the film opened in 1997, two starkly different movies were on sale in the two different nations' trailers.

Based on Russell Banks's novel of the same title, *The Sweet Hereafter* is a stunning if grueling film that examines a small mountain town's grief following a school bus accident that kills all but one of the town's youth. Ian Holm stars as a lawyer come to town in the aftermath, trying to find someone to blame, while he struggles with his own feelings of guilt inspired by occasional calls from his drug-addicted daughter whom he is powerless to help. A film about parenthood, protection, grief, loss, and childhood, it garnered widespread critical acclaim, including the Grand Jury Prize at Cannes, an Independent Spirit award, and Best Direction and Best Adapted Screenplay nominations at the 1998 Oscars. However, while bringing Egoyan one of his largest box office outings, with a little over $3 million grossed, it failed to register with the American public more widely. Inevitably, the question of why it failed to attract a larger audience produces many possible answers: audiences may have considered it too bleak, too slow, too dark, "too Canadian," not star-studded enough; it may have been released on too few screens; or any number of other reasons. Another possible answer that I want to advance, though, is that the American trailer sold a different film with a different genre, one that was formulaic and uninteresting. Especially when compared to the Canadian trailer, the American trailer hijacked and augmented the film, confusingly offering audiences a different product than the one they would actually have received should they watch the film.

The American trailer includes a voiceover in typical Hollywood style, offered by one of its typical voice talents. As images from the film shoot by, with interspersed dialogue, the announcer reads:

> In a town where no one is a stranger, in a place where everyone feels like family, something has happened that will change their lives forever. Now, one man must find the truth. But who can you trust when everyone has a secret? Who can you blame when no one is innocent?

At no point do we see the bus veer off the road and crash, nor do we see the obvious aftermath; rather, we are left with oblique references to something awful that has happened, likely involving children, and the viewer's attention is pointed toward one man's quest for "the truth." Ian Holm's Mitchell appears to be one part lawyer, one part detective, and in the absence of the knowledge of exactly what sort of accident or incident took place, one is left to assume a murder of some sort. The trailer poses a lone investigator stuck in a town in which "everyone has a secret," yet "no one is innocent," implying widespread complicity in whatever has happened. Numerous snippets of dialogue suggest a cover-up, with the trailer giving particular prominence, through muting all background sound when spoken, to Mitchell's declaration, "As far as I'm concerned, there is no such thing as an accident." This is *The Wicker Man* (1973) with snow, or, given that the trailer ends with Sarah Polley's Nicole reading the "Pied Piper of Hamlin" fairytale, possibly a *Children of the Corn* (1984) scenario. When

I showed the trailer to a class of 250 undergraduates at University of California, Berkeley, none of whom had watched the film, the clear consensus among the students was that the town as a whole had committed a ritualistic murder. Or, taking their cue from the final interior shot of Nicole approaching a window at night, only for a blinding light to be emitted from outside, some students felt that supernatural, even alien causes might lie behind the "accident."

The trailer slots Mitchell into a long tradition of American detectives trying to "cut through the crap," vaguely referencing their forerunner in the Western hero nobly taking on the bad guys and the environment all by himself. Noir with the blanc of pervasive snow, following in *Fargo*'s (1996) footsteps, but without the humor. The eeriness of the music and the set-up suggest a thriller, complete with the foreboding threat to Mitchell, as made explicit by a scene in which Bruce Greenwood's Billy demands that he stop asking questions. The film's title suggests death has occurred, but also suggests a continuing threat of more death, with a promise from Nicole that she will not lie offering the hero his only shred of help, and yet another nod to a seemingly formulaic thriller, in which the nice young girl helps the tired old detective. The trailer announces the various awards won by the film, but viewers are left to suppose that this was due to its artful camerawork—of which we see plenty in the trailer—or Holm's performance, or the gimmick of moving this old Hollywood formula into the snow, since little else about the film seems original or award-worthy. Without much apparent originality, and without star power or sex appeal, it promised to fall too easily into the no-man's-land between art-house and multiplex viewing cultures.

As should be clear, though, the movie that the American trailer offered hardly resembles the actual film. For a closer approximation, we must turn to the Canadian trailer, which while using many of the same shots and dialogue, is markedly different in tone, detail, and hence generic delivery. Eschewing the standard Hollywood "In a world where . . . " voiceover style, the Canadian trailer uses voiceover only at the end to announce the film's director and title, and instead uses title cards, reading, "Sometimes the past can't be forgotten. Sometimes justice can't be found. And sometimes the truth is just the beginning." Importantly, since Egoyan was a known quantity to Canadians, and known for dark, peculiar characters and plots (*Exotica*, for instance, follows a taxman's obsession with a stripper who once babysat for his child, who was abducted and killed), the trailer had the luxury of not needing to place this ungeneric, original

Fig. 2.3. *The Sweet Hereafter*'s Billy watches in horror as his children's school bus sinks into ice. Decontextualized in the American trailer, the reason for his horror is considerably clearer in the Canadian trailer.

director's work into a generic box, as did its American counterpart. Instead, then, this is advertised as "an Atom Egoyan film," a quantity that would have more meaning for its Canadian audience. Moreover, the Canadian trailer uses considerably more shots of the school bus, at first full of children, and later hauntingly empty and destroyed. The trailer also adds the sound of children screaming in the background to one shot, and it adds shots of the bus cracking through the ice, and of it driving off the roadside, followed by a fade to white. Thus, whereas American audiences were being encouraged to imagine an eerie detective thriller, Canadian audiences were offered the shock of the actual accident from early on.

I distinctly remember audience members gasping in horror during many of the trailers' showings in 1997 in Vancouver. Billy's reaction shot, as the father of two children who is riding behind the bus when it crashes (fig. 2.3), though used in the American trailer, now gives the audience an immediate point of identification, and a set of parents' eyes through which they can watch the incident. With this shot added, with the intertextual knowledge of Egoyan's past work alluded to, and with the title cards focusing on the *absence* of meaning and announcing that "sometimes the truth is just the beginning" instead of promising the truth, audiences could now immediately understand Mitchell's mission as futile. Similarly, Billy's act of threatening Mitchell is recontextualized as giving voice to desperate anger and grief, and the entire film is framed as being about dealing with loss, not discovery. Meanwhile, the title now gains a grim quality—this is anything but "sweet"—and the Pied Piper tale becomes quite clearly about loss, childhood, and parenthood, not about cultish killings or alien abductions. The trailer speaks to us in a markedly different tone, capturing the spirit and genre(lessness) of the film with considerably more accuracy.

Here, then, we have a stark example of how two different trailers can offer two different films. Interestingly, though, if one watches *both* trailers, the genre-refusing nature of the film becomes all the more impressive, precisely because the American trailer shows the genres and formulas that Egoyan's film frustrates: this is clearly *not* a film where the detective will get his man, and it is clearly *not* a puzzle movie with an answer at the end. The American trailer, as such, shows the backdrop to the film, while the Canadian one shows the development and foreground. Such a reading, though, is left mostly for the Egoyan or *Sweet Hereafter* enthusiast watching both trailers on the DVD. At the time of release, with YouTube several years away, and barring a jet-setting lifestyle, North American viewers would have been left with only one of the two trailers. Initially, viewers would have made a decision to see the film or not based on their reactions to the trailer they saw, and perhaps based on discussions with others who had seen the trailer. Without Egoyan's past films serving as active intertexts screaming out that the director's films aren't usually so simple, American viewers would likely make this judgment with faulty "advice." If a trailer is a window into a movie, windows point in different directions, giving us different angles of vision, some refracting or otherwise distorting. And in case my above account suggests that the Canadian trailer encapsulated the film perfectly, we could certainly envision another trailer that would accurately encapsulate elements of the film, yet focus on different themes; for instance, the incestuous relationship between Nicole and her father might feature more prominently, as might Mitchell's relationship with his daughter, likewise pointing to a film about parenthood, childhood, damage, and loss, but now highlighting the threatening, tenuous nature of the parent–child relationship. While I hesitate to write in hypotheticals, were viewers to watch this imaginary third trailer, they might watch the film with such themes more firmly in mind, yet again shifting their expectations and changing the nature of the text that they experience. Therefore, while Egoyan directed the film, the stark differences in trailer editing gave the studio significant powers of authorship that in part superceded his own, and would likely have proven constitutive of the frames with which viewers would watch the film.

Hence, trailers and promos not only question how textuality works, but also how the author works. If the author, director, or writer is assumed to be s/he who creates a text, scripting its characters, themes, genre, and so forth, trailers and promos may rob this figure of some of his or her creative powers. Admittedly, we would be foolish to regard any cinematic or televisual creation as coming from a single creative figure, and even when fans talk of creator figures in reverential terms, they nearly always recognize film and television to require communal acts of creation. When we speak of authors, as will be discussed further in chapter 3, we often speak of what Michel Foucault dubs the "author function"—not a real figure but a projection, "in more or less psychologizing terms, of the operations that we force texts to undergo, the connections that we make, the traits that we establish as pertinent, the continuities that we recognize, or the exclusions that we practice."[34] This author function may prove its own powerful paratext at times, as chapter 3 will examine. However, at the same time, the trailer's or promo's power to create an initial interpretive framework for a text—sometimes as much as a year before the show is delivered to its audience—or to propose a new framework later in the text's life, means that a considerable component of textual creation comes from neither the author figure nor the author function, but from the studio's hired marketing staff and the editors who compose the trailer or promo. These editors must work with footage filmed by the film or program's creative personnel, so they do not have carte blanche, but as the case of *The Sweet Hereafter* illustrates, editing allows one remarkable freedom of creation and re-creation.

The power of the trailer editor is often most evident with generically complex films and programs, such as *The Sweet Hereafter*. Similarly, for instance, M. Night Shyamalan's movies have also posed a challenge to their editors. Shyamalan's films (*The Sixth Sense* [1999], *Unbreakable* [2000], *Signs* [2002], *The Village* [2004], *Lady in the Water* [2006], and *The Happening* [2008]) are renowned for their plot twists, but they all mix genres too. Trailers for *The Village* tried to peg the film as horror, focusing on creatures in the woods, and including several standard horror film scenes, such as the creature's apparent stalking of the young female lead, and the listing of rules for avoiding the creature. Granted, *The Village* draws from the horror genre, as Shyamalan uses horror as decoy for the movie's twist, but ultimately it is not horror, and audiences who went to the film expecting that genre—primed as they may well have been by the trailers—would have been sorely disappointed. By contrast, Shyamalan's next films, *Lady in the Water* and *The Happening*, had suitably vague and generically open trailers that more accurately pegged the films as odd mixes of, respectively, drama, character study, fairy tale, and horror, and horror, sci-fi, and bio-disaster.

Ultimately, a film need not mix genres for a trailer to play with or augment its framing. Trailers for dramedies notoriously tend to include all the film's funniest lines, thereby suggesting an out-and-out comedy; trailers for thrillers can suggest an action film by focusing only on the more high-paced moments; character-rich films might be pitched as plot- or action-based; trailers for sequels might fail to acknowledge a change in tone; films designed for a niche audience might deliberately be pitched as for the whole family; in the wake of the *Lord of the Rings* trilogy's success, many films in the fantasy genre are pitched as action films even when they are not; and so forth. A great deal of movie-going in particular is about expectation, and since trailers play a key role in setting expectations, they become a key contributor to a text's meaning and can be central to an audience's reaction to that text.

Trailers' contribution to meaning may even be growing, given their increasing presence in all forms of media. Many cable providers now offer a free Movie Trailers On Demand channel, while many a commercial break contains at least one ad for a film or television program. YouTube, Hulu, Facebook, and MySpace, meanwhile, all circulate trailers and previews, as does IMDb. Movie trailers regularly attract more views on video-sharing sites than do even some of the most popular viral videos,[35] and television promos can easily top a million views. Thus, where trailers were once limited to the space before movies (whether in a theater or on a VHS tape) or to television ad breaks, they can now be found in various other locations, as Hollywood has used new media to circulate ads for its shows far and wide. In such an environment, producers and marketers may well be gaining considerably more control over the meanings of a text. When trailers were limited to a few minutes before movies, or a few television ads, their effect may have been more muted, but today's proliferation of trailers means that most of us watch each one multiple times, often unable to escape them even if we wanted to do so. Today's culture of trailers sets the stage for parodic items such as The Onion News Network's on the *Iron Man* trailer discussed in the Introduction, or Stephen Colbert's occasional segment on *The Colbert Report* called "Trailers That

Are Ruining America." Their constructions of meaning, suggested modes of viewing, and tailored calls to specific viewing audiences are repeated incessantly, and are constantly available for repetitive viewing. With each viewing, the director's text potentially dissolves yet a little more, with the marketing team's text replacing it. Final cut is relative, as the high trade in trailers and promos over YouTube and similar sites puts ever more power into studios' hands to pre-purpose and repurpose films and television shows.

The Twenty-Second Text: Opening Credit Sequences and "Proper" Interpretations

So far in this chapter, many of the examples have been of promos or trailers as entryway paratexts, either setting up the initial framework(s) for viewing or establishing a new framework years later for a different audience. Many trailers and promos on television in particular, however, work in medias res. Ads for rerun television shows and replayed films may just as likely address themselves to repeat viewers. Even beyond reruns, after a new show is up on its feet, its network hardly stops advertising it, nor do networks direct their continuing ads for a show only at non-viewers, attempting to convert them into viewers or fans. Rather, many ads preach to the converted, welcoming longtime viewers back, and serving both as continual reminders of a show's time and place in the weekly schedule and as narrative lures. When addressing new audience members, promos can set frameworks for expectation, can give a text a definite character, and can generate a text prior to viewing. When addressing returning audience members, promos can on one hand begin to construct the text of the individual episode, while on the other hand, at the level of the show in general, they offer producers the chance to reiterate their version of a text, and rerun broadcasters the chance to recontextualize the text. In the wake of Stuart Hall's Encoding/Decoding Model and its reliance on a notion of a text's "preferred reading,"[36] Justin Lewis answered David Morley's question regarding where the preferred reading originates—with the text, audience, or analyst[37]—by stating, "The answer must inevitably be: *the audience*."[38] Instead, I would pose that paratexts often tell us how producers or distributors would prefer for us to interpret a text, which audience demographics they feel they are addressing, and how they want us to make sense of their characters and plots. In short, promos offer "proper" and "preferred" interpretations.

Working in a similar fashion, moreover, are opening credit sequences and recaps. Like promos, opening credit sequences and recaps serve an entryway function for new audiences, introducing them to the characters, genre, themes, relationships, and general subject matter. Take, for instance, the opening credits for *The Simpsons*. The camera pans down from the clouds to Springfield Elementary, and into a classroom window, where we see Bart writing lines on the blackboard before he leaps on his skateboard and heads home. Next, we find Homer working at the nuclear power plant, so excited to get off work that he doesn't notice the glowing uranium ingot attached to his clothing till he is halfway home, an ingot that he simply tosses out the window. Mother Marge is shown buying the family groceries and losing sight of Baby Maggie, who gets scanned for a price, before they too head home in the family station wagon. Meanwhile, Lisa is shown playing saxophone in the school band, and is banished by the band teacher for interjecting a virtuoso solo performance into an otherwise typically cacophonic school band song. Unfazed, she leaves the room and cycles home. Then all the family members converge on their living room to watch television, allowing the animators a quick moment of play, as each week the "couch gag" involves doing something silly to the family, such as when they "beam" onto the couch, *Star Trek* (1966–69) style. All the while, Danny Elfman's theme song, a rather frenetic orchestral piece, plays in the background, until finally, as the song crescendos, we cut to the family's television, to creator credits, and then the sequence is over.

Though only seventy-five seconds long, the sequence serves as a formidable introduction to the characters, tone, genre, and style of the show. Famously, each episode begins with Bart writing a different set of lines, giving a sense of him as a serial mischief-maker, as does his reckless skateboard trip home. Marge's momentary loss of Maggie codes her as a busy mother, while Lisa's introduction codes her as gifted, soulful, and, per force, solitary. Homer's introduction visually references the opening sequence to *The Flintstones* (1960–66), thus establishing him as a similarly dumb but well-meaning comic hero. The upbeat tone of the background music, the 2.5 kids, the numerous comic moments in the intro, and the final destination of the family living room all clearly announce the text as a family sitcom, though some of the quirks, such as Maggie being scanned for a price or Homer discarding a uranium ingot, allude to the show's intent to play with the rules and tone both of family sitcoms and of realistic depiction. While Homer is presented as somewhat stupid from the outset, and Marge as simply flustered, Lisa's sax solo and the suggestions of Bart's intelligence from some of his lines written on the blackboard (such as "I do not have power of attorney over first graders" or "I am not the new Dalai Lama") immediately tell us that these kids are not normal sitcom kids. Occasional blackboard lines also announce the show's meta approach, as, for instance, when Bart writes "I will never win an Emmy" or "I should not be 21 by now." And with the final shot being of the television, the credit sequence subtly suggests the degree to which the show will be about television as much as it is about family life. Thus, by the end of the seventy-five seconds, viewers know the central characters and genre, have been adequately warned of its offbeat, subversive nature, and know to expect the unreal.

The Simpsons' opening credit sequence is a particularly effective one, but all opening credit sequences work in similar ways to create genre, character, and tone. Many involve remarkably fast editing, with more frames per second employed than anywhere else on television, as characters and character relationships are introduced. Colors, background music choice, and relative use of naturalistic or computer-doctored images can tell prospective viewers a lot. Watch *CSI: Miami's* (2002–) opening credits and one knows to expect a style-conscious, sexed-up procedural, just as *ER's* (1994–) pulse-like music and somber tones announce a more realistic, gritty drama, *Desperate Housewives'* (2004–) opening credits announce a playful, tongue-in-cheek tone, *The Wire's* (2002–8) discordant theme song penned by Tom Waits prepares one for a dark and uncompromising look at Baltimore's drug trade and at urban poverty in general,[39] and *Dexter's* (2006–) eerie tight close-ups of the titular character cutting his bacon and eggs, flossing his teeth, shaving, and squeezing a blood orange (fig. 2.4) put one on edge and ready for a show about a serial killer. So central are opening credit sequences in offering "proper interpretations" of genre and character that some of the recent class of genre-mixing serial dramas such as *Lost* and *Heroes* have eschewed using them, relying instead on a simple title-card and a "previously on . . . " segment, thereby refusing to pin down a broader sense of genre, character, or theme.

However, credit sequences are also powerful in medias res paratexts. Raymond Williams's account of televisual flow is famous, his argument being that broadcasting's "defining characteristic" was the "planned flow" between program and program, program and ad, ad and channel identification, and so on, so that "these sequences together compose the real flow, the real 'broadcasting.'"[40] He contrasts this to meetings, concerts, or games

Fig. 2.4. A close-up image of a blood orange being squeezed from *Dexter*'s opening credits looks distinctly fleshy, hence contributing to an unnerving and disturbing sequence.

that we might attend elsewhere, all of which set up their own internal conditions and responses so that one's "most general modes of comprehension and judgment are then closely linked to these kinds of specific and isolated, temporary, forms of attention."[41] But opening credit sequences frequently serve an important function of setting the tone for programs as they begin, and thus of redirecting the nature of the flow and setting up their own "specific and isolated, temporary, forms of attention." Opening credit sequences, in short, serve an important ritual function. Earlier I wrote of the trailer's role in transitioning us from a noisy theater to the world of celluloid, and most performative events require similarly obvious, repetitive rituals to signal their beginning. In live theater, it is the dimming of the lights and raising of the curtain. In classical music performances, it is the orchestra's tuning of their instruments. In a sports game, it is the playing of the national anthem. And in television, it is the opening credit sequence. Opening credits help to transport us from the previous textual universe to a new one, or out of "real life" and into the life of the program (even if a growing number of shows are opting for cold starts to throw the viewer right into the action). Hence the importance of tonal shifts in opening credit sequences, and hence the utility of story-style opening credits (as in *The Simpsons*, *The Fresh Prince of Bel Air* [1990–96], or *The*

Brady Bunch [1969–74]). If trailers frequently announce "In a world where . . . ," imploring us to move with them to that "world," an opening credit sequence is similarly entrusted to take us to its text's world.

Thus, David Johansson notes that the opening credit sequence to *The Sopranos* (1999–2007) is "a 'road movie' in miniature,"[42] taking us as viewers alongside Tony Soprano in his ride through the urban, sterile environment of New Jersey. He notes that the "Drive Safely" sign on the turnpike "grows in absurdity every time the viewer sees it since this is a world where no one is ever 'safe.'" He also writes of the toll booth as representing "impersonal bureaucracy and a faceless government—the system. Tony must enter it like anyone else who wishes to drive down the highway of the American Dream."[43] And he states of the trip with Tony:

> He's a bad guy certainly—but we're with him, inside the frame with his face, his hairy hands, his brute strength, his air of danger, but within the intimate bounds of the car we get a sense of strength in repose, the alpha male at rest, his guard down, vulnerable. And this deepens the viewer's sympathy for the "hero" because, even though he *is* a bad guy, we're *right there* with him, in tight proximity, where the sense of Tony's physical presence—his aura—feels private, as though we are being trusted. He may be a tough guy but for now he's alone, as naked as the rest of us.[44]

I am less interested here in the universality or "correctness" of Johansson's rather close reading than in how it illustrates the degree to which opening credit sequences inspire close readings from all viewers, thereby becoming spaces for the projection of personal interpretations. Or to change metaphors from projection to uploading, we might think of the opening credit sequence as providing time for our memories and preferred reading strategies to be uploaded, preparing us for the episode at hand. This role also pertains to theme songs, which over time similarly come to represent the entire program, and the joys and memories of that program.

Through repetition, opening credit sequences may also reaffirm what a show is about, how its characters are interrelated, and how we "should" make sense of them. Precisely because it and its theme song can represent the show, standing in for it metonymically, its constituent parts declare what a show is about. This is most obvious when performing what Barthes calls the "commutation test" of replacing one or more elements to see how the meaning of a text changes,[45] and many stark and clear examples are offered by *Buffy the Vampire Slayer's* (1997–2003) opening credit sequence. To begin with, this sequence is one of the most densely packed in television history, using more than one shot per second to introduce the show's large cast and novel concept at lightning speed. As the show aged, though, it frequently remixed the intro, so that new characters, character details, and character relationships could be reflected. Indeed, it is worth speculating on the degree to which *Buffy* was aided in picking up many fans later in its lifespan— as was required, given that its original ostensible genre of high school soap meets gothic horror was not an immediate and easy fit with the "quality television" label for which it would soon come to be known—by its remarkably comprehensive "cheat sheet" opening credit sequence. By contrast, opening credit sequence–shunning serial dramas such as *Lost* and *Heroes* can prove deeply confusing for newcomers (leading to the former's need to play reruns with pop-up style background notes). *Buffy*'s opening credits adequately introduced, for instance, the complexities of Angel, the vampire with a soul, showing both his kinder, somewhat stock tall, dark, brooding romantic lead character, and the killer Angelus. In time, too, the sequence would adapt to suggest the depths of Spike, another vampire seeking a soul. *Buffy* would also play with its opening credits occasionally, as in "Superstar," an episode in which local nerd Jonathan casts a spell to make himself revered by all, thereby producing a remixed intro in which Jonathan replaces Buffy in many shots. Or, when the show added a sister for *Buffy*, the opening credit sequence added her seamlessly, as though she had always been present.

Similarly, Victoria Johnson is able to rest much of her analysis of *The Mary Tyler Moore Show*'s (1970–77) construction of a proudly urbane American Midwest "Heartland" on its developing opening credits. Over several pages of rich close reading of *The Mary Tyler Moore Show*'s first five seasons' credit sequences—wherein, for instance, the first season's lyric, "You might just make it after all," in the second season becomes the more famous, "You're gonna make it after all," while images of Mary encountering the city are replaced in later seasons by images of her integrating within the city and as a single head-of-household—Johnson shows how these intro sequences

"evolved" to offer a "balanced" view, portraying Minneapolis as a site of public liberation and private self-actualization. In this sense, the program promoted an idealized vision that suggested 1970s downtowns might be "reclaimed" (particularly for young, white, female professionals) as liberating, joyful spaces of tourism, labor, and consumption in an era post-1960s upheavals and political traumas.[46]

As did *Buffy* years later, *The Mary Tyler Moore Show* communicated *and framed* its title character's and its setting's "evolution" as well as the "evolution" of its theme, argument, and hence "proper" interpretation through its evolving opening credit sequence, such that Johnson can chart these varying evolutions largely through the sequence alone.

Arguably the greater commutation test, though, can be witnessed by watching multiple fan-made opening credit sequences. After all, if production personnel can "prefer" certain meanings through official opening credit sequences, fan edits can prefer their own readings, while at the same time illustrating the many different introductory frames and filters that can be provided for any one show. One *Buffy* fan-made intro sequence, for instance, removes the Nerf Herder rocked-out theme song, replacing it with *Buffy* spinoff *Angel*'s (1999–2004) more somber strings and rock theme, thereby setting the show up as darker and less frenetically peppy. Various other songs replace the original theme song in other fan-made trailers, too, each giving the show a decidedly different spin. Similarly, the fan-made trailers string together different frames from the series, in the process offering different interpretations of the characters and their interrelationships: some downplay Buffy; others show her to be a more tortured figure; some show her to be an angry, vengeful character; and yet others suggest a romantic bond between Buffy and Spike, Buffy and Willow, or Angel and Spike. In this way, as will be explored in considerably more detail in chapter 5, viewer-end paratexts can repurpose the "proper" interpretation, posing their own frames for viewers, and shrugging off the official frames that (in this case) Mutant Enemy Productions put forward. But to repurpose the proper interpretation requires that it has already been stated, and the television industry's opening credit sequences often make this interpretation clear, underlining and repeating it on a weekly basis.

Conclusion: More Show than the Show Itself?

Whether in their fan-made or more official varieties, opening credit sequences, trailers, posters, and ad campaigns often build the text at its outskirts. In saying this, I do not mean to suggest that films and television programs will prove unable to overcome or to challenge these meanings in due course, for undoubtedly a viewer who eventually watched *E.T.*, *Six Degrees*, *The Sweet Hereafter*, or *Buffy the Vampire Slayer* would find quantitatively more textuality on offer, and a more coherent, realized narrative, than their respective poster, ad campaign, trailer, or opening credit sequence offer. The point, therefore, is not that paratexts necessarily kill or become their texts. Rather, in preparing us for the text and offering us our first encounters with it, entryway paratexts hold considerable power to direct our initial interpretations, telling us what to expect and establishing genre, gender, style, attitude, and characterization. Working in medias res, paratexts also attempt to police proper interpretations, insisting on how they would like us to read the text. At the same time, though, while paratexts do not necessarily become their texts, especially for eventual viewers, it would be a trap—and a trap into which media studies analysis often falls—to concentrate only on what texts mean to their eventual close viewers and fans. In the case of casual viewers, paratextual frames are likely to rise in importance, precisely because there is less countervailing textuality on offer from the film or television program itself to challenge the paratextual frames. And in the case of non-viewers, of the millions who saw the *E.T.* poster, *Six Degrees* ads, *Sweet Hereafter* trailers, or *Buffy* opening credits, then decided to take their media consumption elsewhere, now there is no countervailing textuality to challenge the paratext, meaning that the paratext may well be, for such (non)viewers, the entirety of the text. Regardless, then, of whether they address eventual fans, eventual casual viewers, or non-viewers, and regardless of whether their meanings dovetail with or diverge from those of the film or television program, introductory paratexts are a vital part of the interpretive and consumption process, the first outposts and the beginning of textuality.

3

Bonus Materials

Digital Auras and Authors

As examined in chapter 2, Hollywood and its marketers often mobilize paratexts to proffer "proper interpretations," some preceding the show's arrival in the public sphere, thereby setting up pre-decodings, and some working in medias res to subtly inflect the public understanding of an ongoing and open text. Many such paratexts will aim to strike a balance between simile—insisting that a show is "just like X," or "a mix of Y and Z"—and metonym—encapsulating in microcosm the fuller diegetic world that exists in the show. In doing so, as I have argued, they are not always successful or even uniform, sometimes employing similes or metonyms problematically, and thus setting up unrealistic expectations that cannot be met, and offering various versions of what therefore becomes only nominally the "same" text. In all cases, though, they allow the text to be created in part outside of its supposed borders, so that public understanding of the film or program is generated in multiple sites by multiple paratexts. However, while chapter 2 offered numerous examples of paratexts creating or maintaining frames through which we are invited to make sense of what a text is ostensibly "about," who it addresses, what are its basic themes, and who populates its diegesis, paratextual frames can also prove remarkably important for how they assign *value* to a text, situating it as a product and/or as a work of art. Tony Bennett notes that "value is not something which the text has or possesses. It is not an attribute of the text; it is rather something that is produced for the text."[1] This chapter argues that paratexts are the source of much of this production.

Here we reach a dilemma for hype, promos, and synergy. For on one hand, media producers have found them to be absolutely necessary to attract audiences and encourage them to enter their textual worlds. Given the considerable textual clutter and the easy availability of endless shows in multiplexes, in video stores and libraries, on television, and on a mushrooming number of other devices and technologies, marketers must find ways to cut through the clutter to announce their show(s) as offering a better viewing experience than the thousands of other available options. Hype, promos, and synergy, with their pre-decoding scripts and either promises or reminders of diegetic pleasures, are thus imperative. However, on the other hand, hype, promos, and synergy contribute to the clutter that often bothers many a would-be audience member, thereby devaluing the show and losing would-be audiences with their mere presence. This dilemma proves particularly challenging for films' and television programs' claim to artistic status. Hype, promos, and synergy can easily remind us that a film or program is first and foremost a product of a studio machine, especially when their pitches start to look and sound remarkably similar. Many a film trailer, for example, "invites" one to "journey to a world where _____, and one man must fight for _____. But how do you succeed when all the odds are against you?" . . . and so on. If Hollywood itself often proves to be a paint-by-numbers industry, with recombinance and outright copying behind much of its production,[2] the hype, promo, and synergy industries can be even more obviously standardized, as in the above instance of Mad Lib trailer-making. As I explained in the Introduction, one of the motivating factors in writing this book has been that too often we in media studies do not bother to look beyond paratexts as instances of crass consumerism that detract from a business that could and should be about art, not industry. The fact that work on paratexts has often stopped at this obstacle speaks to the degree to which many viewers, and not just media studies analysts, detest and/or resent many paratexts.

Nevertheless, if hype campaigns, advertising, and merchandising can engender such skepticism about paratexts as being meaningful, complex entities, and about their accompanying texts as being legitimate art, other forms of paratexts try to offset the damaging effect of their culturally suspect counterparts. Just as some paratexts label a film or program as yet another mindless industrial product that "if you only see one this summer" absolutely *must* be this one, other paratexts actively create artistic aura for their associated text. In an impressive act of alchemy, numerous paratexts create an author figure, surround the text with aura, and insist on its uniqueness, value, and authenticity in an otherwise standardized media environment, thereby taking a heretofore industrial entity and rendering it a work of art. It is to these paratexts that this chapter turns.

Before I examine how paratexts attempt to give artistic and aesthetic value to fictional texts, I will first explore how they can similarly attempt to surround even nonfictional programming with greater aura and authenticity, thus attempting to increase such programs' moral and civic value. This process could be charted in the fetishistic invocation by any number of news programs of their websites or blogs, an act which draws attention to the supposed excess of facts, information, and opinion that they can marshal, and suggests a mastery of news and an overflowing concern for their citizen-viewers. Instead, though, in keeping with the book's interest in entertainment media, I will look at how makeover and improvement shows rely on their paratexts to battle pervasive critiques of reality television as exploitative, excessive, unreal, and pointless with an image of the shows as philanthropic, caring, and important.

If paratexts can change one's understanding of the authenticity of supposed reality programming, their powers to change one's appreciation of fictional, artistic texts are even starker. Hence, since I have spoken of paratexts as alchemists, I next turn to DVD "silver," "gold," and "platinum" editions, complete with their extensive bonus materials. Many of these bonus materials, such as "restored" scenes, interviews with creative personnel, commentary tracks, production stills, and making-of documentaries, stamp their texts with authenticity, insisting on that text's claim to the status of great art. While Walter Benjamin famously noted that "that which withers in the age of mechanical reproduction is the aura of the work of art,"[3] today's DVD digital reproduction often proves constitutive in assigning a text a sense of aura. Thus, I will study how the *Lord of the Rings: The Two Towers* Platinum Series Special Extended Edition DVDs append aura, author, and authenticity to the text. Such is the success of DVDs in creating authenticity that they are regularly regarded as containing the true version of the film (the "Director's Cut"), the real work of art, and I will examine how DVDs have managed to lay discursive claim to the real text. Following my extended example of the *Two Towers* DVD, I will then examine how this discursive claim has proven particularly important for television programs. I will explore how television authors can be "born" in paratexts, and how they conduct their, the industry's, and the audience's bidding in this realm, working as signifiers of value for all in question.

Ultimately, though Benjamin declared the death of aura, and Roland Barthes declared the death of the author,[4] this chapter argues that, mixing alchemy with necromancy, various paratexts have resurrected both aura and author, becoming primary sites for the generation of both as discursive values in today's mediated environment. I do not mean to imply that artistry, authenticity, aura, and authority exist *only* in paratexts, nor that such values will be acknowledged equally by all audience members: speaking personally, for example, I cannot imagine how any amount of paratextual pomp and pageantry could convince me that *Deuce Bigalow: European Gigolo* (2005) is anything other than a cinematic crime. Nevertheless, to a certain degree, paratexts can often determine what counts as cinematic and televisual art, aura, and authority, necessitating our close attention to them.

The Doctors' Rounds: Becoming the Real Deal

Since reality television hit the American market in full force in the early 2000s, the genre has commanded little respect, more commonly spoken of as hurting society than helping it, and as appealing to escapist and de-valued impulses, not reflective and valued ones. However, in recent years, a variety of shows dedicated to the improvement and "making over" of participants have sought to counter the image of reality television as con-trived, exploitative, and a waste of televisual space by touting themselves as contributing to the bettering of the nation. In their recent book *Better Living through Reality TV*, Laurie Ouellette and James Hay link the ex-pansion of shows promising to change the lives of guests, subjects, and viewers alike to a trend toward off-loading welfare, social services, and citizenship instruction to television. Through such programs as *Extreme Makeover: Home Edition*, *Supernanny* (2005–), and *The Biggest Loser* (2004–), reality television, they argue, is "being reinvented as an instruc-tional template for taking care of oneself and becoming self-enterprising as a path to (among other things) 'empowered' citizenship."[5] The shows in question stage "interventions" in order to give explicit and implicit in-struction on issues as varied as how to dress, eat, decorate, exercise, and raise one's children, taking as their premise the curing of bad personal behavior, style, and/or living environment. I argue that if the supposed bastard child that is reality television can muster the chutzpah to purport to be helping and educating Americans, its paratexts have often proven vital in making this rhetorical move possible. Makeover and improvement shows' paratexts, in other words, have given their texts value.

Many of these shows, after all, risk collapsing at their supposedly warm and fuzzy centers due to four intrinsic dilemmas. The first, as noted above, is that reality television has a bad reputation, its shows being coded as a waste of time. The second is a result of their frequently hyperbolic mode of address, which boasts of their supreme philanthropy. As networks and cable channels have realized the potential for makeover shows (broadly defined) to serve as sterling corporate public relations, their boasts regarding their shows' positive, transformative effects on society have become commonplace. However, most shows help a statistically insignificant number of people, while rejecting a statistically significant number of applicants for "help." Especially when the show's home network or channel is one of the world's more profitable companies, clearing millions or billions of dollars each year in profits, and when they have proven so resourceful in pawning off most fees to corporate sponsors and selfless volunteers, these shows run the risk of seeming callous, exploitative, and uncaring at worst, or irrelevant and inconsequential at best. A third dilemma centers on these shows' ethos of surveillance. As Ouellette and Hay note, a paradox exists when shows balance their message of civic education on the value of the free society, yet flagrantly violate personal freedoms by using Big Brother–like surveillance techniques to reach their goal.[6] Finally, and relatedly, they must assuage the viewers' potential guilt at being reduced to passive voyeurs of a spectacle, who are complicit with its surveillance, when the shows' call to improve oneself seemingly demands that audiences be more active and "do something."

Of course, contradictions exist throughout television and televisual pleasures, and many other shows similarly promise a value, then undercut that same value. But central to reality television's attempts to solve the above dilemmas are its paratexts, as the interventions that the shows perform frequently overflow into web pages, mailing lists, books, merchandise, and other platforms. For instance, writing of NBC's weight-loss competition, *The Biggest Loser*, Ouellette and Hay observe:

> The "text," in the old sense of broadcast media, is only one element in a network of cultural technologies that coalesced around the *Biggest Loser* concept. Viewers are invited to take part in its interventionist ethos by applying an array of technical suggestions and motivational strategies to their own weight-loss regimes. NBC has constructed an interactive website complete with nutritional guides, dieting tips, sample recipes and menus, customizable exercise regimes, and weight-loss tools, including a body mass index calculator. Tie-in merchandise—including workbooks and the *Biggest Loser* exercise DVD—is available for purchase, and participants are also urged to join the *Biggest Loser* email club and sign up for informative podcasts. Finally, for people on the go there is also the

much-promoted *Biggest Loser* wireless service. For only $2.99 per month, anyone with a cell phone can sign up to receive a daily health tip, an exercise pointer, or inspirational message.[7]

The "old sense of broadcast media" they allude to is, I would pose, that of the show-based model. In the "new" model, the text is now dispersed across not only the show, but also its multiple paratexts. The website serves as a portal into various sites of *The Biggest Loser*, of which the television show is merely one (fig. 3.1). Similarly, ABC's hit *Extreme Makeover: Home Edition* lives on in its Better Community website; NBC's short-lived *Three Wishes* (2005) tried to circulate dollar bills with *Three Wishes* stickers on them so that audiences would use them to help others' dreams come true; and *Supernanny* Jo Frost wrote a best-selling book on raising children. All of these paratexts encourage viewers to act upon the messages learnt, to continue the process of learning and self-evaluation, and/or to extend the philanthropic ministry beyond the shows and across multiple spaces of everyday life.

Many of these paratexts, then, *broaden* the shows' mission to countless others, asking for viewers to transform themselves into versions of the shows' contestants and self-help gurus, revolutionizing their or others' lives. Importantly, too, they also afford promos the opportunity to boast of this broader mission. By doing so, they address the first and second dilemmas noted above by suggesting a huge, "nationwide" pool of prospective recipients of help, recoding the show as mere catalyst, not as the sum total, of a philanthropic endeavor that goes well beyond the television screen. As for the third dilemma, the paratexts recode the surveillance as necessary, and as a small cost, so that audiences can "participate" in the push to improve themselves and their surrounding communities. Also, since the paratexts prove constitutive in the attempt to mobilize a broad base of self- and world-improving viewers, the final dilemma is seemingly erased, as the paratexts both call upon audiences to "do something" and give them skills and resources for doing so, thereby allowing viewers the opportunity to feel part of the broader mission. The paratexts, as such, aim to "cure" the texts.

Across reality television, paratexts have frequently attempted to make texts more accessible, more welcoming, and hence more popular, but they have also worked to "solve," or at least gloss over, seemingly inherent problems with the genre. It is at the level of the paratext where much improvement television attempts to refine its address. Importantly, no guarantee

Fig. 3.1. *The Biggest Loser*'s website offers multiple extensions and weight-loss tools, suggesting a *Biggest Loser* mission, not just a television program.

exists that these paratextual valuations will *work.* Moreover, as my liberal use of scare quotes suggests, we need not take the promotional, philanthropic rhetoric at face value; on the contrary, some such paratexts may increase some viewers' cynicism, as the attempt at halo-construction irks them more than the programs themselves. Hence, it is at the level of the paratext where much improvement television *aims* to complete its texts and to become "the real deal," illustrating in the process how paratexts can create value—moral, ethical, civic, and entertainment—for a text. But it is also at the level of the paratext where such shows can lose value and increase or seemingly justify viewers' and non-viewers' skepticism.

The Extra Texts, Bonus Texts, and Ideal Texts of DVDs

If paratexts can brand and recode reality, fictional universes prove an even easier target for branding and recoding. And while fictional films and television shows frequently boast many of the same types of paratexts that makeover shows have, a particularly strong paratext has been the DVD, complete with bonus materials ranging from making-of documentaries to commentary tracks, deleted or alternate scenes, and interactive games. In the first half of 2008, DVD sales and rentals in the United States produced $10.77 billion,[8] serving as further evidence of the market's strength. In an early article on DVDs, Robert Brookey and Robert Westerfelhaus also note their near unique status as paratexts, or, as they call them, extra texts. Many other paratexts are spatially distanced from their film or program, meaning in turn that producers and marketers can never be sure that all audience members will have access to them. Thus, for instance, the *Six Degrees* ad campaign discussed in chapter 2 required a would-be audience member to see the subway ads or the webpage, or to have heard about them from others. By contrast, Brookey and Westerfelhaus observe that "by including such interrelated [para]texts in a self-contained package, the DVD turns this intertextual relationship into an intratextual relationship."[9] Barbara Klinger writes that DVDs have an "instant built-in and changeable intertextual surround that enter into [a film's] meaning and significance for viewers,"[10] but as Brookey and Westerfelhaus suggest, this "intertextual surround" can easily become part of the text itself, making the DVD "perhaps the ultimate example of media-industry synergy, in which the promotion of a media product is collapsed into the product itself."[11] Bonus materials' contributions to the text may only be seen by some, and Brookey and Westerfelhaus somewhat overestimate the likelihood that all audience members will bother watching them.[12] But they are nevertheless correct in pointing to the ease with which DVDs bring all sorts of other paratexts—trailers, documentaries, interviews, ads for merchandise and videogames, and so forth—to those audiences who do watch bonus materials, rather than rely on happenstance or active exploration on the audience member's behalf.

Moreover, they note that these paratexts' appendage to the film or program through the DVD lends them and their meanings extra authority, precisely because they are now a digitally integrated part of the show itself. Brookey and Westerfelhaus exhibit particular interest in how this affects the status of the creative personnel's observations in commentary tracks and documentaries. "Individuals involved in the film's production," they argue, "are presented in the extra text as having privileged insights regarding a film's meaning and purpose, and, as such, they are used to articulate a 'proper' (i.e., sanctioned) interpretation."[13] Though DVDs promise the illusion of interactivity, and hence their add-ons and "Easter eggs" can seem like shreds of evidence discovered by the attentive forensic investigation of a given viewer, in fact little real interactivity exists, as instead viewers are given a carefully crafted set of meanings.[14] Using the example of *Fight Club*'s (1999) DVD, Brookey and Westerfelhaus show how the bonus materials and commentary tracks add an authorial voice that instructs readers on how to make sense of scenes and themes, and that in particular downplays the film's obvious homoeroticism, thus constructing a clear "proper interpretation." But their research also examined reviews of the film, and while the movie's post-theatrical release reviews were a mixed bag, its post-DVD release reviews were overwhelmingly positive, with many reviewers turning to the commentary tracks to divine the "real" text and hence the real way to interpret it. Commentary tracks and documentaries were even able to provide retorts to negative post-theatrical release reviews, explicitly attempting to "delegitimate" unfavorable critiques.

Brookey and Westerfelhaus's study of the *Fight Club* DVD once more suggests the potential for paratexts to establish proper interpretations, as well as the degree to which they can at least try to hide or overpower other interpretations (here, a homoerotic reading of the film). But it also suggests that DVDs can enrich the entire textual experience: if DVDs can be seen as offering the real text, then they can perform a quick sleight of hand, reducing the authenticity of the cinematic release or original television broadcast while elevating the paratext in status. P. David Marshall

similarly writes of DVDs' ability to "encircle, entice and deepen the significance of the film for the audience,"[15] foregrounding the degree to which
DVDs add value and meaning to texts, not just interpretive frames. Elsewhere I have examined the peculiarity of *Blade Runner* (1982) fans who
for more than twenty years held out for a "true" director's cut DVD of the
film. The original "Director's Cut" DVD was notable for one particular
added scene that suggested that the central character Deckard was himself a replicant, though this was known not to be director Ridley Scott's
preferred cut, and so fans were often excited at the prospect of Scott finally releasing the film as he wanted it. A paradox therefore existed of
individuals who had remained active fans of the film for years, posting
about it online and basing friendships around the shared love of the film,
yet who maintained that the true object of their fandom—the ideal, legitimate *Blade Runner*—had as yet been denied them. The DVD, as such,
represented the real work of art.[16]

The DVD market has grown so strongly in recent years that proclama-
tions of the DVD's contribution to the text should not seem peculiar. As
Charles Acland puts it, after all, "film texts *grow old elsewhere*," living on
in other venues and on other viewing platforms, and hence "the influence
of individual texts can be truly gauged only via cross-media scrutiny."[17]
Most prominently, Disney and other children's film producers often reap
significantly more profits once a film becomes a DVD.[18] Independent
films, too, Acland notes, regularly view the DVD as the centerpiece of the
marketing strategy. He quotes *Playback*'s description of the release strategy for Lars Von Trier's *The Kingdom* (1995): "It is [. . .] hoped that the
rep release campaign will boost video sales, sort of like running a trailer
for video." Acland also defends Canadian film's success against its many
skeptics, arguing that "focusing on the space of the cinema ignores the
fact that people see far more films in other locations. Indeed, Canadians see far more Canadian films at other locations. As David Ellis notes,
a single broadcast of a Canadian film on television can expect to have
an audience double those expected from theatrical release, pay-TV and
home video combined."[19] While this last example points to the strength of
Canadian broadcasting, not DVDs, in developing the value of Canadian
film, Acland nevertheless reminds us that a film's value, both monetarily
to its producers and popularly to its audience, will develop over time,
with various platforms for re-release and various paratexts playing potentially constitutive roles in creating our understanding and valuation of the
text.

Fig. 3.2. The stylishly designed *Lord of the Rings: Two Towers* Platinum Series Special Extended Edition DVD box immediately aestheticizes the films, suggesting something above the humdrum Hollywood film and/or DVD.

Fellowships of the Disc

To examine further how DVDs assign value to a text, I delved into the four-DVD Platinum Series Special Extended Edition of *The Lord of the Rings: The Two Towers*. While director Peter Jackson's films had received countless accolades upon theatrical release, their DVDs were no less remarkable. Packaged in an attractive "Elven"-designed box set (see fig. 3.2), the discs offer not only approximately one hour of extra (previously deleted) film footage, with scenes worked seamlessly into the cinematic text, complete with visual and sound effects, scoring, and so forth, but also four full four-hour commentary tracks, thirteen documentaries with more than seven hours of material, 1,917 photographic stills (219 of which come with commentaries), and interactive split-screen, map-, and audio-based features. With a credited production crew of 163, and with a total of 113 members of the film's cast or crew interviewed, the *Two Towers* DVDs open up the film and its production to viewers as few other artistic works in history have, creating well over thirty hours of bonus textuality, just as the *Lord of the Rings: The Fellowship of the Ring* DVDs did before them and as would the *Lord of the Rings: The Return of the King* DVDs after them. In watching all this material, I saw numerous themes repeating themselves: the bonus materials seek to enrich the film's quest narrative; they actively construct an aura of supreme artistry around the films that hearkens back to a mythical pre–culture industries vision of art; and in doing so, they create a fantasy realm of cinematic production and reception into which producers, cast, crew, and fans alike can enter. Effectively, they create a Middle Earth of artistic creation, with an author (or two), an aura, and authenticity. *The Lord of the Rings* is an epic tale of an unlikely group of heroes who, through comradeship, resilience, and compassion, manage to overcome the odds and triumph in the face of immense adversity. The DVD bonus material, meanwhile, replicates this narrative continuously, superimposing it onto the cast, crew, director, Tolkien, and New Zealand.

Lending the production of three films considerably more gravitas and mythic resonance, the DVDs' producers paint a picture of multiple other fellowships, innocent and struggling hobbits, charismatic rangers, and sage wizards. Most notably, the cast often transpose their filmic roles onto their own personages, or have the act performed by others. For instance, Orlando Bloom talks of what a privilege it was to come out of drama school and work with the likes of Ian McKellen, who, he notes, brought his "wise old wizard" ways to the cast, becoming a real-life Gandalf. Likewise, numerous cast and crew members discuss Viggo Mortensen's charisma and leadership as if he was his character, the ranger who becomes king, Aragorn. The stuntmen claim that his hard work and dedication on the gruelling Helm's Deep set inspired them. We learn of Mortensen's personal pull in convincing cast and crew alike to camp out the night before a dawn shoot. Colleagues talk of him as an earthy, nature-loving man. And Second Unit Director John Mahaffi even declares, "If I was going into battle and I needed someone to be on my right shoulder, it would be Viggo." Meanwhile, Dominic Monaghan and Billy Boyd provide much of the DVDs' comic relief, reprising their roles as the cheeky, prankster hobbits. In the cast commentary, they constantly toy with the film's register of reality, joking that a dreary, rocky scene looks just like Manchester, for instance, or that the film's huge dragon-like Balrog never bought a round when at the pub with them. Whereas most of the fifteen cast members contributing to the commentary were recorded individually, Monaghan and Boyd are recorded together, hence allowing their back-and-forth banter. Interestingly, too, while Elijah Wood and Sean Astin were recorded with them for the *Fellowship of the Ring* commentary, and similarly joked around as carefree hobbits, the *Two Towers* commentary separates them from Monaghan and Boyd. Paralleling Frodo and Sam's path into darkness, Wood and Astin's commentary takes on a more pensive, reflective nature.

In the *Fellowship of the Ring* commentary, the cast repeatedly referred to their bond with each other as their own "Fellowship," and once again, the *Lord of the Rings* vocabulary is used in the *Two Towers* DVDs. Monaghan notes that it was strange to be split up from the others for *The Two Towers* filming, an act which Wood describes as a "literal breaking of the Fellowship." Yet they and the DVD producers are at pains to describe how much of a complete team they were. Frustrations are downplayed, laughed away, or (likely) cut, as instead we are offered the picture of a group who all respect each others' work incredibly, enjoyed and relished each other's company, and are now sad to be apart. Barbara Klinger notes that despite DVDs' exposé style, "viewers do not get the unvarnished truth about the production; they are instead presented with the 'promotable' facts, behind-the-scenes information that supports and enhances a sense of the 'movie magic' associated with Hollywood production."[20] Here, the script on offer is of a real-life Fellowship. We are even told of a bizarre habit that developed between the cast and stuntmen of headbutting one another and are shown footage of Mortensen and Sala Baker headbutting at a premier, hence suggesting an intimate, ritualistic bond shared by all. What is more, cast and crew remind us continuously of the hard work and dedication that all gave to the project. Bloom, Mortensen, and Brett Beattie suffered broken ligaments or bones and yet forged on, we are told; Andy Serkis braved a frozen river in only a lycra suit; many extras and cast worked countless nights under rain machines in damp prosthetics for the Helm's Deep scenes; Brad Dourif shaved his eyebrows off five times; and all faithfully returned to New Zealand months later for pickups. The bonus materials insist on the cast becoming their own Fellowship, united by compassion, respect, and dedication, and determined to succeed in their own gruelling quest.

The tale of the Little Hobbits Who Could plays out on multiple other levels, too, as Peter Jackson particularly is raised by all commentators to an amalgam of the sage Gandalf, the charismatic Aragorn, the bumbling Merry or Pippin, and the erstwhile Frodo. Elsewhere, writing of George Lucas's image and "role" as independent film producer, Steve Bebout writes of how Lucas "performs" this role by voicing discontent with Hollywood in interviews, but also by keeping public appearances to a minimum, by talking about his work not his life, and by wearing the plaid-shirt-and-jeans "costume" of the American everyman.[21] The *Two Towers* bonus materials similarly assign Jackson the role of humble and unassuming geek next door, depicting a rather hobbit-like man with frizzy hair, no shoes, and no film school training, whose childlike simplicity left him open to practical jokes or the odd tumble into a bog, and yet whose energy, enthusiasm, easygoing and simple nature, and mastery of vision successfully helmed one of cinema's boldest projects to completion.

The design team, meanwhile, is given the role of the rag-tag group of hobbits, dwarves, elves, and humans who make up the foot soldiers who repel Sauron. Conceptual designer John Howe, for instance, talks of how Weta Workshop's creative supervisor Richard Taylor assembled a hardworking group who cared not for the fame, but who just loved the work and were dedicated to the cause. As one might imagine, much of the DVD bonus material studies the great feats of computer programming, set design, artwork, costuming, and other production details that made *The Lord of the Rings* such a lavishly rich project, and we are often hit with remarkable numbers and information: Edoras took eight months to build for eight days of filming, only to be completely dismantled afterwards, while Helm's Deep's set creation was preceded by three months of moving concrete and rock alone. True to *The Lord of the Rings'* democratic interest in all the "little" people who make up the grand front, the DVDs introduce us to many of these crew members who contributed to making it all possible, as the entirety of the Fellowship is fleshed out. From groundskeeper to foley artists, we are shown how huge this Army of the Ring is. Wood enthusiastically declares that "everyone put in everything they had" for the sake of the quest, and others on the DVDs repeat this assertion as if it is religious creed.

Throughout the documentaries, this multi-layering of quests is left not only to cast and crew discussion, as music from the trilogy's soundtrack is also cleverly used to embed certain themes. It is illustrative to focus briefly on the "J. R. R. Tolkien: Origins of Middle Earth" documentary, whose producers use Howard Shore's compositions to welcome Tolkien himself to this Fellowship and to depict his act of writing the trilogy as its own grand quest against publishing norms, academic suspicion, and historical obstacles. The documentary begins by telling us of Tolkien's friendship with C. S. Lewis and their common commitment to a different mode of storytelling, while the soft, inspiring flute of Shore's hobbit theme plays in the background. Then, we are told of these writers' shared experience of World War I, and as several stills of the war are shown, the harsh and throbbing warrior Uruk-Hai theme accompanies them. Later, after Brian Sibley grandiosely describes the completion of the trilogy and its delivery to the publisher as coming "like lightning out of a clear sky," the trilogy's Fellowship theme, or quest music, cues in the background. This piece is again utilized when Jude Fisher describes how the one book was divided into three. Thus, at these four points, musical themes are used to underline, respectively, the camaraderie and nostalgic traditionalism of Lewis and Tolkien, the cruelty and terror of war, and, in the last two instances, the birth of a great epic. At the same time, though, the music serves to *equate* Tolkien's struggle to those of his characters, and in literal concert together, they parallel his life to the trilogy's quest. As in countless other moments in the documentaries (as, for example, when any cast or crew tomfoolery is accompanied by the light and playful music from Shore's "Concerning Hobbits"), the DVDs propose that we view all manner of events and characters associated with the film production predominantly through diegetic *Lord of the Rings* glasses, superimposing Frodo and company's quest and ultimate victory onto Tolkien, Jackson, the cast, and the crew.

Even New Zealand and its inhabitants are painted with a *Lord of the Rings* brush. As the title on one feature, "New Zealand as Middle Earth," suggests, the DVDs engage in a certain degree of conflation (fig. 3.3). Commentary track discussion often insists with awe, for instance, "That's really there," and New Zealand's landscape is imbued with all of the magic of Middle Earth by cast and crew alike, only occasionally interrupted by the revelation that a location was actually constructed in a parking lot or is a matte painting. Meanwhile, from the notable presence of a local accent on many of the crew, combined with little information on their previous (if any) work, to the noted "discovery" of a local acting talent, such as Karl Urban, to the use of cricket fans to record Uruk-Hai chanting for Sauron's Nuremberg-like rally, and to the relatively unknown director himself, regional content in the DVDs is often presented with considerable pride, almost with the suggestion of hobbit-like recluse in the world, mixed with remarkable resourcefulness. Finally, in the DVDs' closing documentary, "'The Battle for Helm's Deep Is Over . . . ,'" Philippa Boyens solidifies the link between the cast, crew, New Zealand, and Middle Earth when she remarks that "anytime you get back together with the cast and other crew, it's great and special . . . especially in Wellington." Boyens thus declares New Zealand as the rightful home of this magic alliance between cast, crew, and diegetic world.

Fig. 3.3. The *Two Towers'* DVDs elide New Zealand and Middle Earth.

This multi-layering results in a formidable "stacking" of the narrative of the film, so that in addition to being a tale of Frodo, Aragorn, and Middle Earth, it is also one of the cast, the crew, Jackson, and Kiwis. Everyone, it seems, lived the movie. Remembering, too, that the *Two Towers* Platinum Edition was released prior to the cinematic release of *The Return of the King*, this stacking imbues the final chapter of the trilogy with significantly more meaning: no longer would we just be seeing Frodo's victory, but also the cast and crew's multi-year quest would come to an end, Jackson's quest would end, and a (coded) Kiwi film would triumph in the almost Mordor-like world of Hollywood. For many who have seen the *Fellowship of the Ring* or *The Two Towers* DVDs, *The Return of the King's* eventual Oscar monopoly would seem only just and deserved, since the DVDs (and other surrounding hype) added more mythic resonance than any of its competitors mustered. Of course, individual viewers may choose not to care about the multiple quests, and may refuse to actualize the DVDs' proposed multi-layering. If primed to accept, though, this is also due to the DVDs' masterful act of bathing the text in aura.

The Aura of the Ring

The multi-layering of the *Two Towers* text by the DVD bonus materials contributes to the steeping of the text in a significance and richness that tries to announce its difference from quotidian Hollywood fare. Taken as a whole, the bonus materials conduct a large-scale project to surround the text with aura. As Walter Benjamin famously declared, the age of mechanical reproduction supposedly killed aura. Benjamin's argument rests on the notion that mechanical reproduction "detaches the reproduced object from the domain of tradition," thereby depreciating its "presence in time and space, its unique existence at the place where it happens to be." "And what is really jeopardized when the historical testimony is affected is the authority of the object."[22] Art, he notes, had aura because of its history, presence, and ritual value. Ultimately, then, his concern is about context and about how contexts of viewing, reading, and listening are created. But context, as I have argued, is created largely by paratexts, and this observation is as true for the original as for the reproduction. For instance, if a painting is widely regarded as a wonderful work of art, a testament to national character, and a landmark in a given family's history, such qualities are in large part figured by its framing, where it hangs, the glowing descriptions and accounts that precede it, and its cost. Or, to rephrase, its value is in large part paratextually constructed. If that same painting is now made into a mousepad and sold in tacky souvenir stores at a discount if three of the same item are purchased, if its aura, presence, and value to the art world plummet as a result, once again paratexts are responsible. Thus, while Benjamin writes of aura as though it is born with the text, aura must be assigned with paratexts; his concern lies with the degree to which aura and value can be reassigned with different paratexts. As Benjamin writes of close-ups or slow motion, they reveal "entirely new structural formations of the subject," so that "a different nature opens itself to the camera [that employs such techniques] than opens to the naked eye."[23] Again, we might rephrase this by saying that different contexts of delivery and the paratexts that often provide such contexts expand the text, in the process offering different possibilities for its valuation. If "aura" is the sense of a text's authenticity and authority—which, by nature, could never be an actual, uncontested quality of a text, only a discursively constructed value—while Benjamin focuses on how reproduction can *lessen* aura, surely we might explore ways in which reproduction might change the text, add context, "tradition," and "presence," and thereby *increase* aura.

The *Two Towers* DVDs wrap the film in aura; housed in an attractive, high-quality box, the discs are filled with explicit and implicit grabs at the title of "Work of Art." If anything, the sheer volume of information, explanation, interpretation, and extra footage suggests an *excess* of artistry from the cinematic release, as if there was far too much to fit into a mere three hours. In the commentary track, for example, Wood explains how much work was put into one scene and yet, "as our luck always is [. . .] it didn't end up in the theatrical edition." At other points in the cast commentary, actors express delight at seeing a scene returned to the text, often expostulating at length the virtues of the scene. They also occasionally discuss the rewards of seeing certain (uncut) scenes in the theater, separating themselves and their involvement with the film to marvel at its artistry. Meanwhile, the cast and crew alike positively gush with praise for one another's performances and work. Wood tells Serkis, for instance, "You're an absolute blessing to that character [Gollum]," continuing, "It's just, uh, it's a marvel, Andy." Similarly, the design team is credited with inspiring many a scene and with themselves being gifted artists.

Beyond merely *telling* us how great the work is in an entertaining if exhaustive manner, the galleries and documentaries *show* us how superb a job everyone did. Revealing painstaking attention to detail in every portion of the film, and the immense amount of work put into getting any one element "right," for example, the galleries present hundreds of stills of sculptures, paintings, and sketches, many with accompanying genealogies by their artists. While allowing the viewer to slow down the film to study its minutiae, these galleries become filmic versions of art galleries with audio tours, rendering the individual works—and, by extension, the entire film—as gallery-*worthy* art. At the same time, the documentaries include film of all of the artists at work and information on the technologies and artwork, how they work, and how the crew revolutionized the forms. The DVDs teach a significant amount of production literacy, familiarizing audiences with the vocabulary of pickups, foley work, mime passes, second units, matte painting, and key frames, even while creating new phrases, such as Big-atures. Much as an art gallery's audio tour or an art history class may, then, the DVDs work to give us the information and teach us to appreciate the work. They also aim to impress with tales of individual artists' creation values. Howe in particular is depicted as a lifelong Tolkien fan dedicated to getting everything as authentically Middle Earth-ish as possible, whether this meant working from archaeological finds from Sutton Hoo to closely approximate a suitably Tolkienesque culture, or placing the stables at the top of the Edoras set to reflect Rohan's love of horses. Klinger notes that DVDs are "in the process of expanding the notion of aesthete [. . .] to include more mainstream consumers,"[24] and true to form, the *Two Towers* bonus materials teach us how and why to admire the film, thereby suggesting the degree to which that film definitively is an object of art deserving of appreciation.

Interestingly, and almost surprisingly, for all the big-budget effects that in many ways characterize the film, neither the documentaries nor the commentaries paint the film as an effects bonanza. Rather, commentators often hold up as sacrosanct the primacy of "the story" and "the way Tolkien wrote it," frequently with a flourish of Shore's Fellowship theme underscoring the sentiment. As described above, the DVDs liken the movie to Frodo's quest, and given the nostalgic simple English countryside ethos this valorizes, especially in the face of Sauron and his dark post-industrial world ethos, the cast and crew often highlight the human's presence in, and placement above, the film's effects. The Gollum documentaries and discussion, for instance, talk at length of how all the computers and programs at Weta could not bring life to the character until Serkis arrived, and a split-screen feature shows how closely the animators based the CGI performance on Serkis's (fig. 3.4). Similarly, we are frequently told of how production staff used "simple" and more "natural" answers for design dilemmas instead of technical, CGI ones. And, of course, the aforementioned narrative of the three-year cast and crew Fellowship suggests its own adherence to an "older, better" way of doing things. In other words, with nostalgic hobbit music in hand, the DVDs depict *The Two Towers* as an organic project, natural in all possible ways, and utterly human. This too, then, contributes to setting it apart from other Hollywood films, and to its obvious desire to be seen as Art with a sense of tradition, Art with ritual value, Art with aura.

The Return to Celluloid Hobbiton

As part and parcel of this construction of aura, the DVDs are keen to offer us an author. To a certain degree, they actually offer two, as Tolkien and his intentions are used as a mantra of sorts. All cast and crew pledge enormous fealty to Tolkien and his wishes, and Christopher Lee and Sean Astin in particular talk of wanting to capture specific scenes' Tolkienesque essence. All diversions from Tolkien's text are met with apologia, in which it is usually explained that the diversion was necessary to remain true to the "spirit" of the books. Beyond Tolkien, though, Jackson is lionized as a true director. Most cast and crew at some time or another glow about how he kept "his own vision" throughout, as Wood states. We are shown and

Fig. 3.4. A split-screen feature shows how Andy Serkis's performance determined the CGI Gollum's performance, further suggesting that special effects followed human ability, not vice versa.

told how Jackson would maintain last say on seemingly everything, checking in on second units or post-production via phone or satellite, acting as final judge on all artwork, set design, and costuming, and finding time to discuss important decisions with all cast and crew. Almost paradoxically, at the same time, the DVDs' act of introducing viewers to the many artists behind the film, including many of those traditionally labeled "below the line" workers, and hence regarded by Hollywood as non-creative by nature, serves to expand our understanding of who "counts" as an author, potentially undercutting the myth of the single author. Ultimately, however, all of these mini-authors are shown to report back to, and serve at the pleasure of, Jackson, the real Author.

As for Jackson's intentions, the DVDs often offer them to us, an act that is itself a powerful sign of the medium's adherence to a pre–Death of the Author world. As Peter Lunenfeld notes—and as Brookey and Westerfelhaus note of the *Fight Club* DVD—the medium fosters the intentionalist fallacy, calcifying the director's version of how to read a film.[25] Moreover, Jackson's stated intentions are all artistic, as neither he nor others (even the producers) violate this claim to authority by framing him as a man with a set "job" in yet another product of the money-seeking culture industries. Likewise, the DVD bonus material is happy and keen to make the film Jackson's, not New Line's or Time Warner's.

Once again, then, the DVDs engage in a nostalgic layering of the text, whereby even their production process claims to suggest a return to a mythic golden age of artistic creation. Pushing against the studio, for instance, the DVDs include several moments when Jackson or others describe clashes between New Line's narrow-mindedness and Jackson's bold vision, such as when Jackson says of New Line's early desire to have less of Gollum, "It's tough to deal with that, really, because they don't quite have the imagination or vision of what's going to be there that we do, so you just have to ignore it simply." Meanwhile, the simple act of including extra scenes, and the general happiness with which cast and crew commentary welcomes them back, implies dissatisfaction with the way New Line "made" Jackson cut the film. Many of the additional or extended scenes are from the books, too, and so the DVDs not only allow Jackson as author to overcome the studio system's desires, but seemingly allow Tolkien as author more presence as well. Characters that were missing from the theatrical version rejoin the film, scenes return, and Jackson's, Lee's, and Howe's Tolkien scholarship is offered in commentaries to fill in gaps with Middle Earth lore and legend. In many ways, the DVDs suggest that, as good as the theatrical version may have been, the DVDs offer the Real Work of Art as ordained by Jackson and Tolkien. Certainly, *The Two Towers* was in a unique position in film history, seeing that the *Fellowship of the Ring* DVDs had conditioned viewers to know that the Real, full-length, Author's version of *The Two Towers* was to be found in the DVDs, not in the cinematic release. One might also note that this division of textuality is in keeping with the nostalgic picture of artistic creation that DVDs revel in, for whereas a cinematic release is an event and an experience,[26] DVDs allow personal *ownership* of the text. Much as an art collector can hang an acquisition in his or her own living room, DVDs better suit this image of austere art in allowing the freedom to see them whenever and wherever their "owner" would like.

We could be amply justified if we regarded cynically this maneuver of conjuring aura, seeing in it and the multi-layerings of the text a deft yet sly move of the culture industries. After all, with few exceptions, film budgets and big-bucks Hollywood visual extravaganzas come no bigger than *The Lord of the Rings*. Jackson may have been a reasonably unknown director handed a huge and daring project, but he was hardly forced to produce it as he did his first picture, *Bad Taste* (1987), baking effects in his parents' oven and starring in it with friends to deal with a tiny budget. *The Lord of the Rings* fits comfortably in a long line of effects-driven blockbusters with big-name actors and the full force of one of the world's richest industries firmly behind it. Thus, to coyly pretend that it is a film from yesteryear, an old-style artistic work (even if this construction of pre-industrial film-making is mythological and ahistorical) aligning itself with the simplicity and wholesomeness of Hobbiton and Frodo Baggins, seems a garish ploy to efface its production history, and, pre-eminently, to act as if it is some-thing it is not. From a marketing standpoint, this is a coup: with the *Two Towers* DVDs acting simultaneously upon release as an ad for the then-upcoming *Return of the King*, they offer the viewer multiple sentimental and nostalgic reasons to "support" the trilogy and its supposedly humble quest by going to the cinema, maybe even multiple times. Likewise, the DVDs' suggestion that *The Lord of the Rings* represents a return to Real and Authentic Art, and to a respect for the craft as it was meant to be practiced, would be a reading its marketers no doubt hoped would attach itself to other *Lord of the Rings* products. On one level, then, the DVDs fully illustrate how multimedia corporations can employ networks of paratextuality to brand their products and increase the salience and depth of their meanings across the synergistic spectrum. Doubtlessly, studio ex-ecutives have discovered of late the powers that DVDs hold.

Nevertheless, to chalk up the *Lord of the Rings* DVDs solely as market-ing tools or ammunition would be to crudely posit multimedia corpora-tions as Sauron-like all-seeing eyes calling to their directors, cast, crew and viewers as the Palantir to Pippin, or the ring of power to Frodo. While this level of analysis tells part of our tale, it does not tell it all. Rather, we must also recognize the utility and attraction of the *Two Towers* DVDs' artistic creation myth to the creative personnel and to the viewers. If *The Lord of the Rings* risks being just another Hollywood item fresh off the conveyor belt, not only does the studio want us to believe it truly stands above and beyond other films, but the entire cast and crew would surely also like to believe that they are involved in something special, and the audience would surely like to believe that they are more than the supposedly average, spectacle-awed, bread-and-circuses crowd. To this end, the DVDs often play with notions of different audiences and posit their own audience as a more knowing, savvy, aesthetically attuned, and sensible lot. At multiple points in the commentaries, cast or crew refer to being aware of Tolkien fans' high standards, but never shirk these off, instead speaking of them with great respect. Sean Astin, for instance, recounts how important it was for him to capture Sam's reaction to seeing oliphants after reading a fan letter that spoke of how much meaning that scene in the book had to the writer. Even the inclusion of Jackson's extended explanations of why he removed certain scenes from the books assume that DVD watchers will be aware of their exclusion; and the insistence on how much attention to detail went into the project, along with the declarations and "outings" of Tolkien fandom amongst the cast and crew, could be read as presentation of credentials to Tolkien fans and discerning cinephiles.

The last and arguably most important Fellowship, then, is forged as the cast and crew ally themselves with the viewers against other filmmakers and audiences (including some theatrical version audiences) as members of a small, elite band. Frequently, the DVDs share intimate "secrets" of the filming as well as jokes, pranks, and gossip from the set. For example, we learn that Howe would sword-fight other designers at lunch, or that Mortensen fell for a beard-wearing stunt woman, and we see most of the cast and crew playing around in the various documentaries. Hence, the DVDs welcome us as viewers into the Fellowship, even to the point of adding a final track to the credits that lists all of *The Lord of the Rings* official fan club's members. The DVDs foster an intimate bond between cast, crew, and audience, one that combines with their construction of the film as Work of Art, and with their construction of the DVD audience as discerning and requiring art aficionados, cloaking the entire circuit of production, text, and consumption in an aura of artistry and excellence. The DVDs allow director, cast, crew, and audience to participate in an elaborate role-play in which they are transporting themselves back in time to an age of true art, pre-mechanical or digital reproduction, and thus preloss of aura—or better yet, that this age has been recovered.

It would be easy to see this role-play as a ruse, ironically befitting its fantasy text's genre. We should by no means underplay or underestimate the political and economic ramifications of such DVD branding, nor should we forget the industry's control over the rings of power that are the *Lord of the Rings* DVDs. However, this role-play also shows us the degree to which both aura and author are not necessarily dead. Granted, as Benjamin and Barthes have detailed, aura and author have changed.[27] But perhaps in a digital era, and under the rubric of new media, we are witnessing an earnest struggle to create a new variety of aura and author and to return (at least symbolically) to "older" models of creation and viewership. Here, I have illustrated how the *Two Towers* DVDs layer the text, so that *The Lord of the Rings* is an even more epic tale, and so that a blockbuster trilogy could be recontextualized as true art created by a rag-tag, hobbit-like group that set out to challenge Hollywood and its logic of production, and that magically found a way to do so.

My focus has been on one particular set of discs, but just as the *Two Towers* DVDs tell their central story multiple times over, so too does this story exist across a range of DVDs and other forms of bonus materials that insist upon their artistry, aura, authenticity, and author. Thus, for example, writing of a *Cinescape Insider* interview between George Lucas and Rick McCallum about their *Star Wars: Episode 1—The Phantom Menace* (1999), Robert Delaney notes Lucas and McCallum's heavy use of "metaphysical codes like 'spiritual' and 'soul' [to] elevate their product to another plane of existence, a level which, according to them, one will find in no other film."[28] Or, Daniel Mackay writes of how a Smithsonian "*Star Wars*: The Magic of Myth" exhibit—bonus materials in lived space—actively creates cultural capital for the trilogy, insisting on its mythological, "timeless" value. Since the Smithsonian is an austere Protector of Culture, Mackay observes that "they must increase the cultural worth of their object [here, a trilogy of popular films] before they use that object." Hence, they are determined to "change the phenomenological experience of the film," and to reveal it as possessing deeper, hidden meanings and cultural value.[29] Albeit to different degrees, many bonus materials claim that their films are from celluloid Hobbiton.

The 4.7-Inch Diameter Canvas: DVDs and Televisual Art

Above, I have discussed the paratextual resurrection of aura and author in terms of film, but if anything, the necromancy of the paratext becomes even more evident when we turn to television. After all, film has now long held considerable aura as a bona fide art form, and film scholarship and audiences have long upheld the value of the author or auteur. With film, then, the industry, cast and crew, and audiences have often needed to mobilize paratexts simply to *restore* or *maintain* aura, authenticity, and authorship where it has been at risk of perishing. Big blockbusters such as the *Lord of the Rings* trilogy risk seeming wholly the products of mass production, necessitating discursive moves to rescue aura, authenticity, and author, while special edition DVDs for "art house" films (the Criterion Collection, for instance) discursively reaffirm a claim to artistry and aura[30] that has already been staked in theatrical release, and through the paratexts of the independent theater playing the film, the high-end magazines or newspaper articles discussing the film, and the academic essays surrounding it. By contrast, since its first days, television has been considered a "lower" form of culture, derided by many, and often regarded as the ultimate exemplar of the accuracy of the Frankfurt School's damning assessment of the culture industries as producing standardized, factory-line mulch.[31] Heavily influenced by this assessment, Todd Gitlin argued, "Although executives may not be allergic to what they deem quality, the networks as a whole aim to create not purposeful or coherent or true or beautiful shows, but audiences. Any other purpose is subordinated to the larger design of keeping a sufficient number of people tuned in."[32] With such criticisms being commonplace regarding television, its surrounding paratexts have often been charged with the task of outright *creating* value and the semblance of art, aura, authenticity, and authorship.

As Derek Kompare notes, a huge obstacle to television being considered truly artistic and meaningful has been its ephemeral nature.[33] Large amounts of early television simply do not exist any longer because they were never recorded, and stories still abound of how little value many networks place on archiving their work. Television has often broadcast programs and then moved on, losing the shows to time and memory. This process also long restricted the development of a vibrant study of television's meanings, for whereas film critics and scholars could obtain copies of the film to study at length and in detail, television scholars were often forced to work with memory alone. And, of course, if scholars and critics had little to hold onto, so did audiences, thereby restricting the degree to which serial television could develop as an art form. As Kompare shows, reruns and the industry's warm embrace of the logic of repetition in the 1970s and beyond therefore did wonders to establish television as something beyond the trivial. Through reruns, television became "a cultural and historical resource for all generations," "a cultural touchstone,"[34] and its programs were recast as classics, as our "television heritage," thereby "validat[ing] the medium in ways that it had never been before, giving it an acknowledged role in the recent life and memory of the nation, and thus an assured place in American cultural history."[35] Ultimately, the impact of the DVD on television would prove equally monumental in the medium's attempt to raise its cultural status.

Kompare observes that DVDs do not just record television, they reconceptualize it.[36] Once television is available on DVD, several changes occur. First, one can now archive television, having it available on command, rather than relying on the vagaries of local scheduling. Admittedly, VHS allowed the same, but issues of relative software size, quality, and ease of use made the recording, storing, and watching of VHS more tricky. DVD availability now encourages viewers to think about which shows they would like to *own*, rather than simply what they would like to watch this week, or what they must remember to record and watch on the weekend. With this comes an increase in the value of television: that which is worth recording, worth keeping, and worth purchasing takes on more artistic value. Second, as Barbara Klinger points out, a "hardware aesthetic" develops among audio-visual aficionados, as some DVDs become valued for their superior sound-editing, picture quality, and bonus materials, independently of the quality of the story recorded on them.[37] Hence, along with HDTVs and home theater systems, DVDs have helped to aesthetically revolutionize the look and sound of television.

Third, pricing issues allow television in some cases to leapfrog over film in stores or in personal DVD collections, in terms of cultural value. Foreign imports and Criterion Collection versions of films are expensive, but most other films can be purchased for about ten to twenty-five dollars, and for as low as five dollars in bargain bins, or even less when pirated. By contrast, a season of a television series regularly costs about thirty to sixty dollars. In other words, TV DVDs are often the ones one must save up to buy, that need to go on wish lists, and/or that are bought as special treats for oneself, while film DVDs—especially at Wal-Mart, Target, or Amazon bargain prices—become more quotidian purchases. At the same time as HBO was staking its claim to high cultural status with the slogan that "it's not TV, it's HBO," ads in the New York transit system around Christmas insisted that DVDs of HBO shows were "the gift they really want." Perhaps it's not TV, it's DVD TV? Box set pricing alone has made television more valuable, even to those who remain true to their VCR or DVD burner, recording off television, since they are now aware that their labor and recording efforts are saving them, for instance, sixty dollars' worth of

DVD purchase. That said, box sets have themselves been aestheticized.[38] *Northern Exposure* (1990–95) comes wrapped in a parka, the original edition of *Battlestar Galactica* (1978–80) comes in a Cylon-head–shaped case, and one can buy the entire *West Wing* (1999–2006) in a portfolio-style design. Meanwhile, external packaging aside, DVD internal packaging is often intricate, as menus open up to yet more menus with original artwork, Easter eggs, and all manner of other goodies adorning the entire viewing experience. And since the average television season takes five or six discs, producers have often had to provide yet more bonus materials, which in turn—as this chapter has already suggested—results in a heightened claim to artistic status and aura. When the Season 1 box set for *Lost*, for instance, includes a series of set photos by actor Matthew Fox, their inclusion demands simultaneously that the show and the set design are true art, and that the actor is a true artist. Or when a DVD of an older show is released brimming with bonus materials, it reframes a show that was likely relegated to daytime television on obscure cable channels as something worth studying closely. In multiple ways, then, DVDs up television's aesthetic ante, surrounding their programs with significant aura and value.

Resurrecting the Television Author

In this regard, however, DVDs are not alone in the paratextual world, for much of what can be found on them are paratexts available in other forms elsewhere. DVDs often present multiple interviews or making-of/behind-the-scenes specials, but versions of these can also be found on television as filler material or as "On Demand" items from premium cable channels, as well as in the programming that plays before movies in the theater. Similarly, the 7 to 8 p.m. time slot on American television is often full of entertainment news programs such as *Entertainment Tonight*, *Extra* (1994–), and *Access Hollywood* (1996–) that give "sneak peaks" and "exclusive" interviews, and these programs have multiple counterparts in the magazine world (*Premiere*, *Variety*, *Entertainment Weekly*), in the entertainment news sections of most major newspapers, and in the ever-increasing number of websites that specialize in entertainment news (such as *ComingSoon.net*). Late-night and daytime talk shows regularly invite stars and directors on to discuss their work, too, making the celebrity interview one of the more common forms of content on television. Moreover, numerous television shows are now experimenting with offering podcasts, as cast and crew record weekly versions of DVD bonus materials, commenting on a range of issues, from production minutiae to their intentions and hopes for various scenes, sometimes fielding fan questions, and releasing extra information. In short, one does not need either to buy, rent, or rip a DVD to be able to access an extensive amount of information made available by cast and crew.

For television in particular, the explosion of websites, the increase in entertainment news magazines and programs, and the advent of DVD bonus materials and podcasting have made executive producers/showrunners considerably more visible than in earlier years of the medium. With this visibility, these individuals are more and more able to add their voice to the audience's understanding of their products, and thus are increasingly able to construct themselves as authors, televisual counterparts to Peter "Frodo" Jackson.

In this light, it is worth returning to Roland Barthes's famous declaration of the "death of the author," especially since it would appear to preclude the existence of authors, even when our media environment seems to be giving us yet more authors. Importantly, Barthes's essay was more of a strategic, rhetorical killing than an actual obituary. He saw the study of texts "tyrannically centred on the author, his [*sic*] person, his life, his tastes, his passions," thereby neglecting the fact that "it is language which speaks, not the author; to write is, through a prerequisite impersonality [. . .] to reach a point where only language 'performs,' and not 'me.'"[39] As discussed in chapter 1, Barthes believed in the need to separate the "work" from the "text" in analysis, yet found the specter of the author to be an impediment to this move, since his or her authority risked presiding over the work, denying audience members the right to create a text. To Barthes, if textual studies were to adequately study language and how it works, how meaning comes to be, and the full range of a text's semiotic and social relevance, the author would forever remain an obstacle, and so, Barthes closed his article, "the birth of the reader must be at the cost of the death of the author."[40]

However, writing on the heels of Barthes's pronunciation, Michel Foucault noted that readers themselves often have multiple uses for the author as concept. Authors, as such, are not solely external authorities; rather, they are texts that audiences utilize to make meaning and to situate themselves in relation to other texts. He argues that "it is not enough to declare that we should do without the writer (the author)."[41] People still talk about authors, he notes, not necessarily as real people, but as projections of our hopes, expectations, and established reading strategies for texts. In particular, the author—or "author function," as Foucault calls it—takes on the role of being classificatory, indicating "a constant level of value," "a field of conceptual or theoretical coherence," "a stylistic unity," and "a historical figure at the crossroads of a certain number of events."[42] Henry Jenkins uses Foucault's schema to analyze the ways in which *Star Trek* "author" Gene Roddenberry is used and discussed. Roddenberry as concept helps classify what is *Star Trek* and what isn't.[43] He also serves as shorthand for a set of values, themes, and aesthetic moves that are seen to be consistent across his work. And to make him an author is to demand that *Star Trek* is of a certain quality: "Seeing *Star Trek* as reflecting the artistic vision of a single creator, Gene Roddenberry, thus allows fans to distinguish it from the bulk of commercial television which they see as faceless and formulaic, lacking aesthetic and ideological integrity."[44] Playing off this last use for the "author function," and following from the above discussions of DVDs, aura, and value, we could add that the value function of authorship can more generally lend weight and substance to an entire medium.

In many ways, we can read Foucault's notion of the author function as responding not only to Barthes's act of murder, but also to the Frankfurt School's own killing of the author. Barthes "killed" the author so that the reader might live, yet Max Horkheimer and Theodor Adorno simply declared that industry had killed art altogether. In other words, while Barthes wanted the author dead, the Frankfurt School would rather s/he was alive, but saw no signs of life. Foucault's concept of the author function allows a middle ground, wherein the author is denied outright authority, but exists as a discursive entity that channels and networks notions of value, identity, coherency, skill, and unity. This is an alternative to believing in Horkheimer and Adorno's faceless "iron system" in which "there is the agreement—or at least the determination—of all executive authorities not to produce or sanction anything that in any way differs from their own rules, their own ideas about consumers, or above all themselves."[45]

Especially when we consider television authors, moreover, Barthes's key objections to the author become less relevant. His complaint about book authors was ultimately one of temporality, as he argued that "book and author stand automatically on a single line divided into a *before* and an *after*. The Author is thought to *nourish* the book, which is to say that he [*sic*] exists before it, thinks, suffers, lives for it, is in the same relation of antecedence to his work as a father to his child." He proposes and prefers a situation whereby we consider that "the scriptor is born simultaneously with the text [. . . and] there is no other time than that of the enunciation and every text is eternally written *here and now*."[46] However, throughout the run of a television series, its author(s) and the text can only exist at the same time: unlike literature (or film), the author rarely writes the material then exits the scene. Instead, a television author or authorial team writes one or more episodes, which are broadcast, then they return to the job, these in turn are watched, and so on. The dichotomy of antecedent author and active text rarely exists with television series, and so the rhetorical importance of Barthes's argument diminishes. Barthes killed the author in order to open the text, but a television series is nearly always already open.

Writing of fan fiction and Barthes's killing of the author, Francesca Coppa notes that "the author [of the source fan object] may be dead, but the writer [of the fan fiction]—that actively scribbling, embodied woman—is very much alive. You can talk to her; you can write to her and ask her questions about her work, and she will probably write back to you and answer them."[47] Film and television still like their *authors*, and interacting with them is rarely as easy as the situation that Coppa describes with fan fiction writers, as authors and readers are separated by PR departments, personal assistants, legalities that ask that television writers not listen to unsolicited ideas, and their own constructed auras. Nevertheless, albeit in the often heavily mediated form of interviews, podcasts, bonus materials, and visits to fan sites or conferences, television authors (and some film authors) engage in significantly more interaction with audiences than did Barthes's "death-worthy" authors.

Television authors still try to exert authority and control over "their" texts, for as I have argued, producer-end paratexts hold significant power in inflecting audiences' interpretive frameworks. When creators try to exert control, the paratexts of interviews, podcasts, DVD bonus materials, and making-of specials are their preferred means of speaking—their textual body and corporeal form—as they will try to use paratexts to assert authority and to maintain the role of author. But rather than serve as gospel, as soon as a show has begun, television authors' words become in medias res paratexts that must compete with all manner of other paratexts, including audience-created paratexts (see chapter 5). Jurij Lotman wrote of reading and interpreting as a "game" between writer and reader, whereby, as one reads, "The audience takes in part of the text and then 'finishes' or 'constructs' the rest. The author's next 'move' may confirm the guess [. . .] or it may disprove the guess and require a new construction from the reader." However, Lotman sees this process inevitably ending in the same way: "the author wins; he [*sic*] outplays the artistic experience, aesthetic norms and prejudices of the reader, and thrusts his model of the world and concept of the structure of reality upon [the reader]."[48] Television texts, by contrast, are continuing "games," with no such easy predictability of outcome. Within these games, each paratext is a move; but whereas in a book or film, most of the author's moves have already occurred, meaning that s/he does not truly "respond" to the reader or viewer's "moves" at all, in television, authors both can and must respond to moves, meaning in turn that audience moves have more importance. With perhaps the lone exception of retrospective commentary offered by a writer after a show has finished, to an audience member who has watched the entire show, the game continues.

Take, for instance, Joss Whedon's response, in a *Science Fiction Weekly* interview, to a question about whether fan commentary influenced how he wrote *Buffy the Vampire Slayer*:

> To an extent it does. For example, when I saw that people were rejecting the Oz character when he was first introduced, I realized how carefully I had to place him. I wrote scenes where Willow falls in love with him in a way where fans would fall in love with him too. You learn that people don't take things at face value; you have to earn them.[49]

Alongside this example, we might add several others, such as Carlton Cuse and Damon Lindelof's reflection on how *Lost* audience reactions have at times shifted their scripting of the show, most notably when Michael Emerson became a quick fan favorite for his portrayal of Benjamin Linus, leading Cuse and Lindelof to write him into the core of the story.[50] *Babylon 5* (1994–98) creator Joe Straczynski posted more than 17,000 replies to fans,[51] illustrating a clear interest in (some might say obsession with) his fans' opinions. Or, most curiously, responding to widespread criticism of the opening episodes of Season 2 of *Heroes*, showrunner Tim Kring apologized to viewers via *Entertainment Weekly*, insisting that "we've heard the [fans'] complaints—and we're doing something about it,"[52] and promising that he and his writing staff would henceforth work on addressing the multiple criticisms of the show. Meanwhile, several writers are popping up on fan boards, and each passing year seems to bring yet more writers to Comic-Con. While both trends are no doubt motivated by a need to solicit fans in a niche broadcasting, post-network era, some writers' presence on fan boards and at fan conventions shows (and is read by some fans as) an earnest interest in fans' opinions. Writers rarely prove wholly responsive to their fans, in part due to issues of chronology (once the fans are watching any given episode, numerous subsequent episodes have already been filmed), in part due to conflicting fan desires, and in part due to personal creative intuition and impulses,[53] but many nevertheless realize the importance of interaction and dialogue.

Whether through posting online, contacting production personnel directly, or simply watching or not watching, audience members and communities regularly play "moves" in the game of television, and any savvy author must now know how to react to these moves, how to counter.[54] Yet far from seeing this necessarily in the framework of "winners" and "losers" that Lotman provides, we might also note that many authors and fans regard the productive act as more communal and participatory. Responding to a question about fan adulation, Whedon notes in an interview with *The Onion AV Club*, "It doesn't feel like they're reacting to me. [. . .] I feel like there's a religion in narrative, and I feel the same way they do. I feel like we're both paying homage to something else; they're not paying homage to me."[55] If we take him at his word, Whedon has internalized the "practical collaboration" of reader with text that Barthes asks for as expected practice.[56] Later in the same interview, Whedon states:

> I wanted [*Buffy*] to be a cultural phenomenon. [. . .] I wanted people to embrace [the show] in a way that exists beyond, "Oh, that was a wonderful show about lawyers, let's have dinner." I wanted people to internalize it, and make up fantasies where they were in the story, to take it home with them, for it to exist beyond the TV show.[57]

Interestingly, then, Whedon positions himself as working toward the same goal as his readers, not "competing" with them. In doing so, he deliberately confuses author and reader roles by adopting part of the reader role himself, and yielding part of the author role to the reader. Admittedly, one might regard this as a discursive move, an attempt to fashion himself as "just one of the fans," when he is decidedly privileged in the relationship. But he both steps away from the author as antecedent role to which Barthes objected, and he reflects on the degree to which, as a public figure, he is an author function, a text/paratext authored by audience members and their uses for him, and a way for people to talk about the artistry of *Buffy* more than he is a specific individual to *Buffy* fans.

Joss Whedon is one of a brand of television authors who have realized the importance of engaging with their fan bases, and *Buffy*'s success arguably was all the greater for this realization, and for his eagerness to at least partly, in Barthesian terms, kill himself as author. As is only fitting for the author of *Buffy the Vampire Slayer*, Whedon was an undead author. But he is by no means alone, joined by others such as Cuse and Lindelof, Straczynski, Kring, Doris Egan, Aaron Sorkin, Jane Espenson, Jason Katims, Toni Graphia, Erik Kripke, Rob Thomas, Josh Schwartz, and others, and preceded by *Star Trek* creator Gene Roddenberry's strong rapport with his fans. All of these figures are known to most audiences only through paratexts. Whether they are "really like that" becomes as much a question for them as it is for Hollywood stars, though, because they and their studios' marketing teams are often able to author them as paratexts, and author some of the paratexts in which they appear, with significant care. They are authored by audiences, too, with their own paratexts. Like Foucault, then, I have little interest (as a scholar) in the "real" Whedon, Cuse and Lindelof, Kring, or so forth, realizing that they are discursive constructions. But as author functions, as signifiers of value, as messages to or from the network and/or to or from the fan, and as paratextual entities that frame both value and textual meaning (see chapter 4 on the latter), they are considerably important. As such, we might regard television authors as mediators between the industry and audiences, and the author function as a discursive entity used by the industry to communicate messages about its texts to audiences, by the creative personnel often conflated into the image of the author(s) to communicate their own messages about these texts to audiences, and by audiences to communicate messages both to each other and to the industry. A considerable danger exists of romanticizing the degree to which *actual* writers mediate effectively between production and audiences, but producers and audiences alike often use them as *discursive* constructions and mediators. Paratexts carry these messages, and thus frequently serve as both the words and the content of discussions among text, audience, and industry.

Paratextual Turn-Offs and Turn-Ons

At the outset of the chapter, I noted that hype, promos, and synergy turn off many a would-be viewer. Thus, while the chapter has examined the role that paratexts play in adding or restoring value, often their mere existence devalues a text. Much hype betrays a text's industrial roots too obviously for some audiences, thereby disqualifying it for consideration as art. Meanwhile, the presence of many in medias res paratexts codes a text as a fan text, thereby invoking the high-cultural critique of the popular that hounds all fan texts. As such, some would-be viewers cling to a heavily romanticized notion of the singular Work of Art that neither needs nor has a paratext, the noble cowboy text riding across the prairies and fighting the elements all on its lonesome. Ultimately, though, paratext-less shows simply do not exist. Granted, some texts claim more paratexts than others, with, for instance, blockbusters and cult texts often sporting sizeable posses. But all shows have paratexts. In discussing paratexts and value, then, we might realize how any would-be audience member or community gives value to certain forms of paratexts in and of themselves, yet is turned off by others in and of themselves. Since genres often address specific communities of viewers, moreover, film and television producers tend to surround their shows only with those paratexts that are likely to add value to their desired audience.

For instance, foreign and independent films often rely upon upscale audiences who flatter themselves as being discerning, (high-)"cultured" viewers. A vigorous hype campaign centered on subways, ad slots during reality television shows, and a videogame could thus harm a foreign film's chances more than help them. But it still requires paratexts to offer value, whether in the form of awards from film festivals, an evocative poster, a director's talk before the film, and/or a positive review in the *New York Times* or other high-end publications. With more than half of the average foreign film's domestic box office coming from New York City alone, as Michael Wilmington has noted, the *New York Times* has "veto power" over a foreign film's future.[58] Or, television procedurals have significant appeal as contained stories that do not require devoted viewing, and thus podcasts or alternate-reality games might ruin some of their seemingly pared-down appeal. But procedurals often rely on special event advertising both for renewing a claim to value and for a sense of realism upon which that value may be based. *Law and Order* (1990–) ads, for example, tout "ripped from the headlines" stories with considerable enthusiasm, as do those for *JAG* (1995–2005) and *NCIS* (2003–). Conversely, favorable *New York Times* reviews or "ripped from the headlines" ads will likely prove relatively unimportant for other genres, such as sitcoms or sci-fi series. Over and above the specific meanings on offer by any given paratext, then, and over and above any given paratext's specific claims to art, aura, and authenticity, sometimes the type of paratext sends its own messages.

All shows have paratexts, and all require their paratexts to create frames of value around them, but different genres will favor or disfavor different types of paratextuality.

Throughout this chapter, I have illustrated the degree to which new media such as webpages, DVDs, and podcasts surround texts with a paratextual veneer of artistry, aura, and authority that aims to be decidedly "old school." Paratexts, and various forms of bonus materials in particular, aim to play a constitutive role in creating value for a film or television show, even if in practice this value is not created equally for all audiences. Some audiences will seek out such paratexts precisely in order to reaffirm their sense of the film or program's value. Others will regard the mere existence of paratexts and hype as the clearest example of the lack of artistic integrity, seeing them as akin to a painter selling his or her work in a shopping mall storefront with a gaudy neon sign. In either situation, the paratext helps create a sense of value (whether positive or negative).

Authority, value, and meanings, however, do not simply circulate via the film and television industries, their stars and directors, and their marketing teams alone. Chapters 4 and 5 therefore turn to other modes of paratextual circulation and function. Chapter 4 explores how films and television shows themselves can come to serve paratextual roles, whether by design or by happenstance. It also explores how, paratextually, audience discussion creates both intertextual networks of understanding that render certain shows as paratexts to other texts, and understandings of the author function that inflect readings of other texts. Then, chapter 5 examines viewer-created paratexts and the ways in which they either challenge industry-created paratexts' "proper" interpretations or otherwise carve out space for personal or communal readings of film and television shows.

4

Under a Long Shadow
Sequels, Prequels, Pre-Texts, and Intertexts

In chapter 1, I offered multiple metaphors by which we can make sense of paratexts—as airlocks, as high priests of textuality, as overflow, as convergence—but on a basic level, we can understand them as intertexts. Intertextuality refers to the fundamental and inescapable interdependence of all textual meaning upon the structures of meaning proposed by other texts. In common usage, *intertextuality* refers to instances wherein a film or program refers to and builds some of its meaning off another film or program, and *intertext* to the referenced film or program. For instance, *West Side Story* invokes the intertexts of *Romeo and Juliet*, *The Colbert Report* relies on its viewers' intertextual knowledge of pundit shows to parody and satirize programs such as *The O'Reilly Factor* (1996–), and *The Sopranos* intertextually plays with and reworks gangster movie tropes. Intertextuality is a system that calls for the viewer to use previously seen texts to make sense of the one at hand. As Laurent Jenny notes, it "introduces a new way of reading which destroys the linearity of a text,"[1] instead opening the text up to meanings from outside, so that often much of (our understanding of) a text will be constructed outside of the text. And while it is more obvious in examples such as *West Side Story*, *The Colbert Report*, or *The Sopranos*, no text creates its entire meaning for itself by itself, as viewers will always make sense of a new text using structures and orders of meaning offered to them by other texts, genres, and viewing experiences. Intertextuality is always at work, with texts framing each other just as I have shown paratexts to frame texts. In this regard, paratextuality is in fact a subset of intertextuality. What distinguishes the two terms is that intertextuality often refers to the instance wherein one or more bona fide shows frame another show, whereas paratextuality refers to the instance wherein a textual fragment or "peripheral" frames a show.

However, paratextuality and intertextuality regularly bleed into and rely upon one another. As Genette uses the word "paratext," he implies a form of subservience to a greater entity. Even if textually the paratext may prove constitutive of that entity, paratexts are generally outgrowths of a film or program. But what of the instance when a show is seen as an outgrowth of another show, as an extension that is functionally subservient and dependent? In such cases, shows can and should be analyzed as paratexts. Paratextuality and intertextuality, though, are also intertwined in that intertextual frames are not wholly personal and insular. Rather, talk and discussion will circulate intertextual frames, suggesting ways that one might interpret a show, or forming an entryway or in medias res paratext that is as fully realized and powerful as are trailers, ad campaigns, or bonus materials. Intertextuality, in other words, often works through the calcified form of paratexts such as viewer discussion. Thus, this chapter will examine various ways in which paratexts do the work of intertextuality, and various ways in which paratextuality and intertextuality combine.

Michael Iampolski notes that "by creating a specific intertextual field as its own environment, each text in its own way seeks to organize and regroup its textual predecessors," thereby also creating "its own history of culture,"[2] but I will examine how paratexts—or shows working as paratexts—operationalize this process. In particular, I am interested in how such "intertextual fields" are created before we even sit down in the cinema or turn on the television. Valentin Volosinov argues that what is important about a text "is not that it is a stable and always self-equivalent signal, but that it is an always changeable and adaptable sign."[3] Tony Bennett explains Volosinov and Bakhtin's intertextual theory by observing that "the position of any single text in relation to other texts, and hence its function, is liable to constant shifts and displacements as new forms of writing transform and reorganize the entire system of relationships between texts."[4] In this chapter, I will focus on how paratexts manage such changes, adaptations, shifts, and reorganizations.

I begin by studying the process of adaptation, specifically how Tolkien's *Lord of the Rings* books established a paratextual perimeter around their filmic adaptations for some would-be viewers, paratextualizing the films even before release. Moving from adaptation to more varied forms of intertextuality, I then examine how these films themselves became powerful inhibitors for audiences' reception of Peter Jackson's subsequent *King Kong* and of Andrew Adamson's filmic adaptation of C. S. Lewis's *Chronicles of Narnia: The Lion, The Witch, and the Wardrobe*. Of interest to me is how audience discussion, as paratext, works to cast a formidable shadow, in the form of the previous film, over the reception of the subsequent films. I then chart how such shadows become prominent enough that they can affect even the production of subsequent texts, as I study how *Batman Begins* maneuvered to escape the darkened shroud of Batman's previous cinematic outing, *Batman and Robin*. Finally, I study how intertextuality becomes a communal game, played in the realm of the paratext. I look at how audience discussion surrounding the release of *Lost* and *Six Degrees* created a paratextual perimeter in the form of notions of executive producer J. J. Abrams's supposed scripting style. Fans and once-fans of Abrams's earlier shows offered interpretive schemas for his recent shows, based on their understanding of how his shows worked. In doing so, they communicated intertextual knowledge (rightly or wrongly) to non-fans and non-viewers of that work, thereby illustrating how intertextual knowledge can reside in and disseminate via paratexts, not solely in and via personal viewing experiences.

Overall, the chapter examines the complex hall of paratextual and intertextual mirrors through which meaning and reception must pass, and how in this hall intertextuality will often work through paratexts. Nick Couldry asks the important question, "On what terms can we go on thinking, and talking, about 'texts' *at all* in a culture where, in a sense, we have too many texts"?[5] As does the book as a whole, this chapter suggests that relational, intertextual and paratextual studies are where our efforts might lie. Finding out which texts, or which parts and iterations of texts, are determinative and controlling of each other can tell us a great deal, and can help us to better understand how and where meaning begins and how it is extended and stretched elsewhere.

A Return to Middle Earth:
Pre-Viewing Lord of the Rings *(with Bertha Chin)*

In the early months of 2001, Bertha Chin and I conducted a somewhat peculiar research project: we examined audience interpretation of Peter Jackson's *The Lord of the Rings: The Fellowship of the Ring* nine months before the film was released.[6] We had not seen the film, nor had any of the audience members under examination; the film, after all, was still in the throes of production. However, though nine months away from cinematic release, the film was at least as many months bathed in hype: amidst continuing and excited press releases, magazine articles, and official website updates, the movie had announced itself long before its Christmas 2001 release. On the Internet in particular, dedicated *Lord of the Rings* web discussion sites were thriving, often with multiple posts a day, producing a curious situation in which people were congregating to discuss a text that seemingly did not yet exist, often in great detail. Thus, whereas chapter 2 argues that texts often begin with their promos, here were individuals parsing and debating all manner of directorial decisions, talking excitedly about particular scenes, and grumbling about poor acting, long before New Line had released a trailer or poster, let alone the movie. Numerous audience researchers have observed the ease and efficiency of conducting their research online, but here we had an audience waiting for us before the film! If not "viewers" discussing a text, they were at the least "pre-viewers" discussing a "pre-text." And if, as Espen Aarseth has argued, "like electrons, [texts] can never be experienced directly, only by the signs of their behavior,"[7] why wait for the text when the "signs of its behavior" were already evident? Chin and I saw this as a golden opportunity to study how textuality begins, where it comes from, and how the text and audience meet.

We were not the first researchers to discuss the consumption of a text before it occurs. As described in chapter 1, Tony Bennett and Janet Woollacott conducted a landmark study of James Bond as a "dormant signifier, inactive most of the time, but capable of being periodically reactivated."[8] Bond's multiple textual appearances, they argued, created an interpretive shorthand for audiences: when a new Bond film is on the horizon, we already have a clear sense of what to expect, and we already have a set of reading strategies and frames ready for use:

> The process of reading is not one in which reader and text meet as abstractions but one in which the inter-textually organised reader meets the inter-textually organised text. The exchange is never a pure one between two unsullied entities, existing separately from one another, but is rather "muddled" by the cultural debris which attach to both texts and readers in the determinate conditions which regulate the specific forms of their encounter.[9]

Performing audience research into the "unsullied entity" of *Judge Dredd*'s (1995) would-be audiences in 1995, Martin Barker and Kate Brooks examined how numerous audience members discussed the film before watching it. In particular, Barker and Brooks were able to isolate various reading frames, ranging from, for instance, Stallone-followers, to action-film aficionados, to fans of the *2000 A.D.* comic books on which the film was based. High expectations and hopes, as well as expectations to be disappointed, were commonplace, and yet as they note, all such reactions pointed to the presence of an *ideal* text, suggesting the degree to which audiences use available intertexts (Stallone as star, blockbuster, *2000 A.D.*, etc.) to project outward an image of the text to come, one that they can "consume" and with which they can engage before the actual film is released.[10] How would the *Lord of the Rings* pre-viewers confirm, further illustrate, and/or challenge these findings?

Given the plethora of discussion in online forums, we felt it unnecessary to contact specific posters. Moreover, whereas media studies have long read viewers and the nature of viewers off the film or program, in a flip of this rubric, here we were attempting to read the text off its viewers. Since our intent was not to make sense of the individual viewers, we did not seek to contextualize their comments within the broader life histories to which one-on-one interviews give researchers greater access. We recorded and coded discussion from the film's official discussion board—www.lordoftherings.net—as well as from two Yahoo Groups boards ("lotr" and "lord_OT_rings_movie") and from www.tolkien-movies.com. Each of these sites is, of course, its own communally authored paratext and could be studied for its general framing of the *Lord of the Rings* books as text, but we aimed to cut a specific path through the wealth of material at each address. Of prime interest to us was any talk that constructed an image of the film, and hence that would provide insight into how a (filmic) pre-text takes form and becomes a text: we were not seeking a representative response or even series of responses, but rather were interested in the form(s) that the text took during early pre-release discussion.

Immediately apparent was that all posters appeared to be devoted fans of Tolkien's books. Elsewhere, Ian McKellen, Liv Tyler, Peter Jackson, or fantasy fans, say, were undoubtedly conducting their own dialogue, but these posters displayed the utmost familiarity with and regard for Tolkien's *Lord of the Rings*. Many posters adopted Tolkien(esque) names, such as Éowyn, princeimrahil, Ms. Took, theprecious, and Mithril1960. Most filled their posts with references to the book, as when, for instance, one poster noted that s/he would "wait and watch carefully, like Elendil waiting for Gil-Galad." Outright statements of fealty to the books and/or to Tolkien were also commonplace, as when one poster wrote of how s/he "will always return to the books over and over"; another proposed, "If [the movie] use[s] a narrator I think he should sound like Tolkien." On one level, we might see such verbal tags as expressing a certain sense of "guilt" over posting about the film, as if to do so was to "betray" the books, and thus performed to other posters a faithfulness to Tolkien and the books. On a simple level, though, they also show how many of these posters were longtime Tolkien fans who had come together as an online community with their love of the books as the common factor.

The posters were united by their love for the books, but opinions on the films diverged, ranging from those who raged about the adaptations to those whose excitement could barely be contained: as one poster noted gleefully, "when I found out they were making the movie I could have peed!!!!" To the purists (those who were not peeing with excitement), the films represented a considerable threat to the books, since they saw the story as the books, and any attempt to transplant that story elsewhere as a crime against the text. For instance, one poster explained:

> I'm afraid I'v[11] been gun shy of any movies, etc, of LOTR [*Lord of the Rings*]. Several years ago, I caught an animated version of the hobbit on TV. I couldnt bear to watch it, though, because the elves were purple. PURPLE! sorry, but in my book, they are not purple, or green, or any other color. Then, I had the misfortune of reading a play adaption of the Hobbit, which butchered the story beyond all recognition.

The poster's choice of terms—"gun shy," "butchered beyond all recognition"—signifies the degree to which the television and play adaptations were seen to perpetrate *violence* on the story. Similarly, others wrote of their fear of "Hollywoodification": "you know," wrote one, "having all the women run around with no clothes on, gratuitous sex scenes, getting rid of complicated concepts, etc." To these posters, the text of *Lord of the Rings* was immutable, best honored and respected by being left alone. "I can't help but feel," wrote one poster, "that it's gonna be screwed up and wrong. And be a total veggie effort."

Nevertheless, if only for the fact that these boards had been set up to discuss the film, complete and uncompromising purism was rare. More common was a negotiated position, whereby Tolkien fans *hoped* for three great films and were willing to allow the filmmakers some leeway in translating the beloved books to the screen, but remained somewhat skeptical and fearful. This sense of anxiety was particularly evident in the many postings that made predictions regarding specific scenes or characters.

Of the books' ending, for instance, many felt that New Line and Jackson would cut the last hundred pages or so, ending instead with the great victory at Mordor. "I think," wrote a poster, "that [using Tolkien's ending] will confuse the general film-going public"; another poster echoed, "The filmgoing public likes 'good' closure," and thus "would freak out and cry foul, as they have not the insight to see the true message here." Besides generalizing the "uninitiated viewer" in order to affirm the posters' own roles as acolytes of Tolkien and of Sense, statements such as these expressed an awareness that the text as these Tolkien fans knew and loved it would likely change along with the shift in medium and intended audience. Tolkien fans realized that the text could not translate *as is*, and their discussion and supposed ability to predict such changes became a way of preparing themselves for change.

Numerous postings included expressions of "understanding" why changes must be made. As mentioned above, the general viewing public and their supposed desires for a film were frequently listed as the guilty party, but as one poster stated, "I am not thrilled with the changes [. . . but] I am inclined to be the voice of reason." Along similar lines, another poster wrote, "Everyone should know that to condense such a huge book, with all of the background information into a Movie would be impossible." Or, using a different strategy to predict and reason away differences, many posters engaged in exaggerated and humorous predictions. One board, for instance, had an active thread in which posters offered alternative casting, including the proposal that television's Ally McBeal, Calista Flockhart, might play the shriveled-up monster Gollum. Amidst such anxious play, predictions, expressions of "understanding," and preparations for disappointment, as did Barker and Brooks,[12] we saw the omnipresence of ideals for the film: posters knew the text they wanted to see, often created images of texts they feared they might see, and then had to somehow make these different texts cohabit.

Just as with the coming film's detractors, though, all images and creations of the filmic text were conducted under the long shadow of the *Lord of the Rings* books. While fears and anxiety showed the obvious presence of an ideal text against which the films would be measured, so too did excitement operate under the book's long shadow. Central to the joys of what the adaptation might entail were hopes that the films might "bring the books to life" or "*keep* them alive"—the most commonly noted phrases in our research. "Finally," wrote one poster, "my favorite books of all time are coming to life!!" Another posited, "I'm not interested in details about the movie. I'd rather think that Peter Jackson's work could be a good reason for us to re-think Tolkien's books in today's scenario"; a third poster hoped that "future generations will find enough merit in the story to re-film with special effects 50 years on." Many looked to the movies as breathing new and continued life into the books and reassuring their place in cultural history and their importance for years to come.

There was even an element of self-vindication in these glowing endorsements of the films, a feeling that "our only hope is [. . .] that [family and friends] see the movie. Then we can set back, smuggly and say 'see that's what I'm talking about!'" "I am so glad," added another, "that [the movies] will draw even more attention to the books." A clear desire of many posters, then, was that the movies would contribute further to the *books'* popularity and cultural presence, expanding *Lord of the Rings* with yet more (para)text. One poster in particular offered an analysis of his and his fellow fans' interest in the films as being

> based on a desire to extend, validate and prolong our own experience of the [books]. Having had our imagination fired, our emotions stimulated and our intellect piqued on the journey through Middle Earth, can we then just leave it behind? [. . .] Was Phantom Menace a good film (by Star Wars Standards)? No, It was not. Did it enhance the Star Wars experience? Yes, It most certainly did. Will Peter Jackson's version live up to expectations? I don't know, but come December, I intend to be one of the first people to find out. Will it enhance the Lord of the Rings experience? Look around you, it already has.

What we see happening here is a subjugation of the films under the long shadow of the books, or what this poster calls the "Lord of the Rings experience," accepting the extension of *Lord of the Rings* from a literary tale to a transmediated franchise. Similarly, another poster offers that "the entertainment value of an adaptation is indeed in anticipation," again signaling the degree to which the adaptation is tucked under the wing of the "original" text.

Whether the fans would ultimately revile the films, watch tentatively, and/or enjoy them immensely, the web discussion suggested that their reactions to the films would continue the experience *of the books*. To these fans, the films were functionally junior to the books, and any response to the films, to a large degree, *pre-exists* the films, belonging as much to the books. In Tolkien's *The Two Towers*, our heroes Frodo and Sam have a deeply metatextual discussion about the ways in which stories are told, and to Sam's question, "Why to think of it, we're in the same tale still! It's going on. Don't the great tales never end?", Frodo responds, "No, they never end as tales. But the people in them come, and go when their part's ended. Our part will end later—or sooner."[13] Here, a similar process is at work, as the *Lord of the Rings* books, and reactions to or decodings of them, promised to live on in the shell of the *Lord of the Rings* films. John Fiske refers to intertextuality as "ghost textuality,"[14] a phrase that suggests texts living beyond their time, always with unfinished business to perform. The films might ultimately, as one poster proposed, "inform, expand and improve my vision [of Middle Earth]," but this paratextual vision was first and foremost a vision from, and affiliated with, the books.

The viewers whose responses we recorded may not have been "pre-viewers" of the films as much as they were simply viewers of the books, engaging with a text in a new textual body, anticipating one *with* the other, already reaching to one *by way of* the other. If we asked which text was primary, clearly the films were corollaries to the books. Bennett suggests that intertextuality can work as sedimentary layers,[15] yet these viewers' responses demand that we not limit our analysis of any text to its topmost, freshest layer. Rather, an "underground" layer may prove to be considerably more important to any given audience member, serving as bedrock to any new layer of silt, text to an adaptation's paratext. Of course, the degree to which different layers of sediment become controlling and determinative of the reading process will change from reader to reader, viewer to viewer. Furthermore, audiences will not share all of the same "layers": anyone who had not read *Lord of the Rings* or had not cared for it would approach the films without such "bedrock," just as a diehard Peter Jackson fan would arrive at the films with a completely different bedrock, or as a *Lord of the Rings* reader who is *also* a Peter Jackson fan may arrive with yet more complex striations and sedimentary history. But here, the films were turned into paratexts to the books' text.

The Ten-Ton Balrog in the Room: King Kong *and* The Chronicles of Narnia: The Lion, The Witch, and the Wardrobe

The subsequent worldwide success of the *Lord of the Rings* films hardly needs recounting. According to the Internet Movie Database (IMDb. com), as of early 2009, *Return of the King* held the second spot on the all-time worldwide box office list, *The Two Towers* the ninth spot, and

Fellowship of the Ring the sixteenth, combining for approximately $3 billion. Our research uncovered many Tolkien fans declaring all-out war on the box office record set by *Titanic* (1997), calling on Tolkien fans to unite to ensure that their beloved text would sit atop the textual universe. While ultimately no single *Lord of the Rings* film beat *Titanic*, the trilogy's remarkable success still proved just how lucrative textual shadows can be for Hollywood's balance books: when loyalty to a pre-text sends viewers to the cinema with determination, Hollywood can only win.[16] Meanwhile, as chapter 3 examined, its DVDs became their own sensation. Thus, we might expect that while Tolkien's shadow loomed over the trilogy in early 2001, by the time the films had been released, they had become mega-blockbusters casting their own formidable shadows. In particular, when in 2005 Peter Jackson and New Line were set to release their next film, *King Kong*, and while Disney and Walden were gearing up to release an adaptation of C. S. Lewis's much-beloved *Chronicles of Narnia: The Lion, The Witch, and The Wardrobe*, (pre)fan discussion of both films, and later reviews of them at IMDb suggested that the *Lord of the Rings* films had become their own powerful intertexts, framing and prefiguring the reception of these two new films. Whereas the title *Lord of the Rings* served as the intertextual bridge between books and films, now director Peter Jackson, his effects studio Weta Digital, and actor Andy Serkis bridged *Lord of the Rings* to *King Kong*, while *The Lion, The Witch, and The Wardrobe* was bridged to *Lord of the Rings* by virtue of being a fantasy directed by a Kiwi in New Zealand, and as a result of Tolkien's well-known relationship with C. S. Lewis. Quite simply, too, these were two of the biggest blockbusters to hit the world since *The Return of the King*, and so comparisons to the last big thing were perhaps inevitable.

As we had found with the *Lord of the Rings* films in 2001, for many viewers *King Kong* and *The Lion, The Witch, and The Wardrobe* seemed unable to step out of the shadow of *Lord of the Rings*. A scan through the several thousand reviews of *King Kong* at IMDb, for instance, reveals that for many, *Lord of the Rings* was a natural, obvious, and inescapable intertext for *King Kong*. One reviewer registers disappointment, elaborating that it is "maybe because I love Lord of The Ring trilogy so much that I expect Peter Jackson to make god like creations every time." Another complains that, "while there is no question Peter Jackson is a special effects master this film lacks the intrigue of the Lord Of The Rings series." Again and again, reviewers cannot discuss *King Kong* without reference to *Lord of the Rings*, illustrating the degree to which the trilogy had prefigured their expectations and hopes and/or the degree to which, as reviewers, they assume that their readers *expect* to hear comparisons to *Lord of the Rings*. A reviewer notes sadly that "I didn't feel the same way of what I felt in 'Lord of the Rings,'" as if the new movie *should* have rep-- licated the effects and affects of the trilogy, a response echoed by another reviewer, who asks, "So what has Jackson achieved? A remake which adds nothing, looks bad in places but has great landscapes well shot that just make us wish we were watching Lord of the Rings again. Sorry, I wanted to like this movie but I see little point to its existence."

Even some of those who loved the new film have the vocabulary and scenes of *Lord of the Rings* closest to hand when trying to explain how it succeeds, as when a reviewer glows that Jackson "was also able to master- fully capture some very frightening scenes in the movie, similar to what he did for Shelob's Lair in Lord of the Rings." Over the course of the three *Lord of the Rings* films, many viewers had come to know what to expect, and to like the familiar pleasures, gratifications, and affective registers of these films; the release of *King Kong*, along with its intertextual bridge to *Lord of the Rings*, allowed and encouraged them to project these pleasures onto the new film. Then, whether they found *King Kong* to live up to *Lord of the Rings* or let it down, those projected meanings and pleasures proved at least in part determinative of their viewing, interpretation, and recep- tion of *King Kong*, as *Lord of the Rings* set up a perimeter around *King Kong*. Similarly, many of those who hated *Lord of the Rings* projected their dislike and dissatisfaction onto *King Kong*, forming again a framework for interpretation and reception that could not easily be avoided. Read- ing through IMDb's mass of *Lord of the Rings*–based reviews of *King Kong* thus affirms that long shadows are by no means the sole provenance of adaptations: though *King Kong* was of course a remake, *Lord of the Rings* references proved just as dominant, if not moreso, in reviews as did refer- ences to the previous *King Kong* films.

In such discussion, not only do we see *King Kong* function as junior to *The Lord of the Rings*, but as is similarly evident in the *Two Towers* bonus materials discussed in chapter 3, we also see the construction of Peter Jackson as author. Jackson becomes a brand and hence an inter- or paratextual framing device, a matrix of other (inter)texts that served a paratextual role in directing interpretation. In short, Jackson becomes a paratext that manages a broader textual system.

Meanwhile, however, December 2005's other blockbuster, *The Lion, The Witch, and The Wardrobe*, similarly fell heavy prey to the *Lord of the Rings* effect and shadow. Undoubtedly, *Lord of the Rings'* success was instrumental in opening up a window of opportunity for Andrew Adamson, Walden, and Disney to adapt C. S. Lewis's stories, making *Lord of the Rings* not only an intertext but a precondition for *The Lion, The Witch, and The Wardrobe's* existence on screen. Lewis and Tolkien have often been talked of as a pair, given their friendship, their interest in fantasy from within the hallowed walls of Oxford University, and their mutual interest in using fantasy to serve as religious allegory or national mythology. Just as *Lord of the Rings* helped create room for *The Lion, The Witch, and The Wardrobe*, the latter's producers similarly clearly hoped to tap into the sizeable *Lord of the Rings* market, and thus the film's trailers, posters, and marketing all borrowed heavily from *Lord of the Rings*–type battle scenes, elaborate CGI, and general look. New Line had, four years earlier, actively hoped that Tolkien fans would project their reception of the books onto the films, and now Walden was similarly encouraging a projection of the pleasures and meanings, not just of the *Chronicles of Narnia* books, but also of *Lord of the Rings* onto *The Lion, The Witch, and The Wardrobe*.

To judge from reviews at IMDb, this attempt at setting up an intertextual bridge was highly successful, though ironically perhaps *too* successful, so that *The Lion, The Witch, and The Wardrobe* ended up pinned down under the weight of *Lord of the Rings*. One reviewer declares, "If you're like me you'll find yourself thinking 'why does this feel like a third rate LORD OF THE RINGS?'" This sentiment is echoed by numerous others:

> Adapting a book that so many audience members have read and cherish is surely a daunting task, but I believe it is also a great responsibility. Recently, Peter Jackson set the bar pretty high in this regard with the "Lord of the Rings" trilogy. Unfortunately, Adamson's "Narnia" wasn't quite up to snuff.

> The Lion, the Witch, and the Wardrobe is a wonder, a delightful film, but it hasn't the visual richness of Lord of the Rings, nor has the story the complexity of Tolkien's elaborate mythology, or its immense variety, its real magic.

> Already spoilt by mega war scenes from the Lord of the Rings trilogy, Chronicles doesn't go one up against what audiences already experienced, safe to substitute Uruk-hais and various Orcs with animals and mythical creatures like the centaurs.

Comparisons are inevitable. So here it is: Is this the new "Lord of the Rings"? Bloody hell, no.

The other main gripe I have with the movie is its mimicry of the Lord of the Rings movies. Lots of armor and weapons and posturing and clashing of armies. Unfortunately, it's all pretty dull and hackneyed.

Just as many of Barker, Arthurs, and Harindranth's *Crash* viewers proved unable to watch that film free of the frames posed by critical reviews and the British censorship drive,[17] here *Lord of the Rings* (both films and books) clearly provided a list of demands and expectations for *The Lion, The Witch, and The Wardrobe* that prefigured how at least some audience members would respond to and make sense of it.

IMDb reveals a whole host of other intertexts, though, as did the discussion board at www.narniaweb.com. At the latter, upon early announcement of the film, it was the author or brand function of Disney that concerned many posters more than Tolkien or *Lord of the Rings*. Though Walden would *make* the film and Disney *distribute* it, this distinction was lost on many fans, as a separate thread was set up to gripe about Disney's involvement. Disney was seen to be saccharine, juvenile, and too definitively "mass" media for many at the site who found the books to be more sophisticated, dark, and elite. Yet other intertexts joined the mix, too. One poster maps out her reactions to various intertexts:

First reaction to hearing about the film: awesome! [smiley emoticon]
Then I hear Disney is doing the movie: oh [worried emoticon]
Then I hear Walden is doing the film: yeah! [smiley emoticon]
Then I see the trailer for [Walden's] Around the World in 80 Days [worried emoticon]

Andrew Adamson's selection as director, meanwhile, scared those who felt his previous films *Shrek* (2001) and *Shrek 2* (2004) were unlikely to give him the skill-set needed for a serious live-action film, though his directorial history pleased others. As the release date neared, and as *Lord of the Rings* parallels became more commonplace, so too did *Harry Potter* comparisons race back and forth. Being yet another adaptation of fantasy material by an English children's writer laid *The Lion, The Witch, and The Wardrobe* squarely under the large shadow of the *Harry Potter* franchise, and thus pre-release discussion and post-release reviews often framed

Adamson's film in Potteresque terms. Even *Passion of the Christ* figured heavily in *The Lion, The Witch, and The Wardrobe* viewer discussion, given that both films were Christian epics (and both contain sacrifice on Calvary scenes that many viewers found to be deeply anti-Semitic), and Tilda Swinton fans heralded in other intertextual shadows by discussing her acting and characterization in such films as the gender-bending *Orlando* (1992). *Lord of the Rings* was, therefore, only one of the intertextual framing devices behind *The Lion, The Witch, and The Wardrobe*, as a huge network of intertexts and of audiences' memories of those intertexts converged on the text at hand, invoked and recommended by the paratexts of audience discussion, and making it, as Julia Kristeva argues of textuality, "an intersection of textual surfaces," not a fixed point or meaning.[18]

IMDb and fan discussion boards in general become some of the key paratexts through which many of these intertexts, links, and preferences are offered to the public, serving as the evidence of past intertextual readings at the same time as they share those readings with others. In the next chapter, I will turn to a closer examination of how audiences use paratexts to prefer and proffer their own readings and interpretations.

For the time being, though, and looking back on our research from 2001, alongside viewer responses to *King Kong* and *The Lion, The Witch, and The Wardrobe*, I am also struck by how *competitive* viewers can be with their intertexts. In 2001, Tolkien fans feared that the films might usurp the books, and yet hoped that they would eclipse *Titanic*'s success. Years later, a different set of fans of the *Lord of the Rings* films prickled at the notion that either *King Kong* or *The Lion, The Witch, and The Wardrobe* could "better" their beloved trilogy. And one of the IMDb reviewers of *The Lion, The Witch, and The Wardrobe* notes, "As a loyal Harry Potter fan, *it pains me to say* this film totally blows all four HP films off the map" (emphasis added). Elsewhere, *Star Wars* and *Star Trek* fans have endured a long feud, their divergent textual galaxies seemingly unable to cohabit in one universe. Not only, then, do texts cast shadows, but many viewers become invested in *how much* of a shadow they cast, often wanting their own beloved text to stand tallest, basking in the light as a dominant intertext, and attempting to reduce others to the status of sequels, copies, weak paratexts, and pale comparisons. Hollywood in part conditions us to think in terms of competition via the incessant reporting of box office records and the yearly parade of Oscar, Golden Globe, BAFTA, and countless other award ceremonies, all of which often seem more important for the second-guessing and competitive cinephilia that they induce than for the actual awarding of excellence. The industry is deeply invested in encouraging us to "vote" for our favorite films at the box office. But to reduce a battle of the intertexts to industry programming would be insulting to the intelligence of movie viewers and to the rich affective involvement inspired by well-told stories. Powerful intertexts are those that some audience members find involving and elaborate enough that they can preside over many intertextual interactions, much as the Bible or Homer (the Greek poet *or* the Simpson patriarch) have. In this regard, as much as intertextuality and paratextuality are about framing and the prefiguration of textuality, they are also about, and are motored by, fans' (and others') desires for certain texts to stay alive continuously, reflected off, informing, and inspiring all manner of other texts.

A Dark Shadow over Gotham: Batman Begins

Thus far, I have considered the role of intertexts as pre-texts primarily when they are beloved and when they have inspired fandom and significant affective investment. However, texts can also cast dark shadows when they have been panned and hated. Here, I turn to the example of *Batman and Robin* and the intertextual pall it cast over the Batman film franchise. *Batman and Robin* is by most viewers' accounts an atrociously bad film, too bad even to be camp. At IMDb, the combined ranking of over 60,000 reviewers rates *Batman and Robin* 3.4 out of 10, and as one reviewer caustically comments of director Joel Schumacher:

> He treats the entire Batman franchise like a joke. Even if it was funny, this would be betraying the name of Batman. But here, seeing as it's NOT funny, it only succeeds in becoming the worst of the Batman movies, and, arguably, the worst film ever created[. . . .] Seriously, I'd have more respect for Schumacher if I discovered that he hated Batman, and had intentionally ruined it with this garbage. Then, this might actually be just his own personal joke. Instead, it borders on a travesty of good cinema.

Of course, as the reviewer reminds us, *Batman and Robin* came in a long line of Batman comics, films, television series, and toys related to the much-revered intertext and popular hero.[19] Former Batman screenings suffered mixed reviews, with a general furor surrounding the casting of Michael Keaton for the first film in 1989, and many a fan of the dark, gritty character reinvented by Frank Miller in his 1986 graphic novel, *Batman: The Dark Knight Returns*, grimacing at reruns of the "BAM! KERPOW!" sixties television Batman. Thus, *Batman and Robin* came in an already-turbulent intertextual wake. But the previous films had at least been lucrative for Time Warner, resulting in a steady pace of one film every two or three years and plenty of spinoff merchandising. *Batman and Robin*'s near-universal panning, on the heels of poor reviews for the previous entry, *Batman Forever* (1995), finally appeared to have killed the franchise altogether, even when superhero films became all the rage, with hits such as *X-Men* (2000) and *Spider-Man* (2002). Then, in 2004 came the news that Time Warner was back with Batman, having hired Christopher Nolan to direct *Batman Begins*.

The tale of *Batman Begins* is one of how to escape a dark shadow. Audience and critical reception of *Batman and Robin* had been so near-universally caustic that it had set up a strong paratextual perimeter and a flaming hoop through which any subsequent Batman text would need to pass. *Batman Begins* and Time Warner needed to apologize for *Batman and Robin* and to erase any semblance of an intertextual connection: only Batman himself could remain, albeit radically reconfigured. They also needed to create for themselves a different paratextual perimeter and invoke a different set of intertexts. With this in mind, the studio hired Nolan to write and direct. Nolan was best known for his dark and edgy work on the tale-told-backwards *Memento* (2000) and on his adaptation of the Norwegian serial killer study *Insomnia* (2002), and thus was seen as untainted by big-budget Hollywood, regarded instead as a storyteller with considerable interest in character exploration. Casting similarly sought to veer away from the A-list car crash that was *Batman and Robin*. Nolan hired as his Batman Christian Bale, an actor who had grown up on screen, yet often in independent films and/or character roles, and who was most famous for his eerie portrayal of yuppie serial killer Patrick Bateman in *American Psycho* (2000). A director of a serial killer film and the star of another serial killer film were uniting. Nolan's love of Batman in his Frank Miller–inspired Dark Knight form was widely publicized, as marketing and hiring for the film announced that this movie would be a "return" to the brooding noir aesthetic and sensibility of Batman, skipping over his cinematic and televisual history.[20]

Meanwhile, Oscar winners and highly respected "austere" actors Morgan Freeman and Michael Caine were cast, as were the well-respected Liam Neeson, Tom Wilkinson, Gary Oldman, Rutger Hauer (famous for his villain role in the noir *Blade Runner*), and, hot off their breakthrough roles in *The Last Samurai* (2003) and *28 Days Later*, respectively, Ken Watanabe and Cillian Murphy. Casting and the hiring of production personnel is a deeply intertextual act, as producers bring together a whole host

Fig. 4.1. A prone Bruce Wayne is laid low and punished by Ducard in *Batman Begins*, paying for the crimes of *Batman and Robin* while earning his right to be Batman.

of intertexts through the stars' personae and histories.[21] Many of us create images of a film and its potential based solely on our knowledge of its cast and their former roles. By marshalling a host of "serious" actors and a "serious" director, *Batman Begins* and its early hype strategically overloaded the text with intertexts that they clearly hoped would contrast markedly to the casting of the former film, signaling a new era, and that would overload the film with intertexts other than *Batman and Robin*. Certainly, Batman aside, the prospect for many filmgoers of seeing a Nolan film with Bale, Freeman, Oldman, Caine, Wilkinson, Neeson, Watanabe, Murphy, Hauer, and (for measure) Katie Holmes may have been enticing.

Aside from the pre-production of *Batman Begins*, though, it is also possible to see the weight of the *Batman and Robin* fiasco on the plot of Nolan's film. The film opens with a weary and beleaguered Bruce Wayne struggling with his playboy status and living in the shadow of his father, unable to replicate Gotham City's savior and patron saint. Wayne seeks revenge against the men he believes to be behind his parents' death, but ultimately fails, instead fleeing Gotham. We next see him in a Chinese prison, having wondered aimlessly from home, fighting anyone without concern for his life, clearly a broken man. Liam Neeson's Henri Ducard arranges his release, encouraging him to climb a nearby mountain to a training facility, where Wayne is taught to fight with precision, discipline, and purpose. When Ducard reveals his ultimate plan, to lead an army of highly trained soldiers to destroy Gotham from the inside out, Wayne burns the training facility to the ground and returns to Gotham, where he resumes his playboy lifestyle on the outside, while developing and designing the visage of Batman to wage war on crime and to protect Gotham by night. A running theme throughout the film involves the interrogation of who one "really is on the inside" (with the suggestion that Wayne becomes Batman's mask, not vice versa).

It is easy to read this first hour of the film in the frame of *Batman and Robin*, as a sign of Wayne, Nolan, and Time Warner serving penance for the crimes of Batman's previous cinematic outing. Wayne is a soulless playboy, emblematic of the mindless Hollywood blockbuster that was *Batman and Robin*, lost and without direction, mindful only of how far he has strayed from his father's footsteps, just as the Batman franchise had left its roots and what it "should" be, with films that took away from rather than added to the diegetic world of Batman. The pre-TomKat Katie Holmes serves as moral beacon (and film critic stand-in?), telling him that he is a disappointment. And thus he, Nolan, and Time Warner cannot simply *be* Batman—they must *earn* the right. Removed from home, battered in a prison, left to climb a snow-swept mountain in prison clothes and without equipment, and forced into an arduous training regimen that frequently belittles him, Wayne appears to be paying for Time Warner's past "sins" (fig. 4.1). Fresh from his role as Jedi trainer in the *Star Wars* prequel *The Phantom Menace*, Liam Neeson is seemingly invited to reprise his character, in order to make Wayne (and hence Batman) anew, and Wayne must similarly learn from Freeman and Caine (two wise old men of the film industry) before he is "ready" to become Batman. Of course, the myth of becoming has proven popular in superhero films, but given that this was the fifth film in the franchise, the choice to return to the drawing board was by no means natural. Meanwhile, Wayne is beaten and fashioned into Batman more significantly than other superheroes, many of whom discover their powers and responsibilities quite excitedly. The film is at pains to show us that he is haunted and tortured by his past and struggling to be who he should be. Thus, when Bale finally utters, "I'm Batman," well past the hour mark of the film, he and the filmmakers have performed a long and careful cleansing ritual attempting to earn the right to make such a declaration.

Moreover, the film ends with Batman promising to look into the rise of a super-villain, The Joker. A clear allusion to an impending sequel (*The Dark Knight* [2008]), this scene is also important for its act of trying to completely erase the prior four *Batman* films from the record: the first *Batman* (1989) not only featured the villain, but famously offered Jack Nicholson in the role, and thus for *Batman Begins* to announce its intentions to "do over" both that film and Nicholson's performance is a bold statement that a new Batman exists.

Ultimately, then, *Batman Begins* exhibits the pressure placed on a film, not just in its reception, but also in the casting, hiring, writing, performing, directing, and promotion, when a previous film and its critical panning has cast a dark shadow over it. *Batman Begins* was faced not only with the task of winning audiences, but of winning them *back*, of recalibrating its intertexts, and of reinventing Batman. Influence, allusion, and intertextual borrowing have existed in all forms of art since time immemorial, but here we see an instance of a text that potential audience members arguably *required* to speak back to its intertexts, to delineate and announce its intertextual allegiances (the comic book Dark Knight over Schumacher's Batman), and hence to pull itself out from under a given intertext's long dark shadow.

In the wake of its success and popularity, *Batman Begins* may even have taught a trick or two to the production staff behind *Superman Returns* (2006) and *Rocky Balboa* (2006), two other franchises that returned after lengthy hiatuses and dismal otherwise final chapters. *Superman Returns* forced the diegetically five-year-absent-from-Earth hero to convince Lois Lane that the world once more needed him, while simultaneously bathing itself in the more austere elements of Superman's filmic past. Promotions for the film ignored outright *Superman 3* and *Superman 4* by positing it as a sequel of sorts only to the first two films, and its teaser trailers used little more than a voiceover of Marlon Brando's instructions to Superman from the 1978 film and John Williams's famed soundtrack. For its part, *Rocky Balboa* opened with Rocky emotionally battered by the loss of Adrian. For Superman and Rocky, then, onscreen penance was also required for the sins of the intertexts.

Sharing the Island with Others:
J. J. Abrams and Collective Knowledge

The above examples examine how any given film, while supposedly a singular event, is often framed and interpreted by other films, especially when it is a sequel, prequel, spinoff, adaptation, or part of a series, but also due simply to its actors or other creative personnel. If films prove to be porous entities, however, as was argued in chapter 1,[22] television shows are especially porous and open to inter- or paratextual intrusion, given that we must piece them together bit by bit over long stretches of time during which our reading frames may change. Thus we might expect to see long shadows aplenty on television, and we might expect that some intertexts would act like reference books for television reception, continually offering ways to make sense of what is happening in the here and now. As we saw in the case of Peter Jackson as film author, television authors similarly become paratexts in their own right, constructed by the industry, creative personnel, and viewers alike as signifiers of value—as was noted in chapter 3—but also serving as interpretive decoders and frames for viewers in various ways. Over time, for instance, Jerry Bruckheimer has become shorthand in both film and television for high-concept action populated by rugged, heroic men and petite but gutsy women; David E. Kelley is known for legal dramedies with outlandish cases and often explicitly liberal politics; Dick Wolf is known for a considerably more somber, neoconservative, and morally binaristic vision of law and order; and so forth. Viewers fashion notions of authors out of their previous work, creating an author function that works as a paratext of sorts and as a mediating figure through which intertexts affect current interpretive strategies.

Such was the case for *Lost* and *Six Degrees*, two shows executive produced by J. J. Abrams. In the early days of each show, fans and other viewers congregated to make sense of them online, and there viewers of Abrams's *Alias* in the case of *Lost*, and of *Alias* and *Lost* in the case of *Six Degrees*, offered predictions and evaluations of the new show at hand based largely on Abrams's earlier work. Elsewhere in this chapter, we have already seen how the author as paratext constructs expectations for future viewing, but my interest in the case of *Lost* and *Six Degrees* lies in how, through the prominent online television discussion site *Television Without Pity*, viewers of Abrams's past shows shared various versions of the Abrams paratextual frame with non-viewers. Thus, whereas it may seem that intertexts and paratexts rely on the vagaries of a person's previous viewing experiences, the case of *Lost* and *Six Degrees* shows that through audience and non-audience discussion, paratexts can be passed on to others who do not have the same viewing experiences (at either the film/television or paratextual level), thereby extending the reach of their long shadow. Particularly in the case of *Lost*, *Alias*'s niche fan audience was able to propose and share a series of viewing strategies and expectations with the broader, more mainstream audience that greeted *Lost* in its first season.

Writing of *Twin Peaks* (1990–91) discussion groups in the Internet's early days, Henry Jenkins noted with excitement how the advent of such groups now allowed audience researchers "to pinpoint specific moments in the shifting meanings generated by unfolding broadcast texts, to locate episodes that generated intense response or that became particularly pivotal in the fans' interpretation of the series as a whole."[23] As Stanley Fish had noted with frustration (see chapter 1), too often analysts make sense of a text in its entirety after the fact, but online fan discussion allows a running catalogue and minute-by-minute register of how meanings are circulated, how the text is being interpreted, which intertexts are invoked, and, for our purposes here, how various paratexts are being discussed and activated. This becomes increasingly important in an era in which, as Jenkins has also observed, audiences are interpreting in groups, as a "collective." Drawing on Pierre Lévy's notion of "collective intelligence,"[24] Jenkins explains:

> The fan community pools its knowledge because no single fan can know everything necessary to fully appreciate the series[. . . .] Collective intelligence expands a community's productive capacity because it frees individual members from the limitations of their memory and enables the group to act upon a broader range of expertise.[25]

Yet fans are not alone in this respect, for increasingly, all sorts of viewers regularly "lurk" at supposed "fan" discussion groups, peeking to see what has been said or thought by others, and dipping into this collective knowledge. Hence, though till now this chapter's discussion of intertextuality, paratextuality, and interpretation may have implied a fairly personal, individualistic process of reception, such sites show us how quickly paratexts can spread through talk, making both reception and paratextuality deeply communal processes.

From its beginning in 2004, *Lost* seemingly demanded talk. A genre-bending program, *Lost* opens with a plane crash on a remote South Pacific island. As the survivors gather their wits, they become aware that a strange creature lives in the jungle. Then, as the show develops, viewers learn of a mysterious hatch on the island, leading to a research station, of a series of "cursed" numbers that have caused problems for the "Lostaways," and of a strange group of "Others" on the island who occasionally kidnap, study, and/or kill members of the group. All the while, each episode offers a flashback to the pre-crash lives of one of the characters (or, later, a flash forward to the post-rescue lives), hence adding a chronological element to the already firmly packed mystery. Given this plethora of perplexing plot points and the lack of any definitive answer from the show to its many mysteries, many viewers of *Lost*, as did *Twin Peaks* viewers before them, have turned to the Internet and to others for help. Particularly in the show's early days, though, significant discussion and puzzle-solving at *Television Without Pity* revolved around mobilizing the author function that is Abrams and the intertext of his previous show, *Alias*.

Alias had involved a convoluted mystery surrounding a series of "Rimbaldi artifacts," and thus many fans posited that the set-up and resolution of the Rimbaldi mystery on *Alias* might offer the key to interpreting *Lost*. To begin with, some floated the idea that the two shows might literally be connected, offering, for instance, "Perhaps [the] Island is the Horizon or part of Rimbaldi's artifacts." But beyond such suggestions—often more whimsical than serious—many *Alias* viewers waded into ongoing debates about *Lost*, using *Alias* scripting as evidence of what to expect. Thus, when fans had heard that the show was due to kill off a character, and speculation had turned to its being Charlie, one poster offered, "I've yet to see JJ actually kill off a main character (but please correct me if I'm wrong)." Or, in response to numerous fan suggestions that the Island might be Purgatory, or that the events may otherwise be interpreted within a religious framework, another poster insisted, "I highly doubt that this is what Abrams and Co. are trying to do, because the only 'religious' stuff that they've adhered to in the past is the imaginary Rimbaldi stuff on *Alias*." *Alias*'s use of the occult and mysterious Rimbaldi figure (a sort of Da Vinci meets Nostradamus) led many to look for or expect such thematic crafting on *Lost*. Other posters joined in by noting the presence of supposed Abrams "issues," such as one character's "Daddy Issues," or the love triangle between three others, and both cases required elaboration upon how *Alias* (and Abrams's earlier *Felicity*) might give clues regarding how such issues would be resolved. Frequently, such posts were met with curious replies, by those who had not watched *Alias*, and often lengthy explanations of intricate plot points from *Alias* followed, as posters worked to create a "collective intelligence" with fellow viewers, bringing them up to speed with Abrams's history and intertextual resonance. As Virginia Nightingale has noted, "The text, as work, has a finite quality[. . . .] But there is another text, just as important but infinitely more elusive. It is the text which lives in the community of its users and which 'enters into life.'"[26] Here we can see the second text forming.

Abrams and *Alias* further served to worry many *Lost* fans, who saw *Alias* as having "jumped the shark" with its overelaborate mysteries and prolonged failure to offer answers, and thus this framework was imposed on *Lost*. Early in *Television Without Pity's Alias* deliberations, one poster noted, "If I hear one thing which remotely resembles 'Milo Rimbaldi,' I swear I'm going to shoot someone," clearly signaling intertextually inspired fear. Another echoed that "the [cursed] numbers are going to be *Lost*'s Rimbaldi," implying that the show was headed for doom. A third complained:

"The Swan" and "The Dharma Initiative": Have you learnt NOTHING from doing those horrendous storylines—Rimbaldi and now Prophet Five (pardon if I got the names wrong. I really hate Alias and so obviously know nothing) on Alias? Does that mean Lost would turn into a show like Alias? I'm really scared now.

More generally, multiple posters expressed dismay that they cared about *Lost* and its mysteries but felt that *Alias*'s (to them) overdrawn process of revealing its own answers meant that they may be problem-solving in vain, since "Abrams and Co." may not even have answers to give. Interestingly, though, as is hinted at in the above non-*Alias*-fan quote, through *Alias* fans' drawings of intertextual links, many non-*Alias* viewers were able (and *encouraged*) to work with such intertexts themselves. Here, then, we see the construction of interpretive communities, and the establishment of communal paratextual frames, as viewers share not only viewing experiences but interpretive strategies based on these experiences.

Two years later, when *Six Degrees* was released, again we had an ABC and J. J. Abrams show that attracted viewer speculation based on *Lost* and *Alias*. By this point, some viewers had given up hope that Abrams could ever be trusted to provide answers, or to sustain a show, so that one poster, for instance, griped, "I'm digging this show. I probably shouldn't since [. . .] Abrams is good at creating compelling TV, but sucks at sustaining it. (Everything he touches seems to collapse within two seasons)." Another vented, "If we're supposed to believe that the interconnectiveness [between characters] is meaningful—then I think we'll be disappointed because—hello! JJ Abrams!!" A third noted, "I'm dying to know what's up with Mae though, but knowing JJ, I'll be probably finding out in S[eason] 2." Meanwhile, those for whom *Lost* and/or *Alias* were not worrying intertexts once again invoked Rimbaldi, and now the numbers or the hatch from *Lost*, to make sense of a character's mysterious box, and they culled information from *Lost*'s interconnecting flashbacks to make sense of *Six Degrees*' fondness for interconnection and serendipity. Some posters even bypassed *Lost* and *Alias* to return to Abrams's *Felicity* or looked to his concurrent *What About Brian?* (2006–7) to enable a whole different set of intertexts of urban romance, not otherworldly mystery. Once more, too, the viewer discussion online often involved significant attempts to provide an interpretive decoder for those who had not seen the earlier show(s).

Considerable irony exists in the *Lost* and *Six Degrees* postings, given that, despite being an executive producer of both shows, Abrams was by most insider accounts only tangentially involved in either. As *Lost*'s star rose in popular culture, increasingly it became known as the product of Carlton Cuse and Damon Lindelof, not Abrams, and as *Six Degrees* plummeted, Abrams can be thankful that the press was careful to spell out his lack of involvement. At the time of these postings, Abrams was a strong paratext, even though, in retrospect, his previous work was unlikely to provide answers to how these shows' writers and active producers scripted or planned their series. Watching *Lost* or *Six Degrees* through an Abrams filter would likely have proved unhelpful and misleading. Thus, as was seen with the *Six Degrees* hype and the American *Sweet Hereafter* trailer in chapter 2, paratexts can often lead audiences down blind alleys, and should by no means be considered inherently helpful, just as not every clue that detectives find at a crime scene will aid their investigation. Nevertheless, beyond appraisal of the relative helpfulness of Abrams as paratext lies the fact that viewers not only used them but circulated them to others, creating a perimeter and airlock around the new shows, and proposing set frames of interpretation and decoding.

Managing the Textual Realm

As this case renders clear, paratextuality and intertextuality are not always self-motoring systems. Harold Bloom has written of influence as requiring a text to engage in an Oedipal battle with its forefathers and predecessors,[27] but like numerous literary studies theorists of influence and intertextuality,[28] Bloom sees the intertextual paths and connections between texts as obvious, self-evident, and unavoidable. At times, Bloom is bound to be correct: sequels with numbers, for instance, implore us to consider the former (leading to the apocryphal story that Alan Bennett's play *The Madness of King George III* lost its roman numerals when adapted into a film [1994], lest audience members be concerned that they had not seen the first two films!). Or, even more obviously, adaptations hit us over the head with intertexts, so that presumably few needed tipping off that *The Lord of the Rings: The Fellowship of the Ring* was based on Tolkien's hugely popular book of the same name. However, beyond the simple and obvious intertexts lie a vast realm of other intertexts that any given viewer can reference, and it is paratexts that quite often manage this realm. Intertextuality can play a determinative role in textual reception, and paratexts frequently conjure up and summon intertexts. Hence, the collective intelligence of an online discussion board could inform a would-be *Lion, The Witch, and The Wardrobe* viewer that Disney was behind it, that director Andrew Adamson had previously directed *Shrek* and *Shrek 2*, that Tilda Swinton had been in *Orlando*, that the lion would be voiced by *Phantom Menace* and *Batman Begins* guru figure Liam Neeson, or that they should watch for biblical imagery. So too could reviews, previews, interviews, or any other paratext share such information, and in so doing, invoke intertexts, pointing to all manner of long shadows. As such, paratexts are not only forms of intertextuality, but they can control the menu of intertexts that audiences will consult or employ when watching or thinking about a text.

This chapter has involved consulting sites of audience discussion, both as a sounding board for how viewers are using and constructing texts, intertexts, and paratexts, but also as paratexts themselves. Inevitably, though, once one consults audience discussion, one starts to see both how radically and how subtly it can toggle, dismantle, or revise the careful planning of Hollywood's textual systems. At one level, this should remind us that any film or program's paratexts are no less contingent on the peculiarities of reception than are the films or programs themselves, and that the film and television industries' paratexts must always compete with other interpretive communities and modes of reception already under way. At another level, it also highlights the need to examine in greater detail viewer-created paratexts and their own intricate constructions of the text, a task to which chapter 5 now turns its attention.

5

Spoiled and Mashed Up
Viewer-Created Paratexts

Many of the examples and case studies presented so far in this book examine industry-created paratexts, from hype and marketing, to spinoffs, to introductory sequences. However, audiences create paratexts too, and while they commonly lack the capital and infrastructure to circulate their paratexts as widely—or at least as uniformly—as can Hollywood, their creative and discursive products can and often do become important additions to a text. In its most common form, this audience paratextuality occurs anytime two or more people discuss a film or television program, but audience paratextuality also includes criticism and reviews, fan fiction, fan film and video (vids), "filk" (fan song), fan art, spoilers, fan sites, and many other forms. Type the name of almost any popular film or television program into Google, and beyond the first two or three links for official, industry-created paratexts, one will likely find several if not hundreds or thousands of pages with various forms of audience-created paratexts. In this chapter, I turn to the role that audience-created paratexts play in challenging or supplementing those created by the industry, in creating their own genres, genders, tones, and styles, and in carving out alternative pathways through texts.

I begin with a brief discussion of fan studies' wealth of material on more explicitly antagonistic paratexts, by way of underlining that my interests in this chapter do not reflect the totality of viewer-end paratexts, only one variety. Subversive fan fiction has attracted many a case study, but other viewer-paratexts—particularly spoilers and vids—remain relatively underexplored. My first case study draws on a survey Jason Mittell and I conducted to discover why *Lost* fans who read spoilers of upcoming events on the show enjoy doing so. Mittell and I initially approached the spoiler fans as an oddity, not understanding why they would ruin a good mystery by "cheating" and reading ahead, but we came to see that the circulation and creation of spoilers helped many of those fans to engage with *Lost* on their own terms. The spoilers as paratexts helped carve a more personalized route through the text. This notion of carving out a particular route through a text is also central to my next case study, as I examine fan-made "vids" of popular film and television programs. Focusing on character study and relationship vids, I look at their capacity to create a reflective space in which viewers can engage more closely with the psyches, motivations, and specificities of multiple characters than they might be able to in the films or programs themselves.

However, to talk of viewer-end paratexts such as spoilers or vids is to talk of lesser-known paratexts—indeed, while I do not doubt that my readers are familiar with trailers, bonus materials, and sequels, for instance, I expect that at least some may be unfamiliar with even the terms "spoiler" and "vid," let alone with specific examples. Thus, toward the end of the chapter, I discuss the key issue of paratextual privilege—who gets to make them, and who has the power to circulate their own readings and versions of the text en masse. While the cases of spoilers or vids contrast obviously with the industry-produced paratexts discussed in chapters 2–4, chapter 5's final case study turns to the more liminal example of press reviews. Mass-circulated via newspapers or prominent websites such as *Slate* or *Salon*, press reviews are written by relative insiders who have been allowed advance copies of shows, and yet they are also written outside a studio marketing team's immediate sphere of influence. As such, they enjoy peculiar powers of being able to set up initial frames for viewing—working as an anti-trailer—and to establish value—working as an anti–bonus material. I examine these in relation to numerous reviews for the debut episodes of NBC's *Friday Night Lights*. Throughout this and the other case studies, chapter 5 looks at viewer-end paratexts as traces of an individual's or a community's strategies of reading, as tools for better realizing those strategies, and as frames for others to use.

Viewer Cartographies, Routes, and Marginalia

As a wealth of fan studies literature has argued, fan-created paratexts can facilitate resistance to the meanings proffered by media firms through their own texts and paratexts. The products of fan creativity can challenge a text's industry-preferred meanings by posing their own alternate readings and interpretive strategies.[1] Similarly, fan and audience discussion alone can become a strong paratext, as was examined in the previous chapter. As Henry Jenkins argued in his seminal account of television fandom, *Textual Poachers*, through fan activities and practices, fans "cease to be simply an audience for popular texts; instead, they become active participants in the construction and circulation of textual meaning," and they "actively struggle with and against the meanings imposed upon them by their borrowed materials."[2] As have numerous subsequent fan researchers, Jenkins analyzed the social process of meaning construction that occurs in fandom, whereby a significant portion of a text's value comes from how it is used. Matt Hills notes that "the fan's act of appropriation of a text is therefore an act of 'final consumption' which pulls this text away from (intersubjective and public) exchange-value and towards (private, personal) use value, but without ever cleanly or clearly being able to separate out the two."[3] But fan appropriations are also acts of creation and production that are frequently communal by nature. Challenging this notion of the individual fan's "final consumption," Karen Hellekson and Kristina Busse write of the process by which fan communities distill a version (or versions) of the text—the "fantext"—that includes fan additions to the world (not just "canon" but "fanon" too, source and fan paratexts), so that the multitude of fan-created stories and variations therein becomes

> a work in progress insofar as it remains open and is constantly increasing; every new addition changes the entirety of interpretations. By looking at the combined fantext, it becomes obvious how fans' understanding of the source is always already filtered through the interpretations and characterizations existing in the fantext. In other words, the community of fans creates a communal (albeit contentious and contradictory) interpretation in which a large number of potential meanings, directions, and outcomes co-reside.[4]

Fan discussion of the text, as well as further fan creativity, will hence often prove as aware of the limitations placed on interpretation as of the scope for creative expansion provided by earlier fannish interpretive retoolings of the fantext.[5]

If we analyze Jenkins's key metaphor for fan practice, borrowed from Michel de Certeau's discussion of the practice of reading in general, the notion of "poaching" suggests the complicated nature of cultural consumption.[6] Whereas crude ideas of passive, mindless audiences deal only with the territory on which consumption takes place, Jenkins demands a human geography of consumption, realizing that just as understanding the life of a nation requires more than lists of longest rivers and tallest mountains alongside pretty cartography, so too must textual analysis at some point take account of the readers who populate the text. Within this schema, we might regard paratexts as citizen-made structures that similarly change the nature of the geography, and that must be accounted for.

Much early fan studies work exhibited particular interest in fan activity that repurposed or resisted the territory. Constance Penley wrote of fans as giving a text a vigorous massage that might hurt but is best for it in the long run,[7] while Jenkins wrote of how fans treated the text like silly putty, "stretching its boundaries to incorporate their concerns, remolding its characters to better suit their desires."[8] Fan fiction, for instance, has been seen as a paratext with which fans can repurpose characters, whether by adding reflection on issues absent from the show, expanding the generic repertoire of the show (adding romance to science fiction, for instance), or multiple other strategies that reclaim ownership of the text, its characters, and its meanings. Fan creativity can work as a powerful in medias res paratext, grabbing a story or text in midstream and directing its path elsewhere, or forcing the text to fork outward in multiple directions.

However, in part because multiple fan studies have already mapped lines of textual resistance and rebellion, in this chapter I am particularly interested in paratexts that do not so much work against a show or radically alter the text as much as they invite increased attention to a given plot, character, relationship, or mode of viewing. On one level, viewer-created paratexts are pre-constituted audience research, providing evidence of how viewers make sense of texts. Just as H. J. Jackson notes of studying marginalia in books, paratexts reveal how text and viewer fashion themselves in relation to one another: "A marked or annotated book," Jackson notes, "traces the development of the reader's self-definition in and by relation to the text. Perhaps all readers experience this process; annotators keep a log."[9] On another level, though, since many paratexts are shared with others, a close study of viewer-paratexts can reveal ways in which *communities* of audiences interact with and thereby create texts, not just ways in which individuals fashion them. By nature of its popularity, any popular text must have popular meaning, which in turn means that viewer-created paratexts will surround the text. Those paratexts may echo industry-created paratexts, but they might also, as I will examine here, call for subtle changes in interpretation, valuing the text's various elements differently from industry-created paratexts, and opening up new paths of understanding. Just as outright subversive readings of a film or television program destabilize the show as center of meaning, so too do supplemental paratexts challenge the primacy of the show.

No Crying over a Spoiled Lost (with Jason Mittell)

One such supplemental paratext is the spoiler. Spoilers include any information about what will happen in an ongoing narrative that is provided before the narrative itself gets there. To tell someone who will die on next week's show, what a film's key plot twist is, or what to expect next is to "spoil" the person and/or text. Spoilers can result from some viewers seeing a film or program before others, or from information gleaned through back channels that stands to spoil viewers ahead of time. Given different audiences' uneven paces of progress through many ongoing narratives, spoilers have become an increasingly touchy subject in today's media environment, as some producers have gone to inordinate levels of secrecy to protect news of what comes next, and as fans (or anti-fans) circulate spoilers to a mixture of chagrin, annoyance, disinterest, and enthusiasm. While movies with twists, such as the works of M. Night Shyamalan, or *The Crying Game* (1992), *Planet of the Apes* (1968), or *Soylent Green* (1973), stand out as particularly vulnerable to spoiling, serial television and film have also attracted a spoiler entourage, with their own dedicated websites, such as spoilerfix.com, and their own dedicated sections of fan sites.

As a mysterious show in which few solid answers exist as to why the characters are where they are, who can be trusted, and so forth, *Lost* has a particularly active spoiler fandom online and offline. Spoilers for *Lost* range from leaked plot points, leaked clues, leaked photos of filming, casting information, and plenty of "foilers" (fake spoilers) too. Precisely because *Lost*'s pleasures would seem to rely so heavily upon the enjoyment of its suspense and mystery elements, spoilers would seem to "ruin" *Lost* (hence their name: spoilers). Thus, in 2006, Jason Mittell and I set out with the challenge of working out why people would actively seek out spoilers, and what these paratexts did for or to their consumption of the show.

We approached the topic as outsiders, given that neither of us enjoyed spoilers, yet both of us greatly enjoyed *Lost*. To understand the spoiler world better, we designed an anonymous online survey addressing these issues[10] and posted an invitation to participate on five discussion boards (televisionwithoutpity.com; lost-forum.com; thefuselage.com; abc.com;

losttv-forum.com) and one listserver (LostGame@yahoogroups.com)
dedicated to *Lost* and frequently the site of spoiler threads and discussions. Here, I summarize that research. The survey clearly attracted interest from the show's dedicated fanbase: within a week, 228 people visited
the survey, with 179 completing at least half of its questions. Around 80
percent of respondents identified themselves as American, with seventeen
other countries represented in the survey. Sixty percent of respondents
were female, and respondents' ages ranged from eighteen to fifty-four,
with a mean age of twenty-nine and median of twenty-seven. The survey
combined open-ended questions with more guided choice questions, with
topics ranging from the specific pleasures offered by *Lost* to the ethical
implications of spoiling. While the invitation did not explicitly indicate
that the survey focused on spoilers, as we wished to gather data from
viewers who consume them and those who avoid them, the majority of
respondents did indicate that they consume spoilers to some degree—37
percent frequently consume spoilers, 32 percent sometimes read them,
and 14 percent both consume and disseminate them online, with only 16
percent of respondents indicating that they avoid spoilers as much as possible. Although this should not be mistaken for an accurate portrait of
the spoiling tendency of all *Lost* fans, or even those who frequent online
discussion boards, clearly a good number of active *Lost* fans engage in
spoiler consumption.

In conducting this study, one of the few existing studies of spoiler fans
that we had to work with was Henry Jenkins's analysis of *Survivor* (2000–)
spoiling communities who research where the show is filming and who
gets voted off when, and then post this material online. Jenkins's work
poses spoiler fans as resistive, engaged in "a giant cat and mouse game
that is played between the producers and the audience."[11] *Survivor* producer Mark Burnett, known to some fans as "evil pecker Mark," tries to
hide his reality set and the elimination order, while "brain trusts" of fans
pit their skills against his. Jenkins's study posits these spoiler fans as often
working against the pleasures of the show, resisting both it and the creator,
and as regarding their activities as a game unto itself, a contest between
fans and producers. The fans develop "collective intelligence" and enjoy
the communal relations of the spoiler-circulating community, but there
is little sense of them engaging in reading and/or circulating spoilers as a
way to enjoy *Survivor* itself. In short, their pleasures seem largely external
to the show, even if they rely upon its existence. By contrast, our sense
was that *Lost* spoiler readers often cared deeply about the show, and this

sense was quickly borne out by the data. Few if any spoiler readers pitted themselves against executive producers Damon Lindelof and Carlton Cuse, most were avid viewers, and little comment was made of the joys of the spoiler-circulating community. In other words, every sign pointed toward these fans using spoilers as a way of getting *into* the text.

While Mittell and I have published a fuller-length version of our research findings elsewhere, here I am interested in how spoilers worked as paratexts that negotiated particular ways of reading the text, not necessarily resistive but still less than normative. Given *Lost*'s frequent use of suspense, one might expect that viewers enjoy being surprised, experiencing a fresh plot that grabs them unaware, and that they are likely to focus primarily on plot developments as the source of narrative originality and pleasure. Our research, though, suggested that spoilers allowed some fans to experience the program in other ways, and that the practice of spoiler reading also rendered clear other appeals to this text in particular and to narrative consumption more generally.

First off, we hypothesized that spoiler fans might enjoy spoilers because they preferred to watch in-the-know and were more comfortable with seeing the known than the unknown. A second and accompanying hypothesis was that spoiler fans see the revelatory aspect of the plotline and pleasures of suspense as relatively unimportant, obscuring more enjoyable textual qualities that they seek out, such as narrative mechanics, relationship dramas, and production values. Martin Barker has argued that media studies have been wholly biased toward the specificities of plot, but in doing so have often taken their eyes off other elements of textuality.[12] The normative judgment of spoilers as "ruining" texts stems from this bias, but as Laura Carroll provocatively argues, the underlying assumption behind spoiler avoiding "doesn't imply much respect for anything that a fiction might offer you except abrupt and sensational narrative developments, or much long-term durability of a story. [. . .] A well-constructed story will stand up to decades of use and abuse, won't it?"[13] Carroll reasons that literature professors have long "spoiled" texts in their classes without concern for actually ruining the text, precisely because a text is about more than just surprises and plot-twists. In fact, the long history of storytelling suggests that unspoiled narratives are far less common than spoiled ones—from *Oedipus Rex* to *Romeo and Juliet*, *The Odyssey* to any historical narrative, many of our culture's most revered stories are "spoiled" from the outset. Meanwhile, Derek Kompare observes that much of television is reruns, sometimes new to any given viewer, but sometimes not,[14] while Barbara Klinger notes that favorite movies are often watched again and again, whether on DVDs or on television,[15] meaning that consumption of the familiar often constitutes a considerable portion of our narrative engagements.

The survey data proved less conclusive for the first hypothesis, but stronger for the second. Many *Lost* fans still clearly enjoyed the suspense, with 90 percent selecting "I enjoy the suspenseful plot" as a reason for watching, and 24 percent listing this as their primary pleasure. However, echoing Carroll's commentary, one spoiler fan wrote, "The initial shock value may be ruined, but if a drama has nothing else to offer then it isn't worth watching in the first place." While such outright dismissal of shock was rare among respondents, many clearly allowed their foreknowledge of events to attune their viewing to other pleasures of the text. Spoiler fans noted that knowing what will happen does not take away from their enjoyment of the show's performances, dialogue, production values, humorous moments, and focus on character relationships and development. As one fan wrote, "The words of a quickly written spoiler don't do justice to the actual episode." For some, the reduction of suspense enables greater attention to these details, and even enables a level of emotional connection with characters—one fan wrote that he used spoilers to avoid investing his attention in relationships or characters that are doomed. Thus, for some, learning the events of an episode in advance can yield greater access to the show's other pleasures, allowing them to avoid being distracted by the moment-to-moment suspense. Mittell has argued that a key pleasure for many viewers of narratively complex television lies in the "operational aesthetic," whereby viewers are encouraged to watch the gears of the storytelling machinery while being taken for a ride.[16] For spoiler fans, having already discovered what will happen freed them to concentrate on the formal pleasures of innovative narration and inventive presentation. As one respondent wrote, "It's like reading a book and then watching the movie even when you know the ending."

Spoiler fans were often quick to point out that spoilers reveal the "what" but not the "how," and in doing so sidestep the risks of "ruining" the plot while increasing anticipation. As one respondent offered:

> When the Losties are going to discover something new about the island, and I already know about it, I still want to know HOW they find out. It's still just as exciting, if not more so, to see how they're going to come upon it. For instance, I knew about the Black Rock, and that it was a

boat, before they found it. But that didn't really TELL me anything about it, or why a boat would be in the middle of the jungle. It was even MORE mysterious to KNOW the "answer." That's why Lost is so fun, even with some spoilers.

Here, this respondent reverses commonsense logic regarding spoilers, arguing that they improve, rather than ruin, his experience of the text by focusing his attention on the unfolding story and its telling. Spoilers work to help fans concentrate on what they consider the most important elements of the show. *Lost*'s flashbacks, large cast size, complex narrative, and multiple concurrent mysteries clearly confuse—or at least run the risk of confusing—many viewers, and these viewers spoke of spoilers as focusing their viewing. Spoilers are enjoyable, noted one woman, "because you can pick up on subtle hints and clues between characters, and know what it means," while another talked of the "peace of mind of not having to take all info in at once." We might therefore draw a parallel to another established form of spoiler: study guide summaries of literary texts such as CliffsNotes. Like *Lost* spoilers, CliffsNotes allow a window into future narrative occurrences, so that the individual reader can follow ongoing events more easily: for instance, knowing that Magwitch funds Pip's rise to wealth in *Great Expectations* foregrounds themes of redemption that one may otherwise miss. As such, spoiler fans may not use spoilers to "skip ahead" as much as to "catch up" as they are watching, or to appreciate the fullness of a scene or episode's narrative dynamics. "They give me an idea," wrote one fan, "of what to look for in an action filled show like *Lost*."

Another reason for enjoying spoilers that revealed itself was that many saw *Lost* as a giant puzzle, and their primary interest lay in solving the puzzle rather than in following the plot in linear fashion. *Lost*, after all, is already a slippery, "messy" text[17] that tells its story across time, with the present of the island, flashbacks, and (though not used when we released our survey) flash forwards. Watching requires that viewers piece together information from an erratically drawn timeline. Meanwhile, through the show's transmedia strategies, which have included embedding potential secrets in alternate reality games (ARGs), jigsaw puzzles, a multitude of websites, and spinoff novels, *Lost* has already challenged its own textual boundaries, actively inviting fans to look for clues outside of the program itself.[18] If we think of *Lost* less like a conventional story and more like a puzzle or game, spoilers become appreciably more legitimate:

in attempting to solve any large-scale puzzle or game, players are encouraged to gather as much information and research as possible, not relying on one limited source. Moreover, given that spoiler sources are not always reliable, especially with both production staff and fans circulating foilers to dupe fans, rarely can fans rely on spoilers being accurate, thus rendering them yet one more piece of evidence to consider in fan speculations. Spoilers, as one fan noted, "intensify the mystery-solving aspect of the show"; another offered, "Spoilers make the difference between informed speculation and crackpot theories"; and a third said that she reads spoilers "to find clues to the game." For most spoiler fans, spoilers rarely foreclosed the text's meaning, much less its mysteries; instead, many talked of spoilers *adding* to the mysteries, so that "you find out one thing, but there are 10 new things that pop up from it." Typical spoilers may point to little pieces of the show's major enigmas, but rarely provide information that would reveal the larger mystery of the island. One fan wrote, "I like to know what questions or puzzles will be solved, but not what the *answers* will be"; as did many others, this fan saw spoilers as creating as many questions as they answer, and as enhancing the terrain for speculation about the general puzzle surrounding *Lost*.

Granted, not all shows or films are puzzles, and thus spoilers will work differently for different shows or films, with this study only examining one case that is not necessarily representative. But the audience members who responded to our survey clearly used spoilers to open up the text in ways that were meaningful for them, just as will spoiler fans for any text, even if in starkly different ways. In the case of *Lost* or other shows, paratexts manage the text, allowing fans to make of it what they want rather than simply follow a normative plot-centric approach.

A final way in which they used spoilers as paratexts, we observed, was to take control of their emotional responses and pleasures of anticipation, creating suspense on viewers' own terms rather than the creators'. On one level, spoilers serve to stoke the fires of anticipation for fans, working much as trailers and previews do for continuing texts (indeed, as some respondents felt, "next week on"–style trailers can be seen as industry-circulated spoilers). On another level, though, reading spoilers and debriefing them with friends proved a way of satisfying one's cravings to know what's happening. Serial television comes to us slowly, with weeks or even month-long hiatuses separating episode from episode. In this intervening time, then, spoilers can step in and fill the gaps with textuality. While the show is absent from the scene, the text nevertheless lives on through the paratext (as will be discussed further in chapter 6). While spoilers do not outright cure the desire to reach the next episode, they help reduce anticipation between installments by reducing narrative suspense and giving fans a focus for their speculation, theorizing, and anticipation. Rather than obsessing over this week's cliffhanger, spoiler fans can attend to larger narrative issues and work on piecing together the big picture. And it is in such moments that the blurred line between text and paratext becomes particularly evident. Spoiler fans attempt to eliminate their undesirable anticipation for the next episode by reading spoilers, thereby creating a new form of anticipation for the pre-viewed events while watching each show. Spoilers, as such, become an intrinsic part of the text as experienced by the spoiler reader: the paratext allows a certain type of reading of the text, and in doing so becomes an inseparable part of the text, and a mediator of the spoiler reader's interactions with and reactions to the text.

While we began our project trying to make sense of the unknown, we came to realize the mediating role that spoilers, as paratexts, play in allowing viewers to find their own routes through *Lost*. Of course, the split side to this is that spoiler *avoiders* consciously keep their distance in order to maintain their different routes through *Lost*. From this example, then, one can see how varying paratexts can be consumed, dabbled in, and/or actively avoided as a way to chart different paths through a text, and/or as a way to open up texts to other consumptive pleasures. In this case, we saw that while a good story can be a well-told tale, it can also be a puzzle and a challenge, an object to be marveled at (directing focus to the well-told tale's actual *telling*), a familiar space, a complex network to be mapped, and a site to stimulate both discussion and the proliferation of textuality. Our choice of which paratexts to consume, and which paratexts to create, lets us work out what we want to do with any given tale before us.

"The Ultimate Close Reading": Vidding Character and Relationship Studies

Earlier, I noted a parallel between media paratexts and the marginalia in library books. But surely all of us have had the experience of marveling at marginalia in a library book that made us wonder to what purpose the "vandal" was using the text. When placing books on reserve in my university library for students in a class, I have at times felt the need to instruct the students to ignore the underlinings when the scribbler clearly followed a different path through the text than I wish my students to take. In short, I must plead for them to ignore the paratexts, lest their experience of the text be one that will not help them in my class. Likewise, I have at times hesitated to lend books to a friend, afraid that my own marginalia will betray my odd reading of these texts. And Jackson's careful study of marginalia takes as its data numerous books with famous marginalia writers, noting the titillating nature of reading someone else's marginalia, and thereby gaining a window into their own experience of a text. In a similar manner, all viewer-created paratexts can work as highlighters and underliners, plotting a course through a narrative and leaving tracks for others to follow. To highlight or to underline is to annotate, to choose a specific route through a text. To produce a paratext of any sort is similarly to engage in such route-making.

I have argued that spoilers show how some viewers experience the narrative as a whole. But paratexts can also draw our attention to specific characters and relationships, "highlighting" their path through a tale, and thereby drawing our attention to their peculiarities. In few sites is this process as obvious as in the thriving art form of fan vidding. Vids are music videos, usually made with a selection of clips from a given film or program that the vidder painstakingly juxtaposes with the lyrics of a background song in order to offer an interpretation of and/or argument regarding that show. To the newbie eye, vids can appear somewhat trailer-ish, with rapid-fire and (for the better ones) polished editing; however, with the exception of "recruiter vids," their primary purpose is to comment upon the show, not to sell it per se, and since they are song-length, they usually provide room for a more sustained examination of a show than do trailers. As editing software becomes cheaper and more user-friendly, an increasing number of fans are trying their hand at the art form, circulating their creations within interpersonal fan networks, via imeem (www.imeem.com), YouTube, personal websites, and/or at fan conventions, including Vividcon, an annual vidder convention.[19] Multiple styles and genres of vids exist, but in this section I wish to examine several vids' character and relationship studies and the ways in which these ask the viewer to engage with those characters and relationships.

Vidders Wolfling and Magpie offer a particularly effective character- and relationship-study in "Winter." Set to the slow and mournful song of the same title by Tori Amos, "Winter" edits together footage from the *Lord of the Rings* trilogy that follows Éowyn and her uncle Théoden. Éowyn has a few key moments in the films, most notably when she slays a

Fig. 5.1. Wolfling and Magpie accompany a clip from *The Two Towers* of a solitary and pensive Éowyn with lyrics that suggest her loneliness.

ringwraith in *Return of the King*, but it is otherwise somewhat easy to lose sight of her amidst the multiple other characters and storylines. However, "Winter" studies her relationship with her uncle, a character who we first meet in *The Two Towers* as a decrepit old king under the spell of the wizard Saruman. The vid focuses on tender moments when she tends to her uncle, and shows her as very much alone in Théoden's cold, wintery hall, especially following the loss of her brother (fig. 5.1). The song lyrics ask Éowyn on Théoden's behalf, "When you gonna love you as much as I do?" yet the vid shows no outward sign of his love, instead showing the niece care more for her uncle, and showing her cope on her own as those lyrics announce, "I hear a voice, / 'you must learn to stand up for yourself, / 'Cause I can't always be around.'" Then, when Gandalf frees Théoden from the curse, we are invited to see his return through Éowyn's eyes: where the scene is notable in the film almost solely for the editing and makeup that shows him lose many years of wrinkles before our eyes, the pathos of the song ("I tell you that I'll always want you near, / You say that things change my dear") and the focus on Éowyn now recontextualize the scene as deeply touching for her.

Yet despite the lyrics' brief mention of melting Winter, the joy is similarly brief. Théoden is still distant, as he must bury his nephew, then lead his men and (unknown to him) his niece into battle. As one watches his preparations for battle, one gets the sense of an uncle and niece who are unable to communicate, yet who are, or at least could be, each other's closest companions. Finally, Théoden is mortally wounded on the battlefield, leaving Éowyn to avenge him. Wolfling and Magpie match this act of vengeance to a faster-paced section of the song and show us the uncle and niece's brief moment of togetherness before his death; however, the song's eventual return to a slower, sad pace once more suggests a pervasive loneliness, or Winter, for Éowyn. The song lyrics that "things are gonna change so fast" serve only as a taunt, as little changes for the character. Thus in six minutes, Wolfling and Magpie succeed in providing a masterful, detailed character study of Éowyn that matches the lyrics to a tee. The vid invites viewers to contemplate the character, her motivations, and her relationship with her uncle, and allows viewers the time and reflective space to do so that the films never truly provide. Éowyn is one of only three substantive female characters in the trilogy, too, so this act of highlighting her and her story tries to carve out space for a female character and journey in what can otherwise be quite the boy's story and world, and for readers to appreciate the depths of this character.

Another character and relationship study vid by Wolfling, "Sick Cycle Carousel," examines the anger and rage of Anakin and Luke Skywalker in the *Star Wars* films, and Obi-Wan Kenobi's own entrapment within that cycle using the Lifehouse song of that title. Although this vid focuses on three characters that are at the center of the *Star Wars* trilogies, its deft act of collating and juxtaposing many of the films' scenes of Skywalker anger and of Skywalker–Kenobi conflict invites viewers to contemplate Luke's, Anakin's, and Obi-Wan's inner psyches arguably more than do the films. Moreover, as does "Winter," it provides space for the reflection upon these psyches. The title of the piece immediately suggests a pattern of cyclical rage, as do Lifehouse's alternative rock sound and lyrics about an unhealthy relationship and the singer's struggle to end it:

> So when will this end?
> It goes on and on
> And over and over and over again
> Keep spinning around
> I know that it won't stop
> Till I step down from this for good.

Yet gradually we see Luke and Anakin triumph over this rage, and thus where the films contextualize Anakin's eventual, dying act of heroism in macro terms, as saving the universe and defeating its prime evil, "Sick

Cycle Carousel" contextualizes his triumph as a personal and familial one, a last-ditch attempt to end the "sick cycle" that has enveloped him and his son.

This ability of vids to drill deep into a character's psyche leads to many of the form's better offerings. For instance, while the show *Dexter* is remarkable for being one of the few on television to study one character's psyche in depth, and for using voiceover from Michael C. Hall and flashbacks to open the character's mind up to the viewer, Luminosity's vid "Blood Fugue" arguably opens that mind up yet further. Drawing heavily from clips at the end of the first season that revealed Dexter's horrific past—watching his mother be slaughtered with a chainsaw in front of him, before staying locked in a cargo container in a pool of her blood—"Blood Fugue" offers a three-minute examination of Dexter's bloodlust and of the genesis of a serial killer. While *Dexter* itself hardly shies away from creating reflective spaces for the consideration of its titular character, never has it offered such a sustained period of introspection, more commonly employing dark comic relief and/or subplots to break up its journey into the passages of Dexter's mind. All the while, too, "Blood Fugue" is set to Dog Fashion Disco's "Mature Audiences Only," a frenetic string piece that puts the viewer on edge with mumbled phrases such as "there was blood everywhere," "I'm losing my mind," "these dark sexual urges," and "there are many demons I face every day" sampled into the music. As Kristina Busse writes:

> There are many quick cuts between past and present, job and secret life, victim and killer, interspersed with slower moments of Dexter's introspection, often accompanied by images of water/blood/drowning. The voice over the heavy violins (sounding like saws?) whispers of blood and dark sadistic urges, and the screams mid-vid offer a vision of Dexter that the show whitewashes to a degree. In fact, the entire vid seems to resurrect the violent unconscious that somehow, even amid all the blood and torture and murder isn't quite present on the show itself.[20]

Luminosity makes it darker still, then. And what Luminosity does for a reading of Dexter, obsessive24 does for a reading of *Fight Club*'s narrator in "Cells" or *Heroes*' Sylar in "One of a Kind"; here's luck does for a reading of *Buffy the Vampire Slayer*'s Spike in "Glorious," Willow in "Atropine," or the relationships between Buffy and Faith in "Superstar" or Willow and Tara in "Writing Notes"; Shalott does for a reading of the *Star Wars* trilogies' Amidala in "Kid Fears"; and countless other vidders do for readings of what makes many central or peripheral film and television characters and their relationships tick.

Such is the development of vidding as an art form that several versions of vids have been made with a commentary track overlaid. These allow us access to the vidders' intended meanings and suggest that the casual vid watcher may wish to engage more closely with the nuances of edited storytelling. Of a crucial segment in her vid "Change (in the house of flies)," about the Clark Kent and Lex Luthor friendship in *Smallville* (2001–), obsessive24 notes what her vid dramatically shows and argues, that Superman failed Lex as a friend, a notion that opens up significant ground for new, or at least more nuanced, readings of the two characters and of the Superman mythology more generally. She states:

> And here we come into the crux of this vid, which is: Lex will save Clark, but in the end Clark doesn't save Lex. Sure, he saves him in superficial ways, in the same way that he saves anyone else, but I guess what we're talking about here is a spiritual saving, where Lex propels Clark onto his path as Superman. But what does Clark do in return? He does the only thing that he can do under circumstances, also on his path of destiny, which is to cast Lex down into the abyss[. . . .] Clark is really almost a villain in this story, because they made each other who they are. In Lex's case, he made Clark great, but in Clark's case, he kind of failed in making Lex the man that Lex had originally set out to be. He wanted to be good, but later, much later in the future, Lex couldn't remember this, and I doubt that Clark could either, but the audience can, and I guess that's where the tragedy lies.[21]

When television shows have multiple seasons behind them, the visual catalogue open to the average vidder is huge, allowing significant ground for character and relationship studies, arguments, and observations that pull together scenes and moments from across the series, as does obsessive24, meaning that some of the more thoughtful and thought-provoking commentary on such longrunning shows as *Buffy the Vampire Slayer* and *Smallville* exists in the world of vids.

In an email interview, obsessive24 wrote to me of the importance of using trusted betas (editors), but if repurposed, her comments provide a way of thinking of the relationship between the film or show and the vidder for character study or relationship vids. She wrote:

I'll try to take on all of their suggestions even where I don't personally agree. This is because I think the artist him/herself has blind spots when it comes to actually communicating to the audience what s/he wants to say; it's a beta's job to point out the bits that don't work and force you to change it, even if you love it personally.

Perhaps, just as betas help vidders to communicate more clearly, so too do vids help the film or show to communicate more clearly. Or, as obsessive24 also notes of her own character study and relationship vids, many are "trying to 'read deeper' into what's already there and [are] bringing it out so that other people can see it more easily." In another email interview, here's luck observes, "Vidding is the ultimate close reading: a vid sends the vidder, and possibly the viewer as well, back to the text in a profound and literal way." As all of the vidders and vid-fans to whom I talked noted, many of the better vids have something interesting, substantive, and/or revelatory to say about the show. Many of the better vids send us "deeper" into and "back to the text," having said something of substance about it.

here's luck's declaration of a vid being "the ultimate close reading" is highly apt, given a good vid's ability to unlock and make sense of parts of a text while being considerably more entertaining and affectively gripping than are most close readings. To this end, here's luck notes, "I'm not sure that vids allow me to say things I otherwise couldn't; [but] they do allow me to say some things more elegantly or persuasively or quickly. And they allow me to invite an audience to collaborate in making meaning with me, which I think is pretty cool." Vidding's "elegance" lies in the fact that it is its own art form, presenting its case in a visually and aurally pleasing manner. Hence, just as Jenkins notes that spoilers might become the text itself for spoiler fans, as those spoiler fans circulate them and engage in a giant "cat and mouse game" with the producers more for the sake of it than for the enjoyment of the text being spoiled, so too have vids become texts in and of their own right, watched closely, parsed for meanings, eagerly anticipated, traded in fan communities, given commentary tracks, and becoming the basis for their own conventions.

Another helpful way to understand vids, both as texts in their own right and as paratexts, is offered by academic, fan historian, and vidder Francesca Coppa, who argues that fan fiction in general follows dramatic rather than literary modes of storytelling. Responding to the endless and frequently facile criticism of fan fiction being "merely derivative," Coppa states that in literature, fan fiction's repetition is strange; [but] in theatre, stories are retold all the time. Theatre artists think it's fine to tell the same story again, but differently: not only was Shakespeare's *Hamlet* a relatively late version of the tale [. . .] but we're happy to see differently inflected versions of the tale. Moreover, there's no assumption that the first production will be definitive; in theatre, we want to see *your* Hamlet and *his* Hamlet and *her* Hamlet; to embody the role is to reinvent it.[22]

Coppa's argument suggests that we could see gifted vidders as thoughtful actors or directors working with a script, not simply repeating the lines of a "derivative," stale performance, but trying to make new sense of a character or characters. Meanwhile, just as many theater buffs attend multiple *Hamlet*s, *Macbeth*s, and *King Lear*s over the course of their lives, each hopefully further fleshing out the plays' enigmatic figures, vid audiences similarly watch to see and hear new or developing interpretations of characters. Fan fiction, writes Coppa, "is community theatre in a mass media world,"[23] a staging and therefore a reading of a text.

Further echoing this notion of vids as performative, Luminosity explained to me, "Vids allow me to *show*, which is better than tell," and she later added:

All of my vids are personal expressions. [. . .] I don't know if it's my age or the fact that I have been an artist all of my life, but I "own" everything about my vids. They're moving paintings of my thoughts about specific issues or events within the universe of the show or movie—or maybe about just one thing, or maybe even about a universal thing that I choose a specific source to explore. For example, my father died in 2004, and I was very close to him. Part of my working through my own grief included making the vids "Art of Dying" and "Serenity." If I had been painting then, I would have painted my grief instead, but I was vidding. When I look back at those two vids, I'm able to see how I channeled my sense of loss into them. I suppose that's where "personal expression" really lives, and it's something that I do a lot. [. . .] I tend to explore my own psyche when I vid (as well as the imaginary characters' motivations, etc.).

Luminosity's narrative suggests a complex yet energizing relationship between text, paratext, fantext, vidder, and audience member. She suggests a process whereby her personalized construction of and relationship to *Kill Bill*, vols. 1 and 2 (2003, 2004), and *Firefly* (2002), respectively, based in part on a grieving process following her father's death, is worked into her own artistic performance and act of creating the vids, and is thus communicated to and shared with a broader audience or community of vid watchers. She therefore in part close-reads those texts and directs her audience to resonances of *Kill Bill*, *Firefly*, and *Serenity* that they may have overlooked, and in part adds new meanings and resonances to them, broadening viewers' understandings of the texts.

Given the degree to which vids carry resonances and messages that will prove more meaningful for a particular community of fans with the necessary fannish and interpersonal knowledge to decode them in full, some vids operate within these communities and not more broadly for a wider audience. While some observers may see the result as an insular art form, it also shows how paratexts can domesticate texts to specific communities (as does community theater), offering the prospect for those communities to construct a more intimate relationship to what may otherwise seem a "mass" text. Moreover, not all are so insular. Vids, after all, are also vehicles for some fantastic songs, for small stories and arguments, and they can also exhibit significant editing prowess, none of which necessarily require knowledge of the fan object. For instance, a particularly famous vid, "Us" by Lim, juxtaposes numerous clips that are often used in vids or that have become iconic for fans, but it also uses a catchy song by Regina Spektor and shows off Lim's significant editing and animation skills, making it visually stunning for the uninitiated viewer. Others approach the level of parody, and thus have comic potential in and of themselves, as is the case, for example, with Luminosity's "Hopeless," which playfully examines the love affair between various *Lord of the Rings* characters and the ring, while set to the cheesy Olivia Newton-John song. Regardless of their intended audiences, however, vids can offer fascinating close readings that energize many of a text's elements, lighting up the vidder's path through a text while also cutting deeper, often more nuanced paths into the text for others to follow, and thereby contributing to what Hellekson and Busse call the fantext.

"You" and Your Limits: Privileged Paratexters

While the vids that I focused on above illustrate viewer-paratexts' abilities to study characters and relationships, of course other viewer-paratexts will study other aspects of texts, illustrating considerable variety in paratextual focus. The fanvid itself is a diverse form, and character study and relationship vids are only two related genres within a wider catalogue. Other viewer-paratexts change focus too. Fan-written episode recaps, for instance, can range from those that function strictly as plot recaps, to those that treat the characters as eye candy and focus on the show's erotic elements,[24] to many of *Television Without Pity*'s recaps that call for a playful, ironic reading of the episode. Each style will simultaneously provide evidence about how any given community or individual watches the show in question, and it will serve as a paratext that encourages others to watch in a similar manner. By contrast, some media-related wikis (such as *Lostpedia* or *Wookieepedia*) tend to treat texts as expansive universes with dense histories and sociologies that require archiving and the constant oversight of a fandom's collective intelligence. Other wikis actively invite audiences to continue the creation and performance of the text themselves, as with *Wikiality* (fig. 5.2), a wiki based around *The Colbert Report*'s slyly satiric celebration of style over fact, and of white conservative American chauvinism.[25] Posing itself as a *Wikipedia* for "truthiness" (Colbert's term for opinions that hold no factual basis but that "feel" true), and claiming to host 10,747,142 articles in "American" at last visit (early 2009), *Wikiality* includes entries, for example, on "Global Warming" that at present calls it "a complex consumer confidence scam put forth onto the American public by Al Gore and the Weather Channel," and on Colbert's parodic target and conservative pundit, Bill O'Reilly, that calls him "a godlike killing machine, liberating the world from the liberal, ivy-league media elite and their front politicians known as democrats." Here, fans are invited to continue Colbert's brand of ironic punditry and to enjoy each other's wit. Indeed, since Colbert's satire relies quite heavily upon the ironic juxtaposition of his own supposedly cult-like fans—"the Colbert Nation"—to the allegedly unthinking, sheeplike fans of self-worshiping American conservative pundits such as O'Reilly, the wiki's removal of Colbert from this supposed altar to the character, and its fans' ability to produce a similar brand of humor without Colbert present, is arguably important in assuring that the ironic contrast holds. These and countless other examples of viewer-created paratexts all invite different relationships to the associated film or television program, and all stand to recalibrate the text's interpretive trajectory as a result.

However, while audiences and fans can and regularly do create their own paratexts that privilege their own readings of texts and their own interpretive strategies, we must avoid the trap of seeing these as necessarily of equal presence and power as those created by film and television

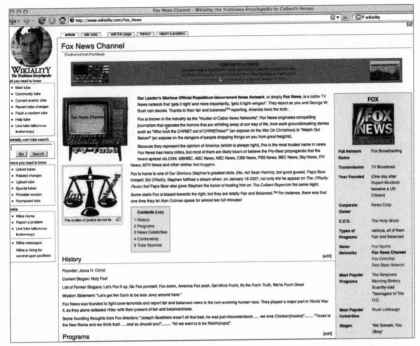

Fig. 5.2. A page from *Wikiality*, a wiki playing along with and honoring *The Colbert Report*'s satiric take on the state of American politics and media.

producers and their marketing teams. Bruce Leichtman, president and principal analyst of Leichtman Research Group, Inc., while presenting at 2008's National Association of Television Production Executives convention in Las Vegas, was particularly keen to dispel some of the digital era's utopian rhetoric, noting the fact that on an average day, YouTube attracts as many viewers as does one episode of FOX's prime-time karaoke competition *Don't Forget the Lyrics* (2007–). Even on YouTube and imeem, viewer numbers suggest that many more people have seen the *Iron Man* trailer than even the most-watched vids, while on the average day *Lost* spoilers likely reach fewer readers than did *Six Degrees'* New York hype campaign at its peak. The recent advent of online communities, social networking, and video-sharing sites, as well as various digital platforms and technologies that assist in ripping and burning video, has led to much "You-topian" rhetoric of which we should be wary. In 2006, *Time* announced that its Person of the Year was "You," thereby repeating many popular and academic accounts of the rise of audience power. Much of the hoopla surrounding Web 2.0's multiple sharing sites, such as YouTube, MySpace, and Facebook, has focused on how they challenge corporate culture and logic, opening up cultural production, authorship, and distribution to seemingly anyone. In the face of such excited rhetoric, though, we must remember that "You" still require significant technology and communications infrastructure to be able to enjoy this new era, and hence "You" often excludes all of those on the other side of the digital divide who do not own computers with editing software and high-speed Internet service. Also, media multinationals frequently have considerably more time and resources than do "You" to produce, publicize, and circulate paratextual entourages.

Legally, these multinationals also have considerably more clout to police the acceptable edges of textual universes. Trailer editors, hype campaign designers, and other industry-made paratextual artists rarely have their names attached to their work, but no litigation would likely follow from the release of such names. By contrast, most vidders use aliases, some admittedly for other reasons, but some in fear of reprisal from a grumpy and aggrieved media production company's law firm. Carlton Cuse and Damon Lindelof's publicly voiced distaste for *Lost* spoilers[26] and J. K. Rowling's elaborate legal attempts and threats to keep *Harry Potter* news under wraps till her publisher's release dates[27] further warn of the acceptable limits of paratextual production for insiders (whether *Lost* cast or crew member, or Bloomsbury or Scholastic typesetter). Even some reviewers have been threatened, not with lawsuits but with blacklisting, when their caustic comments stand to damage a show's public reputation. And though legal scholars have argued for fan fiction's legality,[28] the lack of case law to serve as precedent has notoriously enabled media firms to send cease-and-desist letters with wild abandon, and with little consistency as to what constitutes (to their mind) acceptable use of a show's diegesis.[29]

Hence, if media multinationals and individual audience members or communities have varying interpretative, framing strategies that are built into their paratexts, media multinationals have a significant advantage in both blanketing the media environment with their own images, and making that environment inhospitable for others' images. Despite the enthusiastic discussion of YouTube's or Web 2.0's prospects for developing grassroots politics, everyday creativity, and a more democratic version of cultural production, then, YouTube and friends are also home to thousands of film and television trailers, many with viewership in the millions, while the Internet more broadly is populated with hundreds of glitzy official film and television show web pages, complete with their small armies of paratexts. Moreover, rather than see media firms' paratexts and fans in competition or contrast, we should also acknowledge the increasing incidence of media firms creating policed playgrounds for fans, setting up fan sites that invite various forms of fan paratextual creativity and user-generated content, yet often imposing a set of rules and limitations and/ or claiming legal rights over the material. Thus, several companies have experimented with releasing clips from shows and encouraging fans to edit together a montage or trailer to be entered into a competition at the show or film's official website. Similarly, fan film and fan fiction have at times been brought under the "protective umbrella" of various media firms, while representatives of the producer's or marketer's staff regularly expunge fan discussion at official fan sites when they deem it to be offensive or inappropriate.

The power to create paratexts is the power to contribute to, augment, and personalize a textual world. Thus, many media firms' frequent acts of filtering acceptable content from fan creations (whether film, fiction, or simple discussion) seek variously to outright deny fans the right to contribute, augment, or personalize; seek to co-opt and profit from fans' paratexts; and/or seek to strictly limit the scope of possible meanings that fans can attach to a text. Most notoriously, slash fiction and fan film—those that posit a same-sex relationship between two characters—are often met with disapproval by media firms' moderators. But on the less overt end of the scale, media firms can still subtly reinforce their own preferred meanings by privileging certain fan products whose meanings wholly conform to those of the firm, and hence that effectively echo the firm's own paratexts and paratextual meanings.

Many media firms' restrictive reactions to fan creativity tellingly reflect on the degree to which they realize the power of paratexts. For instance, when Lucasfilm drew a hard line that fan creativity could be parodic but not expansive of the *Star Wars* universe, their decision was likely forced on one hand by precedent regarding the legal status of parody, and on the other hand by the knowledge that fan creations could hijack "their" text.[30] Viewer-made paratexts are resources with which, whether through creation, consumption, or both, viewers can add their own voice, interests, and concerns to a textual world. They give partial ownership of a text to those other than the initial creators. And thus Hollywood has often come down hard on paratexts, or on certain types of paratexts, in order to maintain ownership privileges and rights. Of course, such proprietary acts are often futile. As discussed in chapter 1, a text only becomes a text, only gains social meaning and relevance, at the point that it comes alive with its audience. Therefore, a text is always already a collaboratively created entity, and regardless of how media firms rewrite copyright law to give them power of attorney over a text, the only texts incapacitated enough to be ownable are those that have absolutely no social relevance or audience attention. At the moment that audiences care about a text, it has multiple creators, and that creation is often maintained by paratextual creation and consumption. Along with Henry Jenkins, then, I am depressed by some media firms' dogged refusal to accept what is already occurring, and by their desperate attempts to keep proprietary status over their texts. As Jenkins notes, "Over the past several decades, corporations have sought to market branded content so that consumers become the bearers of their marketing messages," and yet, he also notes, the same corporations have a tendency to cry foul "once consumers choose when and where to display those messages, their active participation in the circulation of brands" now stunningly becoming "a moral outrage and a threat to the industry's economic well-being."[31] Never will such legal maneuvers ever truly exclude audience readings and strategies altogether, but their ramifications for the scope of fan paratextual creativity can often be significant.

Moving the Goal Posts: Press Reviews and Friday Night Lights

Beyond media firms, though, we might also look to other privileged paratextual creators. Audiences, after all, are by no means equal. A prominent vidder with a large audience will enjoy privileged status as a paratextual creator over someone whose viewing circle of friends is small. A person with a fancy, well-funded website with thousands of viewers can similarly enjoy privileged status. Anyone with the capacity to reach a large audience will have greater potential power to offer his or her interpretive strategies to others and to gain converts. A particularly prominent example of such a privileged decoder is the critic. Critics occupy a hybrid space between the media and the audience, frequently receiving copies of shows before the rest of us, yet not officially affiliated with any media firm and thus supposedly neutral and objective. Prior to the release of a new film or television show, press reviews can catch the audience at a decisive pre-decoding moment, just as the text is being born. But even for longrunning television shows, as Amanda Lotz points out, in a post-network era with hundreds of channels in many homes, "Critics become increasingly important as their reviews and 'tonight on' recommendations provided promotional venues to alert viewers of programming on cable and network channels they did not regularly view and as legitimate, unbiased sources within the cluttered programming field."[32] Of course, just as audiences might miss or ignore the hype, they might miss or ignore critics' reviews. Nevertheless, upon release, as does a network's marketing machine, reviews hold the power to set the parameters for viewing, suggesting how we might view the show (if at all), what to watch for, and how to make sense of it.

Barbara Klinger clearly illustrates the subtle power of reviews in her discussion of *Home Theater* magazine's regular feature, "Snacks, Wine, and Videotape." Here, the editors review films by way of suggesting food pairings. As Klinger notes of their pairing of *Shawshank Redemption* (1994) with filet mignon and exotic marinade, the effect is to suggest a decidedly more upmarket film, whereas their pairing of *Ed Wood* (1994) with hamburger

> suggests that the film's concerns (i.e., cross-dressing, drug addiction, and bad filmmaking) give it a more questionable, campy status that detracts from its consumption as "serious." However, even here, hamburger is made more respectable by associating it with Dijon mustard, Thousand Island Dressing, and chilled grapes. Thus, the hamburger is rescued from ordinariness by accompanying relishes and food items.[33]

Albeit in less graphic or appetite-inducing manner, all reviews similarly try to pair a film or television program with an image. Labeling *Ed Wood* as a "hamburger with Dijon and chilled grapes"–type film firmly places it on a value hierarchy, but also suggests something of its meanings and the attitude with which viewers should approach the film. While it is a frequent retort from aggrieved creators to harsh critics to "do something" rather than "just" criticize, their criticism very much "does something," mediating and hence co-authoring a media text at the constitutive moment when it becomes a text and launches itself into popular culture and/ or an audience member's mind.

Seeking other examples of where reviews dictated textual meaning, in the fall of 2006, I collected multiple reviews for several of NBC's new shows using an online review aggregator—Metacritic (www.metacritic.

com)—and later I examined them for the rhetorical and hermeneutic moves they make in trying to position the shows. My interests lay in how paratextual authors play an intermediary role between production and reception, as part author/encoder, part privileged reader/encoder. Elsewhere, I discuss the reviews of *Studio 60 on the Sunset Strip* (2006–7) and *Heroes*,[34] but a particularly stark attempt at recoding the marketing rhetoric was evident in the reviews of *Friday Night Lights*. Though the show's interest in high school football allowed reviewers plenty of opportunities for football puns, most reviewers were also quick to insist that the show is not "just" about football, or not *even* about football. Thus, the reviews tried to move the show's generic goal posts.

Reflecting quite openly on the opportunity that the football show allows him, for instance, Matthew Gilbert begins by noting:

> One way to praise NBC's "Friday Night Lights" would be to say, "It's a stand-up-and-cheer drama about football!" And then to use football metaphors such as "Catch this TV forward pass." Because, as the show's Dillon High Panthers wrestle for a Texas state championship on the field, you'll want to stand up, cheer, and program the series onto your DVR. But "Friday Night Lights," which premieres tonight at 8 on Channel 7, is more than a football drama for ESPN types.[35]

The show was widely praised by reviewers, yet often with surprise. The cause of the surprise is obvious—many thought it would be "just" a football show, "just" a high school drama, or worse yet, just a high school football drama (fig. 5.3). Tim Goodman notes that *Friday Night Lights* "manages to be everything you don't expect it to be—a finely nuanced drama instead of 'Beverly Hills 90210' [1990–2000], a portrait of small town life instead of a cheesy back-lot fantasy, and even a sports story with real authenticity, from the preparation to the game action." The show, he states, "has to overcome so many preconceived notions, so many reasons not to watch, that it's the dramatic equivalent of a Hail Mary pass falling miraculously into the hands of an open receiver." Thus he marvels that what producer Peter Berg "manages to do here is wholly impressive. If you don't care for football, or high school football in particular, or even the concerns of a bunch of high school kids and their fanatical grown-ups—which plenty of viewers probably don't—Berg makes you care."[36]

The litany of "this is not a football show" resounds throughout a reading of multiple *Friday Night Lights* reviews, as many reviewers share

Fig. 5.3. A poster advertising *Friday Night Lights* hails football fans and teen-drama fans, two groups away from which many press reviews seemed determined to shepherd the series.

Goodman and Gilbert's dislike of football and/or football shows, as well
as of high school dramas, yet also share their desire to paint the show as
much more than either genre. Regarding the football, we're told that *Friday Night Lights* "isn't just about the gridiron,"[37] that "football is only the
kickoff,"[38] and that "even skeptics, even people who hate football, could
easily be caught up in the drama."[39] While on one level, this description
is reasonably accurate, the declaration is often intoned with gratitude
and relief, the "skeptics" of this latter quotation clearly including the critics themselves, who furthermore imagine their audiences to be skeptics.
Doug Elfman states point blank that the show "makes me care about a
subject I have zero, or possibly negative, interest in, no matter how rah-
rah I was as a teen: high school daddy ball in rural Texas, where prayers
are reserved for scoring touchdowns."[40]

Yet if the danger of a football show requires a "hard defensive line" to
deflect, Elfman's invocation of his former, lesser teen self also reflects a
general sense in the reviews of the high school drama being a lesser genre.
Gilbert glows, for example, that "there's nothing corny or precious about
Dillon—none of the soapy romanticism of the towns in 'One Tree Hill' or
'Dawson's Creek.'"[41] *One Tree Hill* (2003–) proves a common intertextual
contrast, as a "soapy" program that lacks *Friday Night Lights'* humanity,
grit, and realism. Even if they don't actively distance the show from the
high school drama label, many reviewers are keen to crown it as the best
of the lot, and another variety altogether. Diane Werts states that "none of
this plays as soap opera, or perhaps it actually is soap opera in the finest
sense, as a penetrating moral compass on the way humans privately direct
their lives."[42] Hal Boedeker writes, "Television needs a good high-school
drama, and NBC's Friday Night Lights is a great drama."[43] And Melanie
McFarland observes that *Friday Night Lights* represents a new brand of
family-friendly programming, "stylish, intelligent and blissfully free of
teen caricatures. Granted, the teenagers in 'Friday Night Lights' are TV
beautiful, but the characters are steeped in an authenticity that serves as
an antidote to all the MTV reality images that have been pumped into
our culture."[44]

We therefore have a case of reviewers keen to "rescue" a show from its
low-culture connotations. Perhaps concerned that they need to justify the
presence of their columns in a medium that is mostly regarded as higher
and more literate than the object of their criticism, many press critics
worked hard to frame *Friday Night Lights* as unlike the "low" genres of
football shows and high school dramas. Witness, for instance, Alessandra

Stanley struggling to justify *Friday Night Lights'* inclusion in her decidedly upmarket publication, the *New York Times*:

> [*Friday Night Lights* is] not just television great, but great in the way of a poem or painting, great in the way of art with a single obsessive creator who doesn't have to consult with a committee and has months or years to go back and agonize over line breaks and the color red.[45]

Stanley also invokes *Rebel without a Cause* (1955) and *Splendor in the Grass* (1961) as similar (inter)texts, while *Slate's* Troy Patterson compares the show to *Moby-Dick*,[46] and Elfman calls it the closest thing network television has to HBO's critical darling *The Wire*.[47] The intertexts are mobilized to shepherd the would-be audience toward seeing the text as a very certain product: *The Wire*-, *Moby-Dick*-, and poem-like, not *90210*-, *One Tree Hill*-, or ESPN-like.

Ironically, of course, such reviews might have *lost* audiences as well. NBC's loss of NFL broadcast rights had played a key role in their ratings drop in the previous two seasons, and 2006 marked not only *Friday Night Lights'* premier, but the return of the NFL to NBC; thus, the network would no doubt have loved to capitalize on NFL–*FNL* synergy if possible. Yet when the reviews work so hard to state that the show is *not* a football show, they risk alienating a large segment of the potential audience, and when they similarly try to distance *Friday Night Lights* from high school dramas, they also risk turning off the eighteen to twenty-four demographic, a group that is much beloved by networks. Gilbert and Brian Lowry both almost snidely note that *Friday Night Lights* is the kind of show that middle America longs for—set in a small, God-fearing town, focusing on family relationships—yet never actually watch;[48] however, most of the reviews (Gilbert's in particular) try to sever ties between a working-class audience and the show by insisting upon its high-culture credentials. Little do they realize that in so doing they may be contributing to the eventual failure of *Friday Night Lights* to reach said audiences. Victoria Johnson has written of the "Heartland myth" that lies at the center of significant discussion about television, whereby "flyover country" is seen as providing "a short-hand cultural common sense framework for 'all-American' identification, redeeming goodness, face-to-face community, sanctity, and emplaced ideals to which a desirous and nostalgic public discourse repeatedly returns," while also functioning "as an object of derision—condemned for its perceived naiveté and lack of mobility as

a site of hopelessly rooted, outdated American past life and values, en-
trenched political and social conservatism, and bastion of the 'mass,' un-
differentiated, un-hip people and perspectives."[49] NBC was undoubtedly
hoping that its show would be received as appealing to the former, uplift-
ing facet of the myth, yet the reviewers seem mindful of the risk that such
an image would involve (or even be swallowed by?) the latter facet of the
myth, and thus they move quickly to recharacterize it as comfortably hip,
gritty, quality fare worthy of an upscale, urban audience.

Admittedly, *Friday Night Lights* is quite boldly innovative at mixing
genres, and subsequently succeeded in attracting a (small) high-end audience. All the same, many critics' odd rhetorical strategy of *excluding* audiences of football and high school dramas is shown to be unnecessary
by Alan Sepinwall's review, a lone exception in my sample that welcomed
and embraced the frame of it being a football show, even as Sepinwall
shares his press critic colleagues' enthusiasm for the program. He writes:

> The best sports movies and TV shows provide us with a kind of certainty,
> the knowledge that you'll get to witness either a clear win ("Hoosiers,"
> "Major League") or some kind of moral victory (Rocky going the dis-
> tance, Rudy getting on the field). So when I say that virtually every devel-
> opment in the "Friday Night Lights" premiere will be telegraphed well in
> advance, I don't mean it as a bad thing. The drama is one of the season's
> best because it makes you care even when you know something big is
> coming—and because it finds pleasant little surprises along the way.[50]

To Sepinwall, the show can be a great football show *and* one of the season's best. It could also be a show that plays to "the Heartland" *and* to an
upscale urban audience. Jason Mittell has written of the rocky path that
genre hybrids frequently walk, as expectations and codings of each genre
might conflict with the prospects for enjoyment and/or understanding of
the other.[51] Many critics' reviews of *Friday Night Lights* expressed anxiety at the prospects for their beloved show to fail, but their subsequent
solution was to try to remove the show from its rocky road and place it
on what they saw to be a safer road called "quality television." Ultimately,
though, this was an act with significant interpretive ramifications, for it
involved framing the show in ways that neglected and/or excluded other
potential ways of enjoying it.

Thus, press reviews provide a clear example of how privileged paratexts
can work to offset or otherwise revise a marketer's paratexts and hype. As

this example also shows, and as argued in chapter 3, paratexts can often position a text on value hierarchies. Television critics occupy liminal space in hierarchies of taste, on one hand writing for newspapers and working in the austere tradition of criticism, yet on the other hand writing of the "low" culture form that is television, and frequently consigned to the same section of their newspapers as reports on Britney Spears's latest antics. In this regard, and as self-appointed taste leaders, they often play a key role in mediating television shows' standing in hierarchies of taste and value, at a key time in the text's birth into popular culture. Individual reviews' powers will of course depend upon the individual reader's own level of interaction with and regard for other paratexts and the show itself. On one end of a spectrum, we could imagine many readers who have eagerly anticipated a show long before the reviews came in, and who do not care about them; on the other end of this spectrum, we should expect to find some readers who have heard little if anything about the program, who greatly value the critics' opinions, and perhaps who do not even watch the show, comfortable to let the critics' opinions at least temporarily substitute for their own. Consequently, realizing the power of reviews to co-create texts does not necessarily allow us as analysts any special predictive powers of how popular culture will receive a text and of what interpretive communities will dominate. Nevertheless, a close analysis of reviews does allow us greater knowledge of the semiotic environment into which new shows arrive, and of the reviews' role both in creating that environment and in co-creating the text.

A Paratext of Their Own

Chapters 2–4 focused largely on how the entertainment industry can fashion a text at its outskirts, using paratexts to set the parameters of genre, style, address, value, and meaning. In this chapter, however, I hope to have shown that audience members are involved in this fashioning of the text not simply as consumers of text and paratext, but as creators of their own paratexts. The industry usually has considerable interest in trying to set its own textual parameters, and it will at times reinforce this semiotic act with legal ones, literally closing off opportunities for its texts to grow in certain directions. But audience members have a built-in interest in fashioning the text themselves. At a rudimentary—though by no means insignificant—level, the paratext of everyday discussion will forever play a constitutive role in creating the text. How we talk about texts affects how others talk about and consume them, as was seen in chapter 4. We can also "talk" through more elaborate forms of paratexts, whether they be spoilers, vids, recaps, wikis, reviews, or other viewer-end paratexts such as websites, campaigns, viewing parties, or so on. Some such forms of "talk" will be louder and more readily accessible than others, some directed at small communities of like-minded audiences, some emanating out to the public sphere more generally. The latter may even in due course come to determine the public understanding of a text. Others allow viable alternatives to the public script to emerge, thereby multiplying the text into various versions. All, though, underline the considerable power of viewer-end paratexts to set or change the terms by which we make sense of film and television, and, hence, to add or subtract depth and breadth to a text and its storyworld.

6

In the World, Just Off Screen

Toys and Games

As I have been arguing throughout this book, a proper study of paratexts and an attention to off-screen studies challenge the logic of "primary" and "secondary" texts,[1] originals and "spinoffs," shows and "peripherals" often used to discuss paratexts. That logic traditionally regards the film or television program as the center of the textual interaction and the only source of authentic textuality, while peripherals are relegated to the role of nuisances cluttering streets, screen time, cyberspace, and shopping malls, and are seen as tacked on to the film or program in a cynical attempt to squeeze yet more money out of a successful product. What I hope to have posed is that the "peripherals" are often anything but peripheral. Instead, they often play a constitutive role in the production, development, and expansion of the text. Granted, the existence of the film or program usually remains a precondition for the paratext's existence, and thus the film or program remains important, but it does not do its work alone, nor will it necessarily be responsible for all of a text's popular meanings.

Inevitably, paratexts will exist on a sliding scale of importance and prominence, whereby the same paratexts will prove meaningless to particular audiences at particular moments in time, but may mean a great deal to other audiences at other points in time. Thus, for instance, as I suggested in the Introduction, for a year or more in the early 1990s, Bart Simpson "Underachiever" t-shirts became active generators of the *Simpsons* text, but their moment has since passed, leaving the average *Simpsons* t-shirt as little more than an interesting totem to most audiences. Trailers, too, likely lose many of their powers on audience members once they have watched the film. However, if paratexts slide along scales of importance and prominence, they do not slide only from irrelevance to middling importance and back; rather, as both Bart t-shirts and trailers illustrate, they can easily slide *past* the film or television show, moving from "secondary" to "primary," or at least working with the film or show as a bona fide part of the text. Furthermore, while many of the paratexts studied so far lend themselves to more fleeting existences—t-shirts likely dying with the vagaries of fashion, trailers enjoying but a brief moment in the sun, spoilers soon rendered moot, DVD commentary tracks probably watched only once, and so forth—other paratexts lay down deeper roots and both encourage and allow a substantially larger time investment from audiences.

This chapter turns to such instances, when the paratext either stands in for the entire text or becomes a key and "primary" platform for that text. First, I will examine one of the entertainment industry's most successful examples of media-related merchandise, the *Star Wars* action figures. While few other paratexts are as denigrated as are licensed toys, and while few others are regarded by cultural critics with as much suspicion, I will argue that the *Star Wars* toys were and are central to many fans' and non-fans' understandings of and engagements with the iconic text that is *Star Wars*. Through play, the *Star Wars* toys allowed audiences past the barrier of spectatorship *into* the *Star Wars* universe, thereby complicating established dichotomies of the authentic text and the hollow, cash-grab paratext. I will then shift from the analog to the digital, examining how various licensed videogames allow audiences to set foot in their various storyworlds' diegetic spaces. As are kids playing with their film or television toys, gamers are offered the chance to perform in and explore both on-screen spaces and those pockets of space just off screen. When they accept such offers, gamers expand the text, changing what it is and how it happens. Following an examination of videogames, I will look at several other forms of games, in particular the increasingly popular "alternate reality games." Using the case of *What Happened in Piedmont?*, an innovative multimedia story, puzzle, and experience that preceded and played through the broadcast of A&E's miniseries *The Andromeda Strain* in 2008, I will explore the degree to which paratexts can either work with or independent from their associated film or program. *What Happened in Piedmont?* did not attract as many viewers or players as did the broadcast, which had an estimated 4.8 million viewers per episode, but many of the former arguably received an experience that was as or more engaging than the miniseries, or that expanded and intensified the experience of the miniseries when both were consumed. Throughout the chapter's various examples, then, my interests lie in exploring how storyworlds can develop and come to life in paratexts, thereby challenging the widespread textual hierarchy that sees films and television programs as necessarily superior to paratexts, and as the center of narrative universes.

Learning to Use the Force: Star Wars *Toys and Their Films*

Though *Lord of the Rings, Dora the Explorer* (2000–), *The Simpsons,* and *Harry Potter* have provided heavy competition, *Star Wars* still has arguably the most voluminous paratextual entourage in entertainment history. Writing in 1992, before the franchise's proliferation of videogames, and before the second trilogy opened the floodgates for yet more merchandise sales, Stephen Sansweet noted that *Star Wars* had amassed over $2.5 billion from merchandise alone.[2] Moreover, though *Star Wars* hardly invented the licensing and merchandising game, with *Lone Ranger* and other properties making considerable profits in previous years,[3] the phenomenal success of its merchandise, along with George Lucas's coup of retaining merchandising and licensing rights, began a new era. Spearheading *Star Wars* merchandising were its action figures, with 250 million selling by the early 1990s, and 42 million in the first year alone, producing profits of $100 million for toy company Kenner in 1977.[4] The host-selling era of 1980s television followed hot on these four-inch-tall figures' heels, and countless other films and television programs would try—with varying levels of success—to replicate *Star Wars'* mastery of the mall.

Ironically, despite its iconic status in licensing and merchandising history, *Star Wars'* merchandising has attracted remarkably little attention within media and cultural studies. The more usual citations for discussions of licensed toys in general are either Stephen Kline's "Limits to the Imagination: Marketing and Children's Culture" or Thomas Engelhardt's critique of "the Strawberry Shortcake Strategy."[5] Both writers note that a toy line can make an entertainment property significantly more profitable, but they see such toys as using and abusing children and parents along the way, offering little more in return than mindless consumerism and hunks of plastic to brag about to one's friends. Another key reference on licensed toys, Ellen Seiter, refreshingly uses a cultural studies approach in *Sold Separately: Children and Parents in Consumer Culture* to discuss the possible meanings and uses that licensed toy buyers might have for them. However, she still sees their uses largely in relation to those of the associated entertainment property. For instance, offering a defense of *My Little Pony* toys, she notes that the program "emphasizes the loyal community of females"[6] and in general values girl culture, but she has little to say of the toys as generators of their *own* meanings and/or as contributors to the meaning of the text. Offering the hint of a theory of the toy as paratext, she notes that "because they are mass-media goods, these kind of toys actually facilitate group, co-operative play, by encouraging children to make up stories with shared codes and narratives," and by way of child psychologist Erik Erikson, she argues for toys' therapeutic value[7] and suggests that they might allow different forms of engagement and consumption than do the film or television program. Nevertheless, this still leaves the licensed paratext as important only because of the meanings inherited from the program, or because of the uses inherited from being a toy. How might toys feed back into the meanings of the program, and/or use their functions as toys to change the nature of the text as a whole?

A more involved set of answers to this question comes from Dan Fleming's study of toys, *Powerplay: Toys as Popular Culture*. Fleming balks at the idea that toys are mere spinoffs of other properties, and instead argues that they generate their own textuality as events in an ongoing process of textual phenomenology.[8] "There may be a great deal going on," he notes, "when a child plays with the [licensed] toy, for which a TV programme cannot be held responsible."[9] Key to Fleming's interest in licensed toys is their ability not only to continue the story from a film or television program, but to provide a space in which meanings can be worked through and refined, and in which questions and ambiguities in the film or program can be answered. Turning specifically to the *Star Wars* films and toys, Fleming notes first that central character Luke Skywalker is "a rather softly defined character," thereby allowing children playing with the toys to give the film's apparent hero a more resolute character in their play, or to identify with any of the other characters/toys instead. Similarly, he regards the toys as providing a relatively open field of play for children, opening up what *Star Wars* meant or could mean with a "deliberate generation of complexity" and an "ultimate refusal of narrative closure."[10] Where the films required set plots, themes, and endings that would in turn aim for resolution, the toys allowed children to play up or down established themes and make their own substantial imprint on the *Star Wars* universe. Thus Fleming sees the toys as variously able to strengthen or weaken established meanings in the films. In particular, for instance, he notes that with a "softly defined" hero surrounded by a motley crew of aliens, creatures, ships, and weapons:

Perhaps unwittingly, what Kenner had tapped into with their original range of ninety-two small *Star Wars* figures (with more for the succeeding films) was precisely those contexts in which the original character of Luke Skywalker had been meaningful. The little plastic version of Luke seems very much at home surrounded by his menagerie of odd associates. And fitting him neatly into a plastic spacecraft with lots of opening panels, movable bits and quirky shapes was precisely the point—the technological environment was being adapted to offer a human "fit" and qualities of human variety.[11]

The toys, in other words, may have accentuated the films' narrative of a youngster coming to terms with difference and with all the technologies that surround him. Luke's mastery of this environment grows throughout the films, but with all the figures under his or her control, the individual child's control would have been significantly more assured, hence strengthening the narrative's theme of growing up.

A closer look at the figures reveals many other ways in which they accentuate the films' themes. We begin with what the figures do and what they do not do. With no bendable limbs, only swinging legs and arms, and notoriously delicate turning heads, the figures hardly offer much versatility or range of positions. Instead, accessories provide this versatility. Most figures come with at least one blaster, lightsaber, or other elaborate weapon. Displayed separately in the plastic bubble that encases the figure on its cardboard backing, these weapons are immediately given considerable power and relevance, firmly positioning many of the characters as warriors, often and even when their film referents appear peaceful. Combined with the packaging's habitual "masculine" color scheme of black, blue, and occasionally dark reds or greens, these figures clearly declare themselves as *action* figures, built not for tea parties, but for conflict (fig. 6.1). Moreover, beyond supplying one's toys with mere blasters, one can also provide them with any number of an impressive array of spaceships and cruisers. Each toy's feet have slight notches, allowing the owner to attach them to any of the battle stations and dioramas available for purchase. At first glance down the list of available toys, it may seem as if everything from the movies has been turned into a toy and is equally represented, but this is not the case. Rather, weapons of war and vehicles predominate. Thus, a Cantina playset was available, but should one have walked through the once large *Star Wars* sections of Hamley's in London or FAO Schwarz in New York, one would have been greeted instead by endless boxes of

Fig. 6.1. Complete set of 1978 *Star Wars* 12-Backs, the first twelve figures released. From the collection of Gary Wines. Photograph by Gary Wines.

fighters, gunships, and gladiatorial attack beasts. In short, the bulk of *Star Wars* figure accessories consist of exactly those things one needs to fight a battle of good and evil, producing a situation in which, although the *Star Wars* movies have a lot going on in them, the action figures underscore the plural in the title, declaring the central frame and theme to be that of a never-ending series of grand and cosmic battles of mythic proportions.

This concentrate of meaning became even more pronounced with the second trilogy's figures, as their packaging now sported character blurbs on the back, which introduced and contextualized the characters. Reading several blurbs, one sees considerable repetition of themes, adjectives, and verbs. Many of the figures, for example, are said to be defending or rescuing others, at war or in battle, or escaping one another. In blurb after blurb, we are treated to two-sentence tales of intrigue, danger, and a perpetual threat of violence, replete with recurring adjectives used to describe the characters such as "powerful," "fierce," "resourceful," "dangerous," "loyal," "deadly," "tireless," and "courageous." Running throughout the blurbs is also the constant threat to peace—the Battle Droids, we are told, "invaded the peaceful planet of Naboo," while "Kit Fisto (Jedi Master)" is "dedicated to the goal of maintaining peace throughout the galaxy." And when war comes, it is intergalactic and all-encompassing. With their buy-me rhetoric, the blurbs situate almost all of the characters in terms of their importance to the battle of right versus wrong and their role in assuring that good or evil triumphs in the end, even when their on-screen equivalents are not depicted at war. Quite apart from the films, the toys establish the war that is waging and what is at stake. Admittedly, the fact that the toys settled on these meanings is unsurprising, and my argument is not that they *transformed* the meanings of the text; rather, I argue that they played a key role in refining and accentuating certain meanings, multiplying them and carrying them beyond the film into the child's play world, while also inviting the child to enlist in the "Star Wars."

In evaluating the potential strength of the toys' messages about the film, it is important to remember that *Star Wars* fans had to wait for three years between films, stringing each trilogy out over six years. Thus, it is equally important to consider the phenomenology of *Star Wars*, since between 1977 and 1983 in particular—a remarkably long time for a child—it was primarily the toys that kept the trilogy alive. The late 1970s and early 1980s came before the ubiquitous presence of VHS in Western homes, and so if *Star Wars* was to live and to be saved from becoming its own cold war, it had to enter the body of paratexts. As Bob Rehak writes of the soundtracks, they were "the closest I could get to 'replaying' the movie— often I listened while poring over the album covers, which featured stills from the films, or while doodling my own spaceships and superheroes or even writing little Star-Warsy screenplays."[12] Toys, too, became ways to keep the series alive. As Matt Hills explains, fan cultures require a text with some form of "endlessly deferred narrative,"[13] and particularly between *Empire Strikes Back* (1980) and *Return of the Jedi*, young fans were left with multiple questions (*is* Darth Vader Luke's father? Will the Rebellion rise again? What's happened to Han Solo? Will Luke become a Jedi?) that necessitated a transference of text to toy/paratext for many young fans.

What happened during those years, as Fleming suggests, is that *Star Wars* invited young fans to take over to a certain degree. With the backdrop of a cosmic battle between good and evil, as Fleming states (here of the *GI Joe* toy line), "what perpetuates the whole line in all its interrelated forms, is perhaps the child's endless pursuit of the story within the story, of what is really going on while the aggression rages."[14] Fans were being asked to fill in the spaces that existed just off screen. With *Star Wars*, no less, George Lucas even allowed for time to have passed diegetically between films, almost as if to respect the young fans' own narratives, and creating the possibility that much of what was played out in the schoolyard might "actually" have happened. A grand, protracted war of mythic proportions had been set up, an army of figures and vehicles sold, and the individual child was left in charge, hence becoming, in play, part of the battle, balancing right and wrong. The child was asked to bring all sorts of concepts—good and evil, science and nature, rationality and intuition, childhood and adulthood, power and responsibility, familiarity and otherness—together to provide synthesis.

Interestingly, too, many of the action figures are of characters who prove entirely peripheral in the films. Characters who literally walk across the screen as alien extras become full-fledged figures, and many characters are named only in toy-ification. Several of the toys' one-man rigs and vehicles, moreover, did not appear in the films, thus suggesting an overflow not only of narrative but of gadgets, weapons, and spaceships into the toy world; as Sansweet notes, they look "as if they *could* have been in the film, but maybe were just out of sight of the camera."[15] Endlessly deferred narratives and "hyperdiegesis"[16] are common in cult texts, but in creating toys for these characters, *Star Wars* specifically offers them up for audience narrativization. To take one example, "Hammerhead" appears briefly in the Cantina scene in *Star Wars: A New Hope*. S/he has no lines, nobody references him/her, and we learn nothing about him/her. Thus, when faced with the toy, the playing child can assign Hammerhead a gender, can make him/her a "good guy," yet another Imperial, or something altogether different, and can perpetuate his/her peripheral status or assign Hammerhead new importance. In his book on *Star Wars* fandom, Will Brooker tells of how as a child he "elevated the trilogy's minor alien characters to a mercenary group called Hammerhead's Gang,"[17] while to others Hammerhead could have been Admiral Ackbar's lover, an ace Rebel fighter pilot, an elementary school teacher, and/or Mos Eisley's town drunk.[18] In no small way, then, these toys allow children to feed meanings back into the proscribed narratives. Here we can draw parallels with what many commentators have noted of fan fiction's expansive capacities,[19] a key difference being that the toys are licensed, as is play, and so presumably no group of six-year-olds were ever in danger of being dragged into court by Lucasfilm.

A fascinating character in this opening up of meaning is that of Boba Fett. Fett has remarkably little screen time in the original trilogy, and all we learn of him is that he is a highly equipped and feared bounty hunter, fond of disintegrating his victims. "He" could even be a she, as an online campaign for a female Boba Fett attested to, and following *Return of the Jedi*'s suggestion that bounty hunters often use voice modulators. More importantly, though, he is a really cool toy: with impressive armor, jet-pack, wrist-harpoons, and various colored platings, Fett rocketed to popularity. Initially, too, one could only acquire Fett by sending in coupons, and the early Fett's missiles could actually fire until redesigned for a safer model. From the outset, then, Fett was a rare and precious commodity, thereby solidifying his peculiarly popular role in *Star Wars* fandom. For somebody so peripheral in the films, I believe the answer to the riddle of his success is in large part the toy. And in a case of this feeding directly back into the text, it appears obvious that Boba and father Jango Fett were featured so prominently in the second trilogy due to Boba Fett's established cult status. Even the news that Fett would be central to the films was announced in a press release by Lucas, and within minutes it was all over *Star Wars* fan sites. The toy was returning.

With such examples, we see how the toys not only intensified several themes of the films—the focus on the cosmic battle, and the voyage of personal discovery especially—but also allowed individual children or communities of children playing together to personalize these themes, situating the child in the middle and as active participant—a true member of either the Rebel Alliance or the Empire—not just as distanced spectator. And perhaps most importantly, they kept those meanings and the text itself alive and thriving. The toys worked to ensure that *Star Wars* and its meanings stayed relevant and kept circulating, being added to and refreshed. It is perhaps no coincidence that in the mid-1990s, as Lucas officially decided to make another trilogy, new toys (and, now, videogames) were sent forward as minions to throw coals on *Star Wars* fans' old flames. The toys, in other words, have never merely been "secondary" spinoffs or coincidental: they have played a vital role in, and thus have become a vital *part of*, the primary text and its unrivalled success. Each movie brought to a head years of play, and characters with long toy histories.

But what of *Star Wars* as a family saga and as shining, nostalgic reminder of youth for those who grew up with it? For many fans, the toys may well have created a significant amount of these meanings. To a degree matched by few other fandoms, to many *Star Wars* is wrapped up in nostalgia for childhood. As Brooker observes, a frequent retort to adult "bashers" of the more recent trilogy has been the "eyes of a child" defense that rebukes such bashers for no longer seeing the film as children.[20] This rebuke suggests that the right and proper way to view *Star Wars* is precisely with children's eyes, and hence it also indicates the frequency with which, more than thirty years on, many original fans still watch with children's eyes. Even in studies of other older cult texts, such as *Doctor Who* (1963–89, 2005–)[21] or *Star Trek*,[22] there is little discussion of childhood nostalgia, little sense that the text engages in such a rewinding of the clock. Something about *Star Wars*, though, fills many of its fans with memories of play with friends or siblings and of being taken to the cinema by mothers and fathers. It would be a true challenge for many of the films' original fans to talk about their fandom without figuring their family into the story at an early point.

Of course, there are roots for this in the films. Both trilogies are, after all, about growing up and going into the wider world. Particularly for boys, moreover, they are tales of becoming an adult, *Lord of the Rings* in space. However, this cannot explain all of the text's magnetic pull, even allowing for the films' mythic, narrative, and visual resonance. Rather, we can again look to the toys for the keystone in the bridge between *Star Wars*, nostalgia, and family. Here we need to ask where toys came from, not in a production sense, but in a "who was this gift from?" or "who paid my allowance / pocket money?" sense, and we soon arrive at family as likely benefactors and providers. Then we can ask where toys were played with and with whom, and the familiar environments of the home with friends or siblings, or of the schoolyard, surrounded by friends, would appear natural answers. At this point, we can start to see *Star Wars* toys as bringing together friends and families, particularly at those times that many of us seem to remember most clearly and when children are most likely to get more toys, birthdays and other holidays. To this end, we should also note that the purchase and display of *Star Wars* figures by adult fans is commonplace, signaling again the importance of the toys themselves. If *Star Wars* can act as a doorway back in time, for many fans toys serve as a key to this door. Building off Hills's work on fan cultures, which poses that fan texts become Winnicottian "primary transitional objects," offering a warm sense of security and familiarity to fans,[23] Cornel Sandvoss has noted that the objects associated with fandom can just as easily work as primary transitional objects themselves,[24] once again illustrating the paratext's capacity to move to "primary" status for any given fan.

With this in mind, it is interesting to speculate about how much stronger the connections between *Star Wars*, moral decision, personal discovery, family, and childhood are becoming now that many of the children of the 1970s and 1980s have their own children, nieces, and nephews who they have introduced to the films. Brooker writes of a young fan whose uncle acted almost Jedi master–like,[25] training him in the ways of *Star Wars*; Brooker's focus is on the child, but what of the uncle? When fans engage in such practices as proudly and happily accompanying them to the second trilogy, or buying them *Star Wars* toys for Christmas or birthdays, surely the adult fans strengthen their own associations between *Star Wars* and family. When these adult fans buy *Star Wars* toys for a child, what they may be trying to hand over as a gift is their own nostalgically remembered relationship with the text that came at least in part from the toys. And in the process, of course, they may well be succeeding, ensuring that another generation of fans will grow up associating the films with family, with childhood, and with moral guidance.

Hills writes, "An important part of being a cult fan [. . .] involves extending the reader-text, or reader-icon, relationship into other areas of fan experience"[26]; I argue that, to its fans, *Star Wars* has not only extended itself but at times *resided* in toys/paratexts. Thus, while to *Star Wars* historian Stephen Sansweet, "If *Star Wars* had taken one visionary to bring the story to life on film, it took another to reduce the characters to under four inches high,"[27] I want to argue that these "visionary" acts may be more linked than they are merely parallels of each other. *Star Wars*, I believe, owes a considerable amount of its success, and of the intensity with which its meanings have been taken on by so many fans, to the toys. In *Star Wars*, Obi-Wan Kenobi explains that The Force is "an energy field created by all living things," and so too has *Star Wars*' textuality been created by multiple entities. As Jedi-like guardians and hosts of the text for considerable portions of its life, the *Star Wars* toys have been as central to what we understand of *Star Wars* today as have the lightsaber or Darth Vader.

Of course, the "we" in my previous sentence needs qualification. On one level, we as analysts should recognize the role that the toys likely played in gendering *Star Wars*, and hence in directing the text's address to boys in particular. In chapter 2, I argued that *Six Degrees*' promotional campaign announced the text as being for women, yet the toys' masculinization of the *Star Wars* universe has been considerably more pervasive and has endured over many more years, working both as entryway and in medias res. Kenner packaged the toys in a masculine color scheme, and their framing of *Star Wars* as battle- and conflict-driven similarly hyper-masculinized the toys, as did their later release of the buff and muscular Power of the Force toy line. Ads then carried this further, as did the packaging itself, which inevitably depicted young boys at play, not young girls. And toy stores often completed the gendering, by grouping the toys with other "boy" toys. For instance, to even reach the formerly longstanding *Star Wars* toys section of New York's FAO Schwarz, one had to voyage through a narrow tunnel of *GI Joe* toys, and while the neighboring Barbie section sported pink floors, the *Star Wars* toy section was all blacks and dark blues. Toys in general can wear their "proper" gender on their sleeve more than many other commodities, giving rise to many liberal parents' concerns about their child's early exposure to gender coding, and *Star Wars* offered no exception. Of course, the individual child could buck the coding or queer the toy, placing Boba Fett in Barbie's summer home, or staging Luke and Han's wedding, so the gendering is not set in stone. Nevertheless, with the toys directing much of their address at boys, it is no wonder that *Star Wars* has the reputation of being a quintessentially male text, and we might expect the textual universe to have literally proven larger for boys and men.[28]

At the same time, however, if one considers the near-omnipresence of *Star Wars* toys in Western society, particularly in the late 1970s and early 1980s, and even the authority given to knowing and involved audiences by other, non-fan audiences to dictate meaning,[29] then the toys, both directly and indirectly, can still be seen as having played an important role in determining what *Star Wars* is and means to society as a whole. Children need not have played with the toys, and adults need neither have bought them or been implored to buy them, for the toys to register as central to popular culture. Indeed, a young girl who had been turned away from *Star Wars* by the hyper-masculinizing of the toys would have relied more heavily, if not totally, upon the toys' paratextual meanings, her understanding of the text created by the toys. As such, the toys and their (apparent) meanings likely figured just as centrally if not more so in many non-fans' and anti-fans' understandings of the *Star Wars* universe as they did for young boys playing with their Chewbacca and Nien Nunb figures.

As has been said, *Star Wars* was by no means the first film to sell licensed toys, or to embed itself within a large collection of paratextual extras. But *Star Wars'* success led to most media companies realizing the gold mine that lay within merchandising. Equally, its success in all likelihood played a part in teaching those who came of age in the 1970s and

1980s that paratextual entourages could and should be expected. To offer an example, Jesse Alexander, former co-executive producer and writer of *Heroes* (to which we will turn in the Conclusion) and a force behind *Heroes*' and *Lost*'s development of transmedia, gives pride of place to *Star Wars* toys in his own personal history of realizing what transmedia could do and why it matters. Similarly, when I asked *Lost* executive producer Damon Lindelof about transmedia's potential at the IRTS and Disney Digital Media Summit in 2008, he began his answer by giving a long history of the Boba Fett toy and of *Star Wars*' mastery of transmedia storytelling. What *Star Wars* represented to many, Alexander and Lindelof included, was a belief that media worlds could and should be somewhat *inhabitable*.

In this regard, we should criticize the self-serving hypocrisy of media firms that hype their licensed toy lines, only to clamp down on multiple other forms of paratextual play. The example of *Star Wars* toys has suggested that we as media analysts should regard toy lines as more than hypercommercialized cash-grabs, and I have argued that toys contribute to the storyworld, offering audiences the prospect of stepping into that world and contributing to it. So too must media firms realize that while a toy line may improve their profits, it also licenses and openly *encourages* play with the storyworld. Though *Star Wars* toys offered many implicit and explicit "proper" uses, in the schoolyard, garden, or on the bedroom floor, children could do anything they wanted with those toys, from the "proper" to the "improper." Having sent such a message, Lucasfilm or other media firms would be both disingenuous and foolishly misguided to try later to close down the prospects for play. Buoyed by the invitations of licensed toys and other childhood merchandising, film and television narratives are open for business—or, rather, for play—and have been for many years, whether media firms and their legal teams like it or not. Paratexts have extended this invitation to play, as they have contributed to the text with their own suggested meanings, and have offered consumers opportunities to contribute further to the text themselves.

Die in the South Pole or Live in the North: Licensed Videogames

Through play, *Star Wars* toys owners could explore and create great expanses of the text's storyworld, thereby making it more accountable to and reflective of their own interests, and ensuring that this storyworld would always be greater than the sum of the six *Star Wars* films. To play with or in a storyworld is to gain more ownership of it, to personalize it, and to move it out of the space of the spectacle and render it a malleable entity. Toys will thus always pry open storyworlds, and, especially when they enjoy huge popularity within children's popular culture, they will offer multiple opportunities for community engagement, not just individual personalization. That said, inhabiting a storyworld is not just a child's game. Rather, multiple forms and styles of media-related games exist, addressing a wide range of audiences.

The most prominent and profitable form of media-related game is the licensed videogame. The videogame industry has become a juggernaut, with U.S. retail sales in 2005 reaching $7 billion and worldwide retail sales estimated at triple that figure.[30] Despite its reputation as a teen's or geeky twenty- or thirty-year-old man's medium, over a third of American and Japanese gamers are women[31] and the Interactive Digital Software Association estimates that 55 percent of regular console gamers are over the age of thirty-five.[32] While many of the medium's popular and more lucrative titles, such as *Halo* (2001–) and *Grand Theft Auto*, stand alone, centering their own franchises and networks of paratexts, games licensed by the television and film industries have also enjoyed a sizeable portion of the market from the medium's early days. Successful films in particular can net a studio approximately $40 million in license fee and royalty revenue.[33] Many of these have also been phenomenal failures, provoking the ire of film and television show fans and game players alike. *E.T.*, for instance, produced a game that to many remains a paragon of poor design and cynical product exploitation. As was the case with *E.T.*, and as will be discussed further in the Conclusion, too many game companies have rushed the design process to capitalize on a film or television show's buzz before it dies down, and as a result, too many licensed games rely on the presence of film or television characters and voiceovers to rescue what is basically an uninspired offering with tepid gameplay. However, even when slightly lackluster, licensed games often succeed at opening up storyworlds in new and interesting ways, and occasional hits excel at doing so. Licensed games allow their players to enter these worlds and explore them in ways that a film or television show often precludes, and/or that amplify the show's meanings and style.

An interesting example of such a game is *The Thing* (2002), presented as a sequel to the 1982 remake of the 1951 classic, *The Thing from Another World*. John Carpenter's 1982 *Thing* is set during perpetual nighttime at a remote research station in Antarctica, where the unearthing of a spaceship

results in the release of an alien life-form-cum-disease. This "thing" in-
habits a person's body, taking them over and first making them homicidal,
then later exploding the host's body. The film relies upon the dual fears of
being stuck in the middle of a remote and hostile environment and being
surrounded by people one cannot trust. The game begins three months
after the end of Carpenter's *Thing*, when two military rescue teams have
been sent to investigate. More than just continuing the plot, though, it
effectively captures the sense of paranoia, horror, and confusion that per-
vades the film by putting the player's avatar in charge of a group who may
or may not become "infected." The pervasive cold means that the player
must hurry when outside, yet moving too quickly results in one's group
members falling behind, off the screen where they may become infected.
Similarly, group members' fear rises over time, and the quickest way to
reduce their fear is to give them a weapon; however, arming an infected
group member could prove perilous. One soon learns, then, to hate the
cold and pervasive darkness, and to trust nobody. The game thereby
places the player within the horror of *The Thing*.

Just as nightmares induced by watching a horror film often heighten its
terror by transporting the viewer-dreamer into the film's world of predator
and prey, uncertainty, anxiety, and visceral fear, so too does the game create a new, arguably more direct relationship between the individual player
and the storyworld. Writing of horror games in general, Tanya Krzywinska notes first of horror films that the genre "derives much of its power
to thrill from the fact that the viewer cannot intervene in the trajectory
of events. While viewers might feel an impulse to help beleaguered characters in a horror film, they can never do this directly."[34] When watching
a horror film, we can only watch in terror as a character heads into the
dark woods, and likely a gruesome death, after hearing a scream. Krzywinska writes of this feeling of losing control, and of the supernatural
force's threatening of human agency, as central to the pleasures of horror.
However, toward this end, she sees horror games as potentially better able
to capture this experience than films, precisely because they can offer the
illusion of control and moments of legitimate control, only to steal them
away at any time, so that though "the player does have a sense of self-de-
termination; when this is lost the sense of pre-determination is enhanced
by the relative difference."[35] While much rhetoric surrounding games talks
of their "interactive" quality, Krzywinska shows how horror games can
heighten the sense of horror by denying that interactivity at any point.
She also sees the game's ability to give us a first-person perspective (only

truly matched by *The Blair Witch Project* and *Cloverfield* [2008] in film) as further placing the player inside the horror, but even when, as in the game of *The Thing*, one watches the action in third-person, the stark vulnerability of one's avatar is arguably more visceral given the player's seeming ability to control him. Moreover, given that Carpenter's *Thing* ends with all but one of the characters killing each other or exploding, its conclusion hangs like a guillotine over the player's neck, creating a sense of the near-inevitability of failure.

Krzywinska also notes the bind in which a horror game places the player, with relation to the exploration of space. As I will elaborate upon below, a common difference between films or television and games is that "games are organised around the traversal of space, to which narrative is often secondary."[36] Space must be explored, often multiple times over, to conquer the game. Hence, one of the appeals of the game of *The Thing* is the ability to explore the story space more fully. However, for a horror game, herein lies a dilemma, since such curiosity in horror films is inevitably punished: the eager teen who goes into the woods to see what that scream was, the young woman who goes into the old house to ask for help, the person who opens a door into another dimension, are all the fools at whom we yell in the theater. But in a horror game, we are forced to become the fool. In games, "the player is encouraged to assert an active, rather than passive, mode of looking, that may endanger them but without which progression through the game cannot be achieved."[37] And since games use ellipses or cuts in space or time more sparingly than do films,[38] the player is left with little external relief from the building tension. *The Thing* game, then, allows players to explore the world, but also further realizes aspects of the film's horror. Just as the *Jaws* poster could begin the text's horror, as described in chapter 2, *The Thing* videogame can continue and heighten its text's horror.

The Thing translates a horror film into the videogame space, but its act of placing the player into the storyworld is duplicated across multiple other licensed games from multiple genres, including gangster (*The Godfather: The Game* [2006]), detective (five *CSI* games to date), comic-book action (*Spider-Man* [2002]), quiz show (the *Who Wants to Be a Millionaire* pub game), espionage (*24: The Game* [2002], James Bond films, *Alias* [2004]), science fiction (*Star Trek: Armada II* [2001]), fantasy blockbuster (*The Lord of the Rings* games), satire/parody (*South Park* [1998], *The Simpsons* games), soap (*Desperate Housewives: The Game* [2006]), children's

(*Dora the Explorer* games, Disney and Pixar games), and sports (EA's *NHL*, *NBA*, *Madden NFL*, and *FIFA* series).

Transporting players to a wholly different storyworld than *The Thing*, for instance, *The Golden Compass* game (2007) offers the player the chance to become Lyra Belacqua, the hero of Philip Pullman's *His Dark Materials* series of books, and of the feature film of the first book, *The Golden Compass* (2007). When Lyra gets to the North Pole and commissions the Panserbjørn (talking polar bear), Iorek Byrnison, to help her, as soon as she climbs on his back, the player then controls Iorek. Whereas the film in particular adopts a breathless pace, moving quickly from event to event, location to location, the game allows the player to slow the progression down and to explore nooks and crannies of the film's and book's spaces, as well as other storyworld spaces that are just off screen or off page.

Narrative, character, and special effects may be primary in the film, but in the game presence, space, and "a protracted sense of projected embodiedness in the virtual world" are also important.[39] While film adaptations of books have long attempted to realize visually the book's characters and events, the pace of and attention to various aspects of that realization remain wholly within the director's hands. Videogames do not open up spaces from within the storyworld with complete freedom, but they do at least allow players to dawdle in some spaces through which a film charges, and they often render these spaces with considerably more attention to detail than do the films. Albeit in restricted and literally preprogrammed ways, then, the player can briefly inhabit both the world(s) of the story and its characters. While *The Thing* throws the player into the middle of the horror, *The Golden Compass* throws the player into the middle of the heroic quest. Lyra's travails and worries now become the player's, as do her successes. We might therefore regard the game as encouraging a different approach to the story. This different approach is less concerned with "narrative" as we often use the term—though, as Wee Liang Tong and Marcus Cheng Chye Tan note (using Stephen Heath's writings on narrative space), narrative is not just about plot, and games such as *The Golden Compass* allow players to visualize their own events and actions, "to re-present and express a moment of narrative significance visually and stylistically."[40] Narrative is still important, then, but games allow players a different entry point into that narrative, and in so doing, as did the activities of *Lost* spoilers, they illustrate how varied viewers' uses for and pleasures from narrative are.

In writing of adaptations, Linda Hutcheon defends their oft-maligned artistic value, insisting that "to be second is not to be secondary or inferior; likewise, to be first is not to be originary or authoritative."[41] Instead, she states, the process of adaptation frequently moves a story across different modes, opening up new possibilities for both the storyteller(s) and the audiences. In particular, she notes three modes of narratives: *telling*, as in novels, which immerse us "through imagination in a fictional world"; *showing*, as in plays and films, which immerse us "through the perception of the aural and the visual"; and *participatory*, as in videogames, which immerse us "physically and kinesthetically."[42] Thus, a videogame adaptation—or at least a good one—is not merely an attempt to rehash or to copy; it moves the story, its world, and its audience to a different narrative mode, wherein the audience can step into (parts of) the storyworld. To understand a videogame "adaptation" or extension, we might ask how well it would fare if its characters, plot, and world were not rooted in a film or television program's diegesis. For players who do not know the film or program, of course, this will be their de facto experience of the game, and the better licensed games may be enjoyed by audiences whose appreciation of the game is based wholly on its superior design. For other licensed games and their players, part of the attraction would seem to lie in the heightened play of being able to "inhabit" the world and its characters and to enjoy a different relationship to them than the film or program allows. Adaptation involves repetition, Hutcheon writes, but it also represents "the comfort of ritual combined with the piquancy of surprise,"[43] as licensed videogames create a bridge to a known storyworld, but also "surprise" the audience by expanding the world, and by changing their relationship to and "consumption" of that world and that text.

Another illustrative example is found in *The Simpsons Hit and Run*. One of several *Simpsons* games, *Hit and Run* loosely follows the *Grand Theft Auto* game model, with third-person control of Homer, Marge, Lisa, Bart, or Apu, the ability to commandeer vehicles on the streets of Springfield, and interlacing missions. The game required substantial amounts of new artwork and animation, was penned by *Simpsons* writers, and includes new voicework from the *Simpsons* voice actors, alongside some fan favorite sound clips from the show. Many of the characters and settings of the television program are encountered throughout the game, from the family's house to lesser-known locations such as Kamp Krusty. And cut sequences offer a plot concerning a new cola that reanimates the dead, involving Simpsonesque tropes such as the evils of advertising, parodic

Fig. 6.2. *The Simpsons Hit and Run* videogame allows one to explore Springfield.

commentary on televisual style, and satiric commentary on American life. One of the more titillating aspects of its gameplay, though, lies simply in the ability to explore Springfield (fig. 6.2). The television show has created many locations, but has rarely shown how they connect. Playing the game, by contrast, allows one to walk, run, or drive between locations, thereby seeing, for instance, how to get from the Simpsons' house to Cletus's farm, or what separates The Android's Dungeon and Krusty Studios. Along the way, one encounters most of the show's regular and semi-regular characters, and one's actions result in various funny comments from one's avatars, as when, for instance, Bart occasionally utters, "Ouch, my ovaries!" when crashing into something with a vehicle, or when Homer insists that "that older boy told me to do it" after he has hit someone. As with the *Grand Theft Auto* "sandbox" style, too, though completing missions advances one through the game to new areas, one has the freedom—with scripted limits, of course—simply to wander the streets and talk to random characters.

With an expansive storyline and space for gameplay, yet also with original animation, original dialogue, and an original script, the game provides significantly more *Simpsons* than an episode of the television program. Just as I have argued of *Star Wars* toys and of the various online ads for *The Simpsons Game*, the game challenges the logic of text and paratext, or of primary and secondary texts, itself occupying liminal space between these classifications. As Hutcheon suggests of games, it also allows one to slow down the rapid-moving world of Springfield, step into it, and engage with it in different ways. Thus, rather than simply acting as another episode offering yet more *Simpsons*—albeit on a game console, not the FOX Network—it expands the world of *The Simpsons* and the modes of engaging with this world. Few are likely to see the game as trumping the television show in importance, so in this respect the game is unlikely to *flip* the rubric of primary and secondary texts, but it does position the game alongside any other *Simpsons* episode as a viable contributor to the world of Springfield.

Another prominent example of licensed games opening up a world comes once again from the *Star Wars* franchise. The sheer range of *Star Wars* titles is amazing, numbering over one hundred, and covering multiple styles and genres, from the early arcade game with simple line graphics that invited players to destroy the Death Star, to today's *Star Wars Galaxies* series (2003–), a massively multiple-player online role-playing game (MMORPG), and to the multi-player military combat games *Star Wars: Battlefront* (2004) and *Star Wars: Battlefront II* (2005), first-person shooters such as *Star Wars: Dark Forces* (1995) and *Star Wars: Bounty Hunter* (2002), flight simulation games *X-Wing* (1993) and *Tie-Fighter* (1994), racing games such as *Star Wars: Episode 1 Racer* (1999), fighting games such as *Star Wars: Masters of Teräs Käsi* (1997), educational games such as *Star Wars: Droid Works* (1999), computerized board games *Star Wars Chess* (1994) and *Monopoly: Star Wars Edition* (1997), real-time strategy games such as *Star Wars: Galactic Battlegrounds* (2001), and even playful-parodic games such as *Lego Star Wars: The Video Game* (2005) and *Lego Star Wars II: The Original Trilogy* (2006). Through these games, the *Star Wars* universe has been able to "colonize" multiple game genres, as the text expands ever outward. Many of these games have also made communal imprints on the universe more possible, as they offer two-player, networked, or online modes that require a group performance of the universe and result in a complex social environment that mixes computer-, game designer–, film or program writer–, and human-generated actions and narrative imprints.

The *Galaxies* series in particular, as the *Star Wars* MMORPG,[44] has made possible daily, evolving exploration of and contributions to the storyworld, profoundly reshaping some players' understanding of the nature of the storyworld in the process, as is subtly alluded to in the title's pluralization of the films' "galaxy far, far away." Even non-gamers therefore now know *Star Wars* as more of a varied universe than a tightly scripted galaxy.[45]

Star Wars' game proliferation is aided by its openness as a text, and by the lack of a master plot that set in and took root following *Return of the Jedi* in 1983. *The Simpsons* is also aided by its form, being a fairly circular world, with no character aging discernibly (save for Apu and Manjula's octuplets), few lessons carried over from one episode to another, and no serialized master plot. But arguably the boldest experiment in videogame licensing and storytelling is *Enter the Matrix* (2003), given that this game actually interlaced its plot with *The Matrix Reloaded* (2003), making it a viable generator of "canonical" plotline. With a storyworld in which all of humankind is revealed to be living an elaborate computer-generated simulation of life, *The Matrix* was a film virtually crying out for a licensed game. As its hero Neo booted in and out of The Matrix, it only seemed natural that a game could seemingly allow the player to boot in and out of the game, and how better to capture the experience of a computer-simulated avatar existence than through a computer-simulated avatar existence? As do several other films that interrogate the borderlands between reality and computerized reality, such as *Avalon* (2001) and *Strange Days* (1995), and with its hyper-slow-mo, ludicrously well-armed action sequence style, *The Matrix* already responds to and invokes videogame play. But rather than simply place the player within the storyworld, the Wachowski brothers and *Enter the Matrix*'s designers made the game a site of the ongoing narrative. Players can choose between two avatars, Ghost or Niobe. Both are minor characters in the film, but cut sequences filmed by the Wachowskis give Ghost and Niobe significantly more dialogue in the game. In a reverse form of avatar identification, then, the game does not offer players the chance to take charge of lead characters Neo, Morpheus, or Trinity; instead, it develops Ghost and Niobe to the point of becoming co-leads in the story. Moreover, the game explains important background to several events in *The Matrix Reloaded*, while also running concurrent to the action, woven into the storyline. Thus, the game rewards players with information and significantly raises the stakes of gameplay. As its title suggests, spatial exploration is still a mainstay of *Enter the Matrix*, but plot development now occurs too.

Enter the Matrix suggests an intriguing step forward in transmedia storytelling, precisely because of this raising of the stakes. Put simply, in plot terms, the game *matters*, with exploration of the game's spaces or networking with other fans who have played the game becoming an almost-necessary element of engaging with the entire story and text. As Jenkins states, "*The Matrix* franchise was shaped by a whole new vision of synergy," making it "emblematic of the cult movie in convergent culture," with its paratexts offering a "more intense, more immediate engagement" for some fans.[46] Certainly, gamers repaid the Wachowskis for this vision, with almost six million sales by the end of 2005.[47] However, as Jenkins has also discussed, while the game may have benefited from this approach, the *Matrix* sequels themselves may ultimately have suffered with other viewers because of it. He argues that the *Matrix* sequels' film critics, "who were used to reviewing the film and not the surrounding apparatus,"[48] thus concentrated only on the films, not the entire "apparatus." But the widespread criticism of the films came from viewers as well, thereby suggesting that many were unwilling to play the videogame, watch the associated *Animatrix* shorts, read the comic, or consult fans who had done any or all of the above. As such, *Enter the Matrix* serves as a warning to transmedia and paratext developers: *allowing* audiences to explore a narrative invites play with a world and an expansion of how it can operate, but *requiring* that they explore that world risks restricting how the film or television program can operate. At root here is an ongoing tension and task for producers of paratexts: how to create and pitch them successfully to address both the general audience and various forms of fans. *Allowing* fans, and giving room to play, is often of vital importance, but *requiring* that all viewers be fans is an immodest and potentially destructive move, even for sequels of cult properties such as *The Matrix*.

Playing Your Own Games

Above, I have discussed videogames, but multiple other forms of game exist for a variety of films and television shows. Role-playing games (RPGs) exist for *Buffy the Vampire Slayer*, *Doctor Who*, *Firefly*, *Ghostbusters* (1984), Indiana Jones, James Bond, *Stargate SG-1* (1997–2007), *Star Trek*, and *Star Wars*, among other films and television shows. In an RPG, several players congregate to work their way through a "campaign" or "module" developed either in concert between professional game designers and the "game master," or by the latter alone. While the game master sets the parameters of the campaign, each player develops his or her own character, and the story develops through the interplay of loose story design, chance, performance, and the luck of the dice. As the name suggests, they are the pre-genesis of MMORPGs, except played in real life; like MMORPGs, they render a pre-designed storyworld open to performance, inhabitation, and hence personalization. Film- or television show–based games—as Kurt Lancaster has written of the role-playing game, war game, and collectible-card game of *Babylon 5*—on one hand allow fans the chance to recapture the original cathartic moment of watching the television show, hence, in performance studies terms developed by Richard Schechner, "restoring" character behavior. They also keep alive (and "restore") some of the escapist and fantasy desires—in *Babylon 5*'s games, notes Lancaster, for humankind to populate space—that form the bedrock for fan engagement with the root show.[49] On the other hand, drawing on Daniel Mackay's work on RPGs, Lancaster notes that such performances are not simply "recapitulations," summaries, or rehashes; rather, they are also "recuperations," *inspired by* the original show, and developing from it, thereby moving the storyworld into a new consumptive and performative space personalized to the assembled group of players, and expanding its parameters much as RPG players force the game master to expand his or her own parameters on the fly.[50] And unlike MMORPGs, actions must not necessarily have been approved or programmed as possible beforehand, opening the storyworld up significantly.

Even within the computerized space, games can be hacked and programs rewritten. Some such hacks come from the production staff themselves, as "cheats" are common in the game world,[51] allowing one unlimited ammunition or infinite lives, for instance. Other reprogramming comes from tech-savvy players capable of entering the game's design structure to make changes in the form of "mods" or "skins," or, more commonly, from players of expansive, open-ended games who use them as engines and sets to tell stories about characters whose actions are restricted in the licensed game itself. Creative productions of the latter sort have resulted in what is called *machinima*, an elision of "machine," "cinema" and "animation."[52] *The Sims* series (2000–), for instance, has served as a particularly useful engine for many such stories, given that the game allows the player to personalize characters and control their actions in a wide-open universe. A machinima creator can generate characters in *The Sims*, make them resemble characters from a film or television program,[53] then use them as children may use their toys or as a director may use his or her actors, "filming" this narrativization to share with others.

Many of machinima's more popular instances exist within the videogame fan world itself, as with, for instance, the remarkably popular *Red vs. Blue* series made with *Halo* and boasting over 900,000 downloads a week.[54] But some machinima creators have used games to create extended narratives set in the storyworlds of popular film and television.[55] The machinima artist Ravensclaw, for instance, has made numerous films with *Sims* "skins" that are set in the worlds of *Buffy the Vampire Slayer* and *Charmed* (1998–2006). When screened for others, machinima works much like vids or fan fiction, adding stories to the text's expanding diegesis, perhaps even giving visual form to the fantext and fan canon, or "fanon." For the individual machinima artist, though, the challenge lies in repurposing a game to create a recognizable storyworld and performing one's own stories within that world. Moreover, as Louisa Stein points out, since *The Sims*' props and settings are predominantly domestic, "the fan generic category of domesticfic, with its concerns with the everyday and the familial, finds a good fit in *The Sims*,"[56] making possible the exploration of the intimate, personal lives of filmic or televisual characters whom fans may ultimately care more about than *Buffy*'s or *Charmed*'s Monsters of the Week. If videogames allow considerable possibilities for the exploration of narrative space, machinima artists, by repurposing them to create machinima, also open up considerable room for the exploration of character.

Games can be decidedly lower tech and much less taxing on one's intellect and creativity, too—as with the drinking game, usually involving a list of events or phrases specific to a film or show, each of which requires that all or some of the party of viewers drink. At the lower end of the spectrum of both game or paratextual complexity, drinking games are nevertheless another viewer-created activity that can recalibrate what matters, opening up a storyworld to the viewers' interests. Often, such games work with a camp sensibility, rewarding a film for its formulaic or repetitive qualities, and drawing attention to them more than to its artistry. Or they might celebrate "improper" interpretations of a show, offering public and communal testament to that interpretation. A *Beverly Hills 90210* drinking game, for example, may call for everyone watching to drink when the character Steve pulls a "concerned" face, or a *Lord of the Rings* drinking game may call for everyone to drink when Legolas looks at Aragorn like a wistful yet aggrieved lover. As was examined with various viewer-created paratexts in the previous chapter, such games cut a personal or communal groove into a text's weft and woof.

Slightly more complex is the sports fantasy league. While most of this book's examples have been of fictional storyworlds, sports fans have long participated in fantasy leagues, thereby staging a remarkably popular game. Such leagues require players to "draft" athletes from across the available teams, and they then gain or lose points as the sport's season progresses depending upon how their personalized "team" fares. As with other games, fantasy leagues allow the player into the textual world, here giving them a greater stake in the nightly or weekly competitions between professional sports players, and making victory or loss a personal possibility, not just a vicarious pleasure or sorrow. Fantasy leagues add new dimensions to sports' competitive atmosphere, hence amplifying aspects of the text. However, like machinima, they also allow players to create new, even rival, pleasures within the textual world. Much of the hype and reporting that surrounds professional sports is based on the narrative hooks of which teams will win and which will lose, with team composition ("Are the interpersonal dynamics 'right' this year?" "Is such-and-such a player a benefit or a curse in the dressing room?") and team wins or losses of primary importance. Fantasy leagues can recalibrate what matters for individual fans, as the personal statistical successes or failures of their players now take center stage. A hockey player could have a fantastic game and be a dominant presence on the ice, for instance, and as a result his team might win, yet he could fail to register a goal or an assist, thereby offering the fantasy league "manager" nothing in return. Or two teams could face off against one another, with television coverage framing the match as a battle of two forces, while a fantasy league manager may have players on both teams, meaning that s/he would prefer a high-scoring affair, but that s/he is ultimately ambivalent about which team actually wins. For such a game player, the other paratexts of team jerseys, bedspreads, and the like may be moot, working against the fans' own method of engaging with the "text" of the game or season, or providing a simultaneous and competing logic that s/he must balance against his or her desire to win the fantasy league when watching.

Popular talk of fantasy leagues and related competitions such as sports brackets is rife with rueful discussion of those uninitiated sports newbies who, having picked their players or teams at random, still clean up the office pool. Such instances illustrate how varied the reasons for participating in any game might be—to win, to engage further in the sport, to have something riding on all games, to fit in with others, and so forth. Learning from this, we cannot assume that engagement with a media-related game is necessarily engagement with the show—the paratext/game may have become the text itself. However, just as chapter 5 showed that spoilers, vids, reviews, and wikis can reflect viewers' preferred modes of engaging with a textual universe, so too do viewers find other ways of personalizing their modes of engaging with a textual universe through games.

What Happens in Piedmont Stays in Piedmont: The Alternate Reality Game's Dual Address

Numerous alternate reality games (ARGs) provide a more dynamic instance in which the game actually trumps the show. The ARG, a relatively new addition to the roster of games, is a multi-site, multimedia puzzle or game, often associated with a television program or film. ARGs have worked as entryway games, introducing an audience to a show's genre and style, building up a fan base, and offering the textual personalization and expansion of play before the show arrives on the scene. They have also worked in medias res, especially during the summer hiatuses of television programs, as a way of keeping an active fan base and layering a storyworld for the truly engaged. ARGs regularly require communal puzzle-solving; for instance, some require players to scour a web page's code for embedded clues, translate passages in obscure languages, refer to ancient history or folklore, or engage in careful freeze-frame analysis. Jenkins has thus expressed interest in their fostering of "collective intelligence" and in their commitment to a truly participatory culture.[57] We might also look at them as viable generators of textuality and storyworld.

　　An intriguing example of the ARG began on April 16, 2008, when a blog called *What Happened in Piedmont?* was started.[58] The blog posed itself as written by Andrew Tobler, a journalism student at University of California, Berkeley. Tobler's initial post, entitled "Not sure what's going on," expressed concern with an answering-machine message he had received from his sister in Piedmont, Utah. Included as a sound file on the blog, the message starts out uneventfully and mundanely enough, until the speaker clearly spots her mother in physical distress. The young girl starts screaming, and the message then cuts out. Tobler slightly downplays the rather shocking audio, saying he might be overreacting, and explaining that his mother has for a while suffered from cardioneurogenic syncope, "which is basically an occasional, brief loss of consciousness due to a decrease in blood flow to the brain. Sometimes she faints or falls down, and a couple of times we had to take her to the doctor after she hit her head.

But it's not the end of the world." Yet he notes that all attempts to call home resulted in no answer, even from others in Piedmont: "Uncle Kyl, Al's, the diner, even the police." The post ends with a request to readers that is simultaneously a pregnant invitation for speculation: "So if anyone has any idea why I can't get in touch with a single person in the town of Piedmont, Utah, can you let me know?"

His next post, offered a day later, casually expresses surprise at the large number of comments and site traffic his blog has attracted. "Tobler" further creates a sense of verisimilitude, establishing the *alternate* reality, or what ARG players and designers often call the "This Is Not a Game" (TINAG) aesthetic. For instance, he explains where his town is to an audience who may well have found out by consulting Google that Piedmont, Utah, doesn't exist. Only those from the town "or the next [unnamed] town" know it, he says, and he notes that its population is 183, "182, since I left for college . . . though the Ritters had a little girl just after Christmas, so I guess that evens it out." Developing the story further, he later informs his readers that he has learned of a possible chemical spill in the area via a Google email alert, and later still he tells of a friend who tried to drive through Piedmont, only to be stopped by the military twenty-five miles away. Successive posts reveal information from a reporter for NNT Morning News and a video intercepted from a secure military digital feed (both available on YouTube), a photo of an object falling from the sky supposedly sent to him from a person who had been hiking near Piedmont, and classified documents that found their way into his hands.

Off-site, Tobler had web presence, particularly on Facebook, where his profile showed a picture of him and his girlfriend Kirsten, also on Facebook. The NNT reporter, Jack Nash, had his own website, sporting a picture of his book, *A Battle to the Top*. So too did Jeremy Stone, a doctor to whom Tobler's research led (fig. 6.3), and Wildfire, a "Bio-Defense" company. And friends that Tobler mentioned on his blog or his Facebook profile also had Facebook profiles. Thus, through various strategies, and despite a discrete disclaimer in the blog's Terms (of Use) that clearly stated that this was fictional, Big Spaceship, the as-yet-uncredited creators of *What Happened in Piedmont?* surrounded the entire ARG with an air of verisimilitude. Occasional "friends" of Tobler would break the fictional frame on his Facebook wall, only for those comments to soon disappear, while the filtered comments to his blog posts stayed wholly within frame. And whether posted under yet more Big Spaceship pseudonyms or legitimately by "players" who wished to contribute to this fictional frame, many

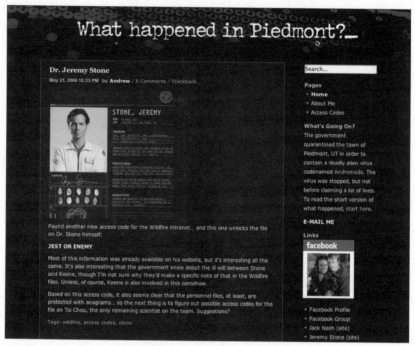

Fig. 6.3. "Andrew Tobler" posts information at ARG *What Happened in Piedmont?* on an individual possibly involved with mysterious happenings in Tobler's hometown of Piedmont, Utah.

of these comments furthered the development of this growing conspiracy theory. One poster, for instance, wrote of similar events in Arizona in 1969, while many others gave advice about dealing with the military, about biochemical disasters, and so forth. Ironically, too, Big Spaceship Creative Strategist Ivan Askwith told me in an interview that the *What Happened in Piedmont?* puppetmasters regularly received posts from readers who clearly did not understand that this was fictional, and from many others whose in-frame postings made it unclear whether they believed in the conspiracy or were simply playing along.

What began as a simple blog and a Facebook account thus quickly picked up momentum. Tobler soon had a small legion of readers trying their best to scour the Internet for information, much of it planted by Big Spaceship. *What Happened in Piedmont?* was an elaborate conspiracy story, somewhat *X-Files*-esque in its mysterious nature and supposed ties to shady government activities. The government, the Army, the media, aliens, the paranormal, elusive companies, and biohazards all figured in the various theories regarding what happened. Those who wished to "play" the game could scour through code, Google, and the documents that Tobler uploaded to find clues (some in Korean) and could post responses and suggestions to Tobler, while others could simply watch the story or game develop and read the blog postings and theories as their own text.

A few days into this game, observant players and readers would have noticed that *What Happened in Piedmont?* bore the fingerprints of the forthcoming A&E two-part special, *The Andromeda Strain*. "Nash" was Eric Mc-Cormack, television's Will from *Will and Grace* (1998–2006); Jeremy Stone was Benjamin Bratt, well-known to many for his four seasons on *Law and Order*; and *Lost's* Daniel Dae Kim also made an appearance as Tsi Chou, a scientist working for Wildfire. *What Happened in Piedmont?* was designed to create buzz for *The Andromeda Strain*. As an entryway paratext, it had established the storyworld and genre, readying viewers for a tale about a deadly alien disease. In this regard, it hearkened back to one of the Internet's more famous stunts, the webpage that set up the supernatural mystery surrounding *The Blair Witch Project* (see chapter 2). Moreover, as did the *Blair Witch Project's* website and accompanying multimedia existence, *What Happened in Piedmont?* became more than just a signal of the genre and a brief taste-test: it worked as its own story, and as a puzzle and a game that tested various players to beat the story to the answers. Should *What Happened in Piedmont?* readers or players have watched the mini-series, its text would already have been operative for them, but should they have simply not bothered, that text—complete with a full story with a beginning, a middle, and an end—would still have existed for them.

What Happened in Piedmont? worked as an "articulated" text in the sense that Stuart Hall suggests when he writes of articulated theory:

> In England, the term has a nice double meaning because "articulate" means to utter, to speak forth, to be articulate. It carries that sense of language-ing, of expressing, etc. But we also speak of an "articulated" lorry (truck): a lorry where the front "cab" and back "trailer" can, but need not necessarily, be connected to one another. An articulation is thus the form of the connection that *can* make a unity of two different elements, under certain circumstances. It is a linkage which is not necessary, determined, absolute, and essential for all time.[59]

Textually, the ARG could quite literally be separated from the mini-series, at no discernible cost to either. Indeed, while *The Andromeda Strain* is at the time of this writing available only in repeat or via fans' tapings, *What Happened in Piedmont?* and many of its links are readily accessible for anyone with an Internet connection. *Should* one have put the two together, however, just as the *Star Wars* toys expanded and developed the text beyond the scope of its six films, *The Andromeda Strain* and its storyworld would have expanded and developed well beyond the scope of the mini-series.

This "articulation" also undoubtedly resulted in the complete invisibility of *What Happened in Piedmont?* to many viewers. Many other ARGs have similarly flown under mainstream popular culture's radar, rarely popping their head out for many casual viewers. As do most games, then, their strength lies in their paradoxical "articulated" power to transform a text for some viewers while remaining totally irrelevant and inconsequential for others. Interestingly, of course, *What Happened in Piedmont?* retold this story, of an important and shocking event that remains covered up to popular culture and knowledge at large, thereby arguably multi-layering the experience of play for players. Their own consumption of the ARG placed them in a position not unlike that of Andrew Tobler, grappling at and occasionally finding shreds of a larger textuality, yet aware that others had no sense of (or interest in) it. Hence, whereas *The Matrix* struggled somewhat to corral its various paratexts in a way that addressed both heavily and lesser-engaged audiences, *What Happened in Piedmont?* (and several other ARGs, many of which are fond of conspiracy theory or mystery formats) built this dual address into its structure and narrative, so that *The Andromeda Strain* did not rely on *What Happened in Piedmont?* yet the latter's more engaged players could experience a broader textual universe.

ARG production has become a minor industry, and was even recently added as an award category (for Interactive Television Program) to the Emmys and British Academy Television Awards. In 2007, the Emmy went to Matt Wolf of D20 (who had also worked on *The Simpsons Hit and Run* game) and Canadian-based Xenophile Media for "The Ocular Effect," an ARG associated with ABC Family's *Fallen* (2006–7). The story, which examined suggestions of fallen angels on Earth and took place across five continents, attracted more than 2.5 million viewers. Xenophile also won an International Interactive Emmy that year for another ARG attached to the Canadian show *ReGenesis* (2004–8) that called upon players to work toward stopping a bioterrorist attack. In such instances—including the most reported-on ARG of recent years, *Lost*'s "The Lost Experience"— ARGs have often worked best with storylines that posit a hidden truth that requires uncovering, as their interactive, puzzle-based nature can prove more conducive to the immersion that some players seek than do their accompanying shows. In a personal interview, Patrick Crowe, founder of Xenophile, talked with considerable passion of ARGs as "a test run for the Holodeck," alluding to the immersive virtual-reality environment of the *Star Trek* series and films, and thus to ARGs' abilities to create text outright. While fan pilgrimages to sets or filming sites have flourished in places such as New York, Vancouver, New Zealand, Hawaii, and Los Angeles, offering, as Brooker writes, acts of creation, performance, disguise, and carnival,[60] ARGs aim to bring these prospects to the viewer, albeit in a starkly different manner.

Rules for Play

In chapters 1 and 2, I described how entryway paratexts establish a perimeter around a text, so that they become our first port of entry—the "airlock," as Gerard Genette poses it—acclimatizing us to the text. Some toys and games will continue to work at a text's perimeter, filling in details at its outskirts and giving meaning to its underexplored portions. Some will also push against the text's borders, expanding its scope, meaning, and uses. However, the risk in discussing paratexts as working at the outskirts of a text is that we reify notions of paratexts as peripheral. Thus, this chapter has argued that for some viewers, the text is at its most interesting, engaging, and/or meaningful at the outskirts. For some, in other words, the outskirts *are* the center. In such cases, the rubric of center and periphery, text and outskirts, must be revised to account for the individual viewer's or community of viewers' migrations to and from the outskirts—or their *sometimes* migration to and from the outskirts—and the concurrent decreased importance of what we as analysts might otherwise be tempted to regard as the "core" of the text, the film or television program. The chapter has also been about how we play with texts; but to talk of play is to talk of the ground rules for that play, and therefore I pose that we might regard paratexts as setting the ground rules for play with the text as a whole. Engaging with any form of entertainment, particularly of a fictional nature, is a form of play, and thus texts are essentially spaces for play and the reflection it inspires. Licensed toys and games frequently amplify, expand, or outright create these spaces, for both themselves and for the text more generally.

Many analysts and media producers alike still see toys and games as wholly peripheral, as they do most paratexts. However, as particularly the cases of *Enter the Matrix* and *What Happened in Piedmont?* illustrate, some film and television franchises have embraced the creative and contributive capacities of paratexts and have moved toward a model of media creation that works across media, networking various platforms, styles, and even textual addresses to fashion a more developed text. Though revenue-generation must of course still be a concern for any instance of commercial media, some have engaged (even if unintentionally) in bold and innovative practices to displace the film or television show as the necessary center of the text and franchise, or as the privileged site of meaning-generation. Since these rare examples have embraced the logic on which this book is based—namely, that the paratext is a vital part of the text—by way of a conclusion, I will now turn to a discussion of textually vibrant and textually void paratexts.

Conclusion

"In the DNA": Creating across Paratexts

Balancing alternate-sized textual universes is rapidly becoming a key task for media producers. Furthermore, since each paratext can toggle or even short-circuit the text (as examples throughout this book have illustrated), another key task is for media producers to streamline their various paratexts. And a third key task is to open sufficient room for storyworlds to be inhabitable, so that viewers have the interest in commandeering portions of the world, as well as the ability and freedom to create their own parts of and paths through this world. Making all of these tasks considerably harder is many companies' and shows' apparent lack of dedicated creative personnel whose job it is to oversee the smooth flow of textuality and meaning between films, programs, and paratexts. Many paratexts fall under a company's marketing and promotions budget, meaning that the show's creators may have little or nothing to do with their creation, thereby producing ample opportunity for creative disconnects, and for uninspired paratexts that do little to situate either themselves or the viewer in the storyworld. Interviews with creative personnel abound with tales of production or promotional personnel tasked with overseeing an established franchise about which they know nothing. At the level of production, relative chaos and piecemeal construction of paratexts on an ad hoc basis can often prove the norm. To conclude this book, therefore, I will now examine the issue of textual *cohesion*, and of how texts are variously put together.

While I argue for the creative potential that is fostered by streamlining shows and their paratexts, and while I am critical of some instances when show and paratext work independently, by no means do I wish to suggest that all texts *should* reign in their paratexts. At times, the push and pull between different meanings among paratexts or between the show and a paratext will be responsible for some of the text's vitality. As chapter 5 examined, paratexts can offer us new ways to make sense of or interact with a world. At other times, a proliferation of competing paratexts will be a text's saving grace, ensuring that its world is varied and disparate enough to welcome a wide range of viewers and interests. Any text that has caught the public's attention and imagination will be surrounded by such a preponderance of paratexts that they could never all agree. Ironically, for all their poor planning and coordination of in-house or commissioned paratexts, many media companies boast legal teams and/or control-freak creative personnel who take decisive action when viewers create paratexts that run counter to their own desires for the text, a move which I do not support. However, to argue, as I have done, that paratexts contribute to the text and are often vital parts of it is to argue that paratexts can be part of the creative process, and not just marketing "add-ons" and "ancillary products," as the media industries and academia alike have often regarded them. To ignore paratexts' textual role is to misunderstand their aesthetic, economic, and socio-cultural roles, and hence I conclude this book by examining what we might call textually "incorporated" and "unincorporated" paratexts.

The Dark Knight's Pepperoni Pizza: Unincorporated Paratexts

In chapter 1, I compared paratexts to ads, which are charged with the task of *branding* the product that is the text. Here, it is worth returning to this comparison, especially since throughout this book I have written of paratexts as textual, not as economic. Such a choice may have sat uneasily with some readers. Writing of ARGs, for instance, Henrik Örnebring complains that "there is relatively little academic concern with how ARGs function as *marketing tools*," and further states that "their primary purpose is not to create new opportunities for interaction, networking and audience participation in mediated narratives, but simply to create an enjoyable experience that will build the franchise brand in the minds of media audiences."[1] He is correct, of course, to point out that most ARGS are designed to advertise and to create buzz; many are allowed to exist because they brand the text. So too are all of the industry-created paratexts discussed in this book in one way or another "marketing tools." But as this book has also argued, Örnebring's hard-and-fast division between marketing and branding on one side, and interaction, networking, and audience participation on the other, ultimately cannot hold. As argued in chapter 1, branding is the process of making a product into a text; thus, when the product is itself a text, branding need not mean anything more than adding sites of construction for that text. What Örnebring calls the ARG's "simple" task "to create an enjoyable experience that will build the franchise brand in the minds of media audiences" will quite often *require* that the ARG works "to create new opportunities for interaction, networking and audience participation in mediated narratives." His division, as such, folds back on itself, illustrating the degree to which much paratextuality confuses the industry's and academia's binary of marketing and creativity.

Örnebring's criticism offers something of a red herring. Of course the profit imperative of an ARG may dictate the course of the story, and may considerably hamper the scope of the narrative. But this is a problem endemic to all commercial media, and hence to films and television programs too, not just to paratexts. We also see "marketing tools" in other seemingly innocuous activities: within academia, for instance, the job talk or any conference paper from an individual "on the market" is a marketing tool, but its marketing prerogative does not necessarily obviate its substance. Anything a head of state does could be regarded as a marketing tool for the next election, but this does not necessarily evacuate it of meaning. In the case of film and television, the profit imperative is bound tightly to the narrative impulse, but this does not necessarily overwhelm that impulse. By no means do I suggest that we should drop our concern with rampant commercialism and with the problematic nature of stories that aim to sell, but once more this is an issue endemic to film, television, and popular culture as a whole, not just to ARGs, spinoff toys, DVDs, trailers, and the like. If it is the marketing that concerns us, since paratexts frequently outpace the film or television show itself in economic terms, in such cases do we criticize the show as a mere marketing tool for the paratext? Or, since ARG creator and game developer Matt Wolf notes the irony that while many within the media industries regard ARGs as strictly promotional, yet these promotions need their own promotions, what are we to make of marketing tools for marketing tools?

Paratexts confound and disturb many of our hierarchies and binaries of what matters and what does not in the media world, especially the long-held notion that marketing and creativity are or could be distinct from one another. As such, I pose that a key concern as analysts should be the textual impact of the paratext. In cases when the paratext adds nothing or harms the narrative or storyworld, we can more easily criticize the paratext for being merely a marketing tool; in cases when the paratext adds to the narrative or storyworld and develops them, we have a more complex entity.

Hype, synergy, and paratexts often annoy consumers. But they are likely to do so only when the consumer does not care about (or actively dislikes) the related text, or when it contributes nothing or takes away from the text. As I write this Conclusion, for instance, following the recent release of *The Dark Knight*, many a television ad break contains a pitch for Domino's "Gotham City pizza." As critics tout the film's dark aesthetic, many impressed that a summer blockbuster superhero film would tread on such dark ground, I am forced to wonder what a pepperoni pizza is supposed to add to *The Dark Knight* as text. *The Dark Knight* was preceded by an elaborate, year-long ARG, in which Domino's and the Gotham City pizza feature, but they add nothing to that story either. The pizza's and the ad's sole contribution, then, is to signal the size of the film ("it even has a pizza named after it"). This move hardly seems necessary, and is trumped by the pizza's and ad's act of taking away from the film, making it seem, well, cheesy. The paratexts are wholly unincorporated, therefore, not a problem because they are an ad and a pizza, but because they are an ad and a pizza that contribute nothing meaningful to the text or its narrative, storyworld, characters, or style. By contrast, such a promotion may have fit *Spider-Man*, given alter ego Peter Parker's stint as delivery man, or *Teenage Mutant Ninja Turtles* (1990), given the characters' love of pizza. For *The Dark Knight*, they are *only* ads and pizzas.

Alongside the Gotham City pizza, we can place countless other examples of paratexts that fail to add anything substantive to the storyworld, or even to sample that world for would-be viewers. We could also point to cases when the paratext's meanings clash with those of the text, as was seen in chapter 2 with *Six Degrees'* promotional campaign and *The Sweet Hereafter's* American trailer. In both cases, while the show was heading in one direction, the paratext was heading in another, likely hurting the text's chances of receiving a wider, appreciative audience in the process.

"360°" Storytelling: Incorporated Paratexts

By contrast, this book has also presented numerous cases of paratexts that were "incorporated," adding to the storyworld and allowing viewers chances to explore that world further or even to contribute to it. The Canadian trailer to *The Sweet Hereafter*, the *Star Wars* line of toys, *What Happened in Piedmont?*, and the *Lord of the Rings* DVDs, for example, all either fleshed or teased out their respective narrative worlds.

I have attempted to offer a wide variety of examples, but we might also turn to several examples of texts whose incorporation extends to numerous paratexts. Kristin Thompson's highly detailed study of *The Lord of the Rings*, for instance, shows how Middle Earth overflowed from books to films to merchandise to games to DVDs and so on, all contributing not only to the franchise's monumental profits, but also to its success at attracting audiences.[2] Another, more recent example of what some in Hollywood have started to call "360 degree" storytelling lies in NBC's *Heroes* (2006–). The show tells the tale of people from around the world who develop super powers, ranging from invincibility to mind-reading or teleportation. Over time, they must deal with various threats from super villains, nefarious organizations, and shadows of the past. In addition to the television program, though, *Heroes* works on various platforms, using a variety of paratexts in innovative ways. Thus, for instance:

- A day after broadcast, each episode appears again online with cast commentary.
- An interactive section on the site's web page allows viewers to catch up on missed information and plot developments.
- The show is accompanied by an online comic, *9th Wonders*, with several pages worth of story accompanying each episode. This comic fills in character background and plot details, tells new stories involving the same characters, and appears within the show's diegesis.
- When enough of the online comic existed, it was published as a graphic novel, with alternate covers by famed comics artists Jim Lee and Alex Ross.
- Another Heroes publication, the novel *Saving Charlie*, examines what happened during one of time-traveler Hiro's jumps to the past, which created a love interest that the show itself did not follow up on.
- Numerous websites exist for organizations within the show's story-world, some mere transmedia window-dressing, some offering helpful information. The character Hiro also has his own blog.
- Viewers were invited to sign up to receive text message clues as part of the "Heroes 360 Experience," later renamed "Evolutions" (fig. c.1).
- A videogame is in the works at the time of writing.

All of these venues, as well as others, have frequently released information not (yet) in the television show. Uniting several of them, too, was the figure of Hana Gitelman, a hero introduced in the online comic and at the center of the show's transmedia presence for a while (fig. c.2). Gitelman has the ability to serve as a transmitter and receiver for virtually any form of electronic message through thought alone. Thus, her powers loan themselves to being situated in the show's complex network of mobile and online transmedia. And while the various paratexts and platforms flesh out the world of *Heroes*, any vital information is later shared on the show itself, ensuring that one can engage with the show alone without feeling left out or confused.

   Lost, too, has become a standard-bearer for today's generation of transmedia world-generation, with ARGs, creative sponsorship extensions,[3] a

Fig. c.1. The *Heroes* "Evolutions" website offers a portal into some of the show's many transmedia platforms.

Fig. c.2. A page from the *Heroes* graphic novel following the adventures of the transmediated hero Hana Gitelman.

videogame, a book written by an in-world character, numerous webpages, DVDs with expansive bonus materials, character appearances on *Jimmy Kimmel Live* (2003–), and various mobisodes or in-world ads. Hannah Montana and Miley Cyrus similarly exist across a broad range of media, as television stars, in concerts, in a 3-D concert video, on webpages, and in mobile media. Disney's other children's media behemoth, the *High School Musical* franchise, has not only traversed television, concert halls, mobile media, and webpages, but has also been remade in various international versions and as a stage musical. The worlds of Marvel and DC Comics can at times appear to be conducting a colonial occupation of the summer box office, while simultaneously developing strong presences in televised animation, videogames, and merchandising. Marvel and DC have trained audiences to expect infinite reboots and alternate universes, a strategy that allows James Bond–like ease of movement across media venues, but also restricts the prospects for a continuing narrative to be told across those venues.[4] As such, just as primetime television hosts both procedural, problem-of-the-week programs and serials, transmedia story-telling also has both rebooted and serial forms. Meanwhile, even shows not known for their paratexts can offer amusing, one-off paratexts, as with Showtime's *Dexter*, which produced a video postcard generator that allowed one to insert friends' names and a taunting message into a mock television news item warning of the serial killer's next likely victim.[5] In such cases, both producers and audiences are encouraged to look upon the paratexts as far more than just a marketing tool, though they may well be that as well. Rather, they are invited to incorporate the paratext into their text, and to see the creation of that paratext as part of the act of creating the text in general.

"In the Bloodstream": Producing Paratexts

Though this book has taken a predominantly text- and audience-centered view of paratextuality, its argument has ramifications for production studies too. Key to an understanding of any given production culture is an understanding of that culture's shared or contested opinions regarding who and what has value. My argument has been that paratexts have significant value, in and of themselves, but also as components of larger units of entertainment. To say this is to say that they are not "just promotional" or "just marketing tools," and thus that we might reconsider which workers are coded as "marketers" and which as "creative." To point to the value of paratextuality is also to call for greater study of the production of paratexts. If paratexts border the realms of promotion and creativity, more work could illuminate how the media industries value or devalue paratexts by categorizing them as creative labor or as promotional and ancillary. Already, significant evidence exists to suggest that the latter is more often the case. During the Writers Guild of America (WGA) strike of 2007–8, though media reports often focused on the issue of DVD and online royalties, arguably as important was the issue of compensation for writers' involvement in paratexts. Currently, creative personnel are not paid for their work on most paratexts, the film and television industries choosing instead to see such work as strictly promotional. When a cast member records a commentary track, when a writer works on an ARG or a mobisode, and when the showrunners of complex, transmediated shows such as *Heroes* or *Lost* try to coordinate and incorporate various paratexts into the grand narrative, they must usually do so for free and for the love of their text; participation in all "promotions" is a part of their contractual agreement. When the WGA went on strike, the only paratext creators who were on strike were those also hired as writers who gifted their time toward creating transmedia. While audiences may be just as if not more captivated by paratextual creativity, Hollywood still tends not to count this as creativity.

A familiar refrain exists throughout my research, which is that successful paratexts tend to be incorporated, while unsuccessful paratexts tend to be unincorporated. Of the latter, for instance, in chapter 6 I noted how often licensed games underwhelm their players. Brian Leake, Vice President of Technology at Disney Interactive Media Group, explained to me that this is because games have often been considered totally secondary and ancillary. Game developers were given too little time to produce spinoff games, which had to be released in tandem with the film or program in question. Producing licensed games could often be "like a starting pistol," therefore, with the developer required to start immediately. Matt Wolf similarly told me that "day and date" productions—those intended for release on the same day as a film, for instance—nearly always suffered. However, Wolf, who worked for *Simpsons* producers Gracie Films to ensure an "authentic" Simpsonian experience on *The Simpsons Hit and Run* game, noted that such games can benefit greatly from not being tied to any particular release date, thus allowing room for real creativity. Leake too felt that game designers will inevitably produce their best, most creative work when allowed the time and chance to "spin" a show, and to add "a little bit extra" to the text themselves. He also suggested that more film and television creators are aware of the importance of games today, and hence that they are getting more involved in the process.

Echoing Leake, Thompson notes that more directors are getting involved in game design, citing specifically Peter Jackson's dedication to the *Lord of the Rings* games. She quotes Neil Young, executive producer of the games, as stating: "Usually here's how games based on movies get made[. . . .] You interface exclusively with the licensing arm of the distributor—the movie studio. Maybe you get a script. You might get some photos from the set. If you're lucky you might get a cuddly toy or a cup. If you're really lucky, you might get a visit to the set."[6] However, Jackson and New Line allowed Young an almost unprecedented level of access to properties from the show. And yet, when Jackson moved on to his next project, *King Kong*, he wanted more involvement in the process himself and hence worked with a different company.[7] Wolf, too, noted Gracie's amenability to work with the game designers, and Leake, who also worked on *Hit and Run*, talked of the huge "Bible" of *Simpsons* information that the designers received from Gracie. Clearly, for licensed games to work, film and television creators need to get more involved, and they need to allow game designers more freedom and more information, inviting them into the creative process of the text as a whole, while not abdicating as much of the narrative foundations to the games as did *The Matrix*.

Writing of the landmark *Lord of the Rings* DVDs, Thompson also notes how important it was to Jackson and their producers that the DVD production arm be just another part of the film, not an independent, isolated entity. Their producer, Michael Pellerin, told Thompson, "We were in the bloodstream of the production, as well as for security reasons, we were given production offices in the film production offices. We literally became another little department of the movie," also insisting that "to this day (even with Universal and *King Kong*) I have never experienced more of a synergy created between the filmmakers, the DVD producer, the menu and package designers than I did on *The Lord of the Rings*."[8] Pellerin and his staff were on set from day one, as opposed to the former tendency in Hollywood to construct piecemeal DVDs after production had wrapped, based on whatever scraps were available to the producer. Again, Jackson was so involved in the process that on *King Kong* he began to produce his own production diary video blog posts, which he later placed into *King Kong: Peter Jackson's Production Diaries*, a set of DVDs released before the film. Meanwhile, David Jessen, Vice President of Blu-Ray and DVD Creative Production at Walt Disney Studios Home Entertainment, told me that standard operating procedure at Disney is now that he is on the set from the moment a show is given the green light, ensuring that he too is, in Pellerin's words, "in the bloodstream."

Given *Heroes'* particular success at crafting a story across various paratexts—winning them an Emmy for creative achievement in interactive media in 2008—I also interviewed the show's former co-executive producer and writer Jesse Alexander, its former associate producer and transmedia head Mark Warshaw, and NBC-Universal's Senior Vice President of Digital Development and General Manager of NBC.com, Stephen Andrade. All three have significant prior experience with transmedia: Alexander worked as a writer on *Lost* and *Alias* before coming to *Heroes*, Warshaw developed an extensive transmedia entourage for *Smallville*, and Andrade has worked in the field at an executive level for many years.

Warshaw told me of needing to run ideas by the showrunners, studio, and network with past projects, while Andrade alluded to some showrunners' disinterest in developing other platforms for their narratives. However, *Heroes* had a dedicated transmedia team (called this, too, following the team's interest in Henry Jenkins's work and use of the term "transmedia"). At the same time, the core of this team, noted Alexander, were the writers of the show, in particular himself, Warshaw, Aron Coleite, and Joe Pakaski. Hence, stated Warshaw,

> the producing team is very transmedia focused so there is more collaboration in the idea generation. Jesse Alexander, who is an executive producer on the series, is obsessed with transmedia and is easily television's foremost thinker in the field. Because of this, the transmedia department on "Heroes" was truly an extension of the writers' room.

The team's love of transmedia is evident: Alexander notes that the writers are "superfans" of transmedia, his personal blog *The Global Couch* (globalcouch.blogspot.com) is all about transmedia, and he and Warshaw have been keen attendees and presenters at MIT's Futures of Entertainment conference (where both introduced themselves to me after hearing of this project). When I asked Alexander if he would be as committed to *Heroes* if it lacked a transmedia component, he responded that he would not, since, in his opinion, "transmedia content is the way of the future of entertainment, and any show—certainly a genre show and a triple-A franchise like *Heroes*—needs transmedia to be part of doing business." "Everything I do," he added, "is gonna have a transmedia component."

While Alexander, Warshaw, and Andrade were all polite in not naming names or expanding upon other less-rewarding experiences, all three clearly felt that a commitment to transmedia must come from above. Alexander spoke of how important NBC's support and follow-through had proven to be, alluding to the need for corporate support, while Andrade spoke both of how much more exciting the possibilities for transmedia development became once NBC head Jeff Zucker was on board with the concept, and of what a treat it was to work with the *Heroes* producers, given their openness and complete commitment as creative heads to offering multiple venues for the *Heroes* story. As a result, transmedia concepts are included in thinking from the beginning, "immediately," Alexander stated, and "in our DNA and so organic to how we tell our stories." Whereas paratexts are frequently conceived of as add-ons, after-the-fact supplements to a preconceived narrative universe, Alexander, Warshaw, and Andrade spoke of the value of creating with transmedia multi-platforms involved in the story from the outset.

At the same time, Warshaw in particular spoke of the structural struggles that transmedia has faced. Transmedia, he states,

> was this square peg that came along when most of what TV had to offer was a bunch of round holes. No one knew if it was marketing or content yet. No one knew a lot of the answers. So there were growing pains during this discovery phase. We had to figure it out along the way. When I was hired on "Heroes," the transmedia storytelling concept was pretty foreign to the studio, network, and some parts of the show. New structures had to be built and ways of doing business defined. They literally created a transmedia production manual. Now there are templates.

A key tension seems to be the push and pull common to television as a whole, between creative and advertising impulses. Andrade offered a telling metaphor in speaking of transmedia as a "three-legged stool," promoting the show while serving as both a vehicle for ads and a site for story development. Transmedia's success and commercial viability, he argued, relies on all three legs being strong. Ivan Askwith has written of how these legs risked breaking with *Lost*'s ARG when advertising took over in the case of Sprite's Sublymonal campaign. Viewers and players were encouraged to visit Sprite's website, with no payoff whatsoever. By comparison, Jeep and Monster invoked less player outrage, and more respect, when the former buried clues and secret documents in a company website, and the latter added a job search website for careers at the in-world Hanso Foundation.[9] Thus, commercial television–centered transmedia operates as does commercial television in general, requiring a careful balancing act between creative and corporate desires. As *Lost's* executive producer Carlton Cuse noted at the 2008 IRTS and Disney Digital Media Summit, the key challenge for paratextual production is how to "embed content in marketing" in a way that avoids the crass consumerism of most advertising and that ensures that the content is still king.

Another huge task for paratextual development is for Hollywood to expand its notion of who belongs to the production team. At the 2008 IRTS and Disney Digital Media Summit, Cuse also noted that he and writing partner Damon Lindelof realized early on in *Lost's* tenure that they were not the people best equipped to make many of its innovative paratexts come to life. Thus, they needed to be able to farm these out. A small group of companies and individuals have started to specialize in such work, from Warshaw to Matt Wolf's D20, Xenophile, Big Spaceship, Hoodlum, Starlight Runner, 42 Entertainment, and others. Film and television have always been collaborative media, but the small, elite club of "above the line" creators may need to open its doors if its members are dedicated to integrating paratexts seamlessly and intelligently. A common complaint from transmedia creators—and one that is evident in many a paratext—is that the network or studio allowed little or no real collaboration or discussion between paratext creators and the film's director or the television program's writing staff.

Nevertheless, Warshaw insists that transmedia remains a particularly exciting space in which to work given that its newness has ensured that television networks do not know exactly how it works or how they *want* it to work:

> Transmedia storytelling has been and still is thrilling and very satisfying to me because there are very few boxes—no rigid pre-established creative structures to work within based on years of data collection and trial and error. There are very few preconceived notions about what does and does not work yet. This has allowed me a lot of artistic freedom and is the reason I leap out of bed excited to go to work most mornings.

Andrade, too, told me, "Everything's a jumpball right now, with all of us [media corporations] trying to invest in everything," until the picture of transmedia's future becomes clear. To this end, and working together, Alexander and Matt Wolf are floating the idea of creating a storyworld that precedes any of its given media iterations, rather than follow the current status quo of letting the transmedia follow the individual show. Whereas the Wachowski brothers may be seen as having done this with *The Matrix*, in truth the original film preceded its paratextual proliferation. By contrast, if incorporated paratexts confuse the boundaries between story and promotion, narrative center and narrative periphery, Alexander and Wolf propose a literalization of this confusion, by creating a storyworld that is from the beginning transmediated, with no paratexts, only textual iterations. Their plan is to start with the DNA code of the story before creating any of its bodies or incarnations.

Videogames, DVDs, and ARGs all present themselves as obvious storytelling extensions for a new brand of media creator, but drawing on chapter 2, we might also wonder about creators' role in streamlining trailers, movie posters, and the like. Further research must also be conducted on production cultures surrounding paratexts, for here I have only scratched the surface and have been forced to take various producers' accounts of their own work at face value. Up-close observation of the day-to-day task of synching films, television programs, and paratexts may well indicate a more complex set of realities. Such analysis might also shed better light on the degree to which the industries' paratext creators work alongside and/ or against the interests of viewer-creators. All of the paid paratext creators to whom I spoke talked of fan involvement with their shows with considerable passion and enthusiasm, with Alexander stating that it shouldn't just be the writers "who get to have all the fun, the fans should get to have fun as well." But surely not all fan practices are equal in all creators' eyes, and production ethnographies and histories would undoubtedly uncover the areas of tension better than have my own questions. Toward these ends, Thompson's *Frodo Franchise*, Henry Jenkins's ongoing interviews with transmedia artists on his blog *Confessions of an Aca-Fan*, and Avi Santo's historical work on the paratextual proliferation of *The Lone Ranger*[10] all provide helpful steps forward, but more still is required.

In the DNA

The production cultures around paratexts still need more study, but I hope in this book to have shown how vitally important paratexts are at a textual level and at the level of the audience's understanding, enjoyment, and use of texts. Paratexts fill the media landscape and can be as responsible for popular culture's encounters with countless storyworlds and texts as are film and television. As media cultures evolve, analysts have often paid close attention to the dominant shifts and newcomers, from the development of photography to that of film, from radio to television, and now to "new media" such as the Internet and mobile telephony. But paratexts have often filled the gaps between media, never a true medium unto themselves, and thus rarely attracting their due attention. As paratexts, convergence, and overflow increasingly bring texts together, however, and as it therefore becomes increasingly difficult to study any one medium in isolation, paratextual study will become all the more important and all the more helpful, and paratextual creation will similarly become all the more vital for any would-be successful text or franchise. In his playful book on literary paratexts, tellingly entitled *Invisible Forms*, Kevin Jackson notes that while there are thousands of books designed to tell one how to write *books*, few if any tell one how to write paratexts.[11] Similarly, while many books ask us to *study* books, films, and television programs, few ask us explicitly to study their paratexts. With this book, I hope to have done exactly that, by showing how these sometimes "invisible," "peripheral," "ancillary" entities are as intrinsic a part of a text's DNA as are the films and television programs that have usually been regarded as the entirety of the text, and that they frequently support, develop, and enrich.

Notes

INTRODUCTION

1. For more, see Shanto Iyengar, *Is Anyone Responsible? How Television Frames Political Issues* (Chicago: University of Chicago Press, 1994); Karen S. Johnson-Cartee, *News Narratives and News Framing: Constructing Political Reality* (Lanham, MD: Rowman & Littlefield, 2004); Diana Kendall, *Framing Class: Media Representations of Wealth and Poverty in America* (Lanham, MD: Rowman & Littlefield, 2005).

2. Charles Acland, *Screen Traffic: Movies, Multiplexes, and Global Culture* (Durham, NC: Duke University Press, 2003), 46.

3. Gerard Genette, *Paratexts: The Thresholds of Interpretation*, trans. Jane E. Lewin (Cambridge: Cambridge University Press, 1997).

4. Julia Kristeva, *Desire in Language: A Semiotic Approach to Literature and Art*, trans. Thomas Gora et al., ed. Leon Roudiez (Oxford: Basil Blackwell, 1980), 36.

5. Tad Friend, "The Cobra: Inside a Movie Marketer's Playbook," *The New Yorker*, January 19, 2009, pp. 41, 46.

6. Kristin Thompson, *The Frodo Franchise: The Lord of the Rings and Modern Hollywood* (Berkeley: University of California Press, 2007), 223.

7. Ibid., 222.

8. Janet Wasko, *How Hollywood Works* (Thousand Oaks, CA: Sage, 2003), 130.

9. Amanda Lotz, *The Television Will Be Revolutionized* (New York: New York University Press, 2007), 108–9.

10. Wasko, *How Hollywood Works*, 164, 162, 166.

11. John Thornton Caldwell, *Production Culture: Industrial Reflexivity and Critical Practice in Film and Television* (Durham, NC: Duke University Press, 2008).

12. See Kevin Glynn, "Bartmania: The Social Reception of an Unruly Image," *Camera Obscura: Feminism, Culture, and Media Studies* 38 (1996): 61–91; Peter Parisi, "'Black Bart' Simpson: Appropriation and Revitalization in Commodity Culture," *Journal of Popular Culture* 27.1 (1993): 125–42.

13. Quoted in Vincent Brook, "Myth or Consequences: Ideological Fault Lines in *The Simpsons*," in *Leaving Springfield: The Simpsons and the Possibility*

of Oppositional Culture, ed. John Alberti (Detroit: Wayne State University Press, 2004), 178.

14. "Archbishop 'May Star in Simpsons,'" *BBC News*, June 20, 2004, archived at http://news.bbc.co.uk/1/hi/entertainment/tv_and_radio/3823541.stm

15. Jonathan Gray, *Watching with* The Simpsons: *Television, Parody, and Intertextuality* (New York: Routledge, 2006).

16. Matthew P. McAllister, "From Lard Lad to Butterfinger: Contradictions of *The Simpsons* in Promotional and Commercial Culture," paper presented at International Communication Association conference, New Orleans, LA, 2004.

17. Ibid.

18. See, respectively, Acland, *Screen Traffic*; and Joshua Green, "What Does an American Television Network Look Like?" *Flow* 7.2 (2007), http://flowtv.org/?p=899.

CHAPTER 1

1. Thomas Elsaesser, "The Blockbuster: Everything Connects, But Not Everything Goes," in *The End of Cinema as We Know It*, ed. Jon Lewis (New York: New York University Press, 2002), 16.

2. Roger Silverstone, *Why Study the Media?* (Thousand Oaks, CA: Sage, 1999), 55.

3. Genette, *Paratexts*, 3.

4. Ibid., 5.

5. Ibid., 408.

6. Celia Lury and Alan Warde, "Investments in the Imaginary Consumer: Conjectures Regarding Power, Knowledge and Advertising," in *Buy This Book*, ed. Mica Nava et al. (New York: Routledge, 1997), 90.

7. Sut Jhally, *The Codes of Advertising: Fetishism and the Political Economy of Meaning in the Consumer Society* (New York: Routledge, 1987), 51.

8. Judith Williamson, *Decoding Advertisements: Ideology and Meaning* (London: Marion Boyars, 1978), 79.

9. Gillian Dyer, *Advertising as Communication* (New York: Routledge, 1982), 116–17.

10. Victoria Johnson, *Heartland TV: Prime Time Television and the Struggle for U.S. Identity* (New York: New York University Press, 2008), 78–79.

11. Roland Barthes, "From Work to Text," in *Image/Music/Text*, trans. Stephen Heath (Glasgow: Fontana-Collins, 1977), 157.

12. Ibid., 162, 163.

13. Valentin Nikolaevic Volosinov, *Marxism and the Philosophy of Language*, trans. Ladislav Metejka and I. R. Titunik (London: Seminar, 1973), 82, 72.

14. Michael Riffaterre, "Compulsory Reader Response: The Intertextual Drive," in *Intertextuality: Theories and Practices*, ed. Michael Worton and Judith Still (Manchester: Manchester University Press, 1990), 76.

15. Michael Riffaterre, "Interpretation and Undecidability," *New Literary History* 12 (1981): 227.

16. Michael Iampolski, *The Memory of Tiresias: Intertextuality and Film*, trans. Harsha Ram (Berkeley: University of California Press, 1998), 2.

17. Kristeva, *Desire in Language*, 66.

18. Iampolski, *Memory of Tiresias*, 3.

19. Stanley Fish, *Is There a Text in This Class? The Authority of Interpretive Communities* (Cambridge, MA: Harvard University Press, 1980), 268, 274.

20. Ibid., 292.

21. Ibid., 171.

22. Laurent Jenny, "The Strategy of Form" trans. R. Carter, in *French Literary Theory Today: A Reader*, ed. Tzvetan Todorov (Cambridge: Cambridge University Press, 1982), 34–63; see also Ferdinand de Saussure, *Course in General Linguistics*, trans. Wade Baskin, ed. Charles Bally and Albert Sechehaye (London: McGraw-Hill, 1983).

23. Gray, *Watching with* The Simpsons.

24. Jenny, "Strategy of Form," 59.

25. See Gray, *Watching with* The Simpsons, chap. 5.

26. Tony Bennett and Janet Woollacott, *Bond and Beyond: The Political Career of a Popular Hero* (London: Macmillan, 1987), 44.

27. Ibid., 262.

28. Jason Mittell, *Genre and Television: From Cop Shows to Cartoons in American Culture* (New York: Routledge, 2004), 9.

29. Ibid., 31.

30. Stephen Neale, *Genre* (London: British Film Institute, 1980), 19.

31. Lynn Spigel, *Make Room for TV: Television and the Family Ideal in Postwar America* (Berkeley: University of California Press, 1992).

32. See Barbara Klinger, *Beyond the Multiplex: Cinema, New Technologies, and the Home* (Berkeley: University of California Press, 2006).

33. Martin Barker, Jane Arthurs, and Ramaswami Harindranath, *The Crash Controversy: Censorship Campaigns and Film Reception* (New York: Wallflower, 2001).

34. Ibid., 86.

35. Janet Staiger, *Interpreting Films: Studies in the Historical Reception of American Cinema* (Princeton, NJ: Princeton University Press, 1992), 39.

36. David Buckingham, *Public Secrets: East Enders and Its Audience* (London: British Film Institute, 1987).

37. C. Lee Harrington and Denise Bielby, *Soap Fans: Pursuing Pleasure and Making Meaning in Everyday Life* (Philadelphia: Temple University Press, 1996), 66.

38. Robert C. Allen, "Home Alone Together: Hollywood and the 'Family Film,'" in *Identifying Hollywood's Audiences: Cultural Identity and the Movies*, ed. Melvyn Stokes and Richard Maltby (London: British Film Institute, 1999), 119, 123, 119.

39. Ibid., 128.

40. Friend, "The Cobra," 49.

41. Will Brooker, "Living on *Dawson's Creek*: Teen Viewers, Cultural Convergence and Television Overflow," *International Journal of Cultural Studies* 4.4 (2001): 456–57.

42. Ibid., 457.

43. Henry Jenkins, *Convergence Culture: Where Old and New Media Collide* (New York: New York University Press, 2006).

44. Fish, *Is There a Text in This Class?* 5.

45. Stanley Fish, "Literature in the Reader: Affective Stylistics," in *Reader-Response Criticism: From Formalism to Post-Structuralism*, ed. Jane Tompkins (Baltimore: Johns Hopkins University Press, 1980), 83, 74.

46. Wolfgang Iser, "The Reading Process: A Phenomenological Approach," in *Reader-Response Criticism: From Formalism to Post-Structuralism*, ed. Jane Tompkins (Baltimore: Johns Hopkins University Press, 1980), 56.

47. Wolfgang Iser, *The Act of Reading: A Theory of Aesthetic Response* (London: Routledge and Kegan Paul, 1978), 112, 18.

48. See Gray, *Watching with* The Simpsons, chap. 3.

49. See also Will Brooker, "Television out of Time: Watching Cult Shows on Download," in *Reading* Lost: *Perspectives on a Hit Show*, ed. Roberta E. Pearson (New York: I. B. Tauris, 2008), 53–78.

50. Will Brooker, *Using the Force: Creativity, Community and Star Wars Fans* (New York: Continuum, 2002).

51. Matt Hills, *Fan Cultures* (New York: Routledge, 2002), 142.

52. Annette Kuhn, "'That Day *Did* Last Me All My Life': Cinema Memory and Enduring Fandom," in *Identifying Hollywood's Audiences: Cultural Identity and the Movies*, ed. Melvyn Stokes and Richard Maltby (London: British Film Institute, 1999), 136, 145.

53. Quoted in Katerina Clark and Michael Holquist, *Mikhail Bakhtin* (Cambridge, MA: Harvard University Press, 1984), 350.

54. See Johnson, *Heartland TV*, chap. 6; Barbie Zelizer, *Covering the Body: The Kennedy Assassination, the Media, and the Shaping of Collective Memory* (Chicago: University of Chicago Press, 1992), 151–52.

55. Scott Dikkers, ed., *Our Dumb Century: The Onion Presents 100 Years of Headlines from America's Finest News Source* (New York: Three Rivers, 1999), 13.

56. Jonathan Gray, "New Audiences, New Textualities: Anti-Fans and Non-Fans," *International Journal of Cultural Studies* 6.1 (March 2003): 64–81.

CHAPTER 2

1. Acland, *Screen Traffic.*

2. Klinger, *Beyond the Multiplex.*

3. Friend, "The Cobra," 41.

4. Wasko, *How Hollywood Works,* 198.

5. John Ellis, *Visible Fictions: Cinema: Television: Video* (New York: Routledge, 1993), 54.

6. Acland, *Screen Traffic,* 23.

7. Friend, "The Cobra," 44.

8. Lisa Kernan, *Coming Attractions: Reading American Movie Trailers* (Austin: University of Texas Press, 2004), 53.

9. See Tom Gunning, "The Cinema of Attractions: Early Film, Its Spectator and the Avant-Garde," in *Early Cinema: Space, Frame, Narrative,* ed. Thomas Elsaesser and Adam Barker (London: British Film Institute, 1990), 56–62.

10. Kernan, *Coming Attractions,* 1, 2.

11. Ibid., 74.

12. See Mittell, *Genre and Television.*

13. See Rick Altman, *Film/Genre* (London: British Film Institute, 1999); Stephen Neale, *Genre and Hollywood* (New York: Routledge, 2000).

14. Barker et al., *Crash Controversy.*

15. Mittell, *Genre and Television,* xi, 36.

16. Kernan, *Coming Attractions,* 178.

17. Ibid., 192.

18. Andrew Wernick, *Promotional Culture: Advertising, Ideology and Symbolic Expression* (Newbury Park, CA: Sage, 1991), 12.

19. Kurt Lancaster, "Immersion through an Interface in The Blair Witch Project," in *Performing the Force: Essays on Immersion into Science Fiction, Fantasy and Horror Environments,* ed. Kurt Lancaster and Tom Micotowicz (Jefferson, NC: McFarland, 2001), 117–23.

20. Such identity games have since become common with the rise of Facebook, and applications that feature multiple "Which character are you?" quizzes; however, while now suitably unrooted from Sex, in the fall of 2006, and pre-Facebook quizzes, the game had distinctly—and, I would argue, obviously—*Sex and the City* roots.

21. Virginia Heffernan, "Serendipitous Connections in the City of Separate Lives," *New York Times,* September 21, 2006, archived at http://www.nytimes.com/2006/09/21/arts/television/21heff.html?ei=5070&en=f7275d1b34d1f7bd&ex=1159588800&pagewanted=print.

22. Amanda Lotz, "How to Spend $9.3 Billion in Three Days: Examining the Upfront Buying Process in the Production of US Television Culture," *Media, Culture and Society* 29.4 (2007): 549–67; Amanda Lotz, "The Promotional Role of

the Network Upfront Presentations in the Production of Culture," *Television and New Media* 8.1 (2007): 3–24.

23. Lotz, "The Promotional Role," 11.

24. Lotz, "How to Spend $9.3 Billion," 549.

25. See http://www.youtube.com/watch?v=sfout_rgPSA.

26. See http://www.youtube.com/watch?v=x25jVzVP1bY.

27. Lynn Spigel, "From the Dark Ages to the Golden Age: Women's Memories and Television Reruns," *Screen* 36.1 (1995): 16–33.

28. Dan Harries, *Film Parody* (London: British Film Institute, 2000), 107.

29. Derek Kompare, *Rerun Nation: How Repeats Invented American Television* (New York: Routledge, 2005), 104.

30. Ibid., chap. 7.

31. Mittell, *Genre and Television*, 57.

32. Ibid., xii.

33. Both trailers can be found on the *Sweet Hereafter* DVD.

34. Michel Foucault, "What Is an Author?" in *Textual Strategies: Perspectives in Post-Structuralist Criticism,* ed. Josué V. Harari (London: Methuen, 1980), 150.

35. The *Iron Man* trailers, for instance, had approximately 12.6 million views logged on YouTube by September 20, 2008, while the "Chinese Backstreet Boys," though up for a year longer, had just under 10 million views.

36. Stuart Hall, "Encoding, Decoding," in *Culture, Media, Language: Working Papers in Cultural Studies, 1972–1979,* ed. Stuart Hall et al. (London: Unwin Hyman, 1980), 128–38.

37. David Morley, "The Nationwide Audience: A Critical Postscript," *Screen Education* 39 (1981): 6.

38. Justin Lewis, "The Encoding/Decoding Model: Criticisms and Redevelopments for Research on Decoding," *Media, Culture and Society* 5 (1983): 184.

39. Moreover, the theme song was performed by different musicians each season, allowing for variations in tone and style, as the show itself shifted focus across various societal institutions.

40. Raymond Williams, *Television: Technology and Cultural Form* (London: Fontana/Collins, 1974), 86, 90.

41. Ibid., 87.

42. David Johansson, "Homeward Bound: Those Sopranos Titles Come Heavy," in *Reading The Sopranos: Hit TV from HBO,* ed. David Lavery (New York: I. B. Tauris, 2006), 31.

43. Ibid., 34, 33.

44. Ibid., 32.

45. Roland Barthes, *Mythologies,* trans. Annette Lavers (St. Albans: Paladin, 1973).

46. Johnson, *Heartland TV,* 133–34.

CHAPTER 3

1. Tony Bennett, *Formalism and Marxism* (London: Routledge, 1979), 173.

2. See Todd Gitlin, *Inside Prime Time*, rev. ed. (New York: Routledge, 1994).

3. Walter Benjamin, "The Work of Art in the Age of Mechanical Reproduction," in *Illuminations*, trans. Harry Zohn (New York: Schocken, 1969), 221.

4. Roland Barthes, "The Death of the Author," in *Image/Music/Text*, trans. Stephen Heath (Glasgow: Fontana-Collins, 1977), 142–48.

5. Laurie Ouellette and James Hay, *Better Living through Reality TV: Television and Post-Welfare Citizenship* (Malden, MA: Blackwell, 2008), 17.

6. Ibid., 65; see also Mark Andrejevic, *Reality TV: The Work of Being Watched* (Lanham, MD: Rowman & Littlefield, 2004).

7. Ouellette and Hay, *Better Living*, 87–88.

8. Roberto Rocha, "DVD Sales Grow, Buck Trend of CDs," *National Post*, July 17, 2008, archived at http://www.nationalpost.com/related/topics/story.html?id=661557.

9. Robert Alan Brookey and Robert Westerfelhaus, "Hiding Homoeroticism in Plain View: The *Fight Club* DVD as Digital Closet," *Critical Studies in Media Communication* 19.1 (March 2002): 23.

10. Klinger, *Beyond the Multiplex*, 72.

11. Brookey and Westerfelhaus, "Hiding Homoeroticism," 23.

12. Peter Dean, for instance, notes that today's "rent—rip—burn" culture relies on programs whose default settings ignore bonus materials, and that Netflix and other direct-mail rental companies' policy of charging per disc frequently leads to renters foregoing additional discs rich with extras and add-ons. See "DVDs: Add-Ons or Bygones," *Convergence: The International Journal of Research into New Media Technologies* 13.2 (2007): 119–28. David Jessen, Vice President of DVD and Blu-Ray Creative Production at Walt Disney Studios Home Entertainment, also noted, at the 2008 Disney/IRTS Digital Media Summit, that audience research reveals widespread apathy for commentary tracks.

13. Brookey and Westerfelhaus, "Hiding Homoeroticism," 23.

14. Ibid., 24–25.

15. P. David Marshall, "The New Intertextual Commodity," in *The New Media Book*, ed. Dan Harries (London: British Film Institute, 2000), 69.

16. Jonathan Gray, "Scanning the Replicant Text," in *The Blade Runner Experience: The Legacy of a Science Fiction Classic*, ed. Will Brooker (New York: Wallflower, 2005).

17. Acland, *Screen Traffic*, 65.

18. See Allen, "Home Alone Together."

19. Acland, *Screen Traffic*, 65, 69.

20. Klinger, *Beyond the Multiplex*, 73.

21. Steve Bebout, "George Lucas: His Roles and His Myths," in *Performing the Force: Essays on Immersion into Science Fiction, Fantasy and Horror Environments*, ed. Kurt Lancaster and Tom Micotowicz (Jefferson, NC: McFarland, 2001), 33–34; see also Christine Witmer on Stanley Kubrick, in "The Mythology of the Stanley Kubrick Image," in ibid., 23–27.

22. Benjamin, "Work of Art," 221, 220, 221.

23. Ibid., 236.

24. Klinger, *Beyond the Multiplex*, 61.

25. Brookey and Westerfelhaus, "Hiding Homoeroticism," 150.

26. See Martin Barker and Kate Brooks, *Knowing Audiences: Judge Dredd, Its Friends, Fans and Foes* (Luton, U.K.: University of Luton Press, 1998).

27. Benjamin, "Work of Art"; Barthes, "Death of the Author."

28. Robert Delaney, "The Myth of George Lucas Surrounding *The Phantom Menace*," in *Performing the Force: Essays on Immersion into Science Fiction, Fantasy and Horror Environments*, ed. Kurt Lancaster and Tom Micotowicz (Jefferson, NC: McFarland, 2001), 42.

29. Daniel Mackay, "*Star Wars*: The Magic of the Anti-Myth," in ibid., 53–54.

30. Klinger, *Beyond the Multiplex*, 66.

31. See Max Horkheimer and Theodor W. Adorno, *Dialectic of Enlightenment: Philosophical Fragments*, trans. John Cumming (New York: Seabury, 1972).

32. Gitlin, *Inside Prime Time*, 56.

33. Kompare, *Rerun Nation*.

34. Ibid., 103.

35. Ibid., 105.

36. Derek Kompare, "Publishing Flow: DVD Box Sets and the Reconception of Television," *Television and New Media* 7 (2006): 337.

37. Klinger, *Beyond the Multiplex*, 83–84.

38. Kompare, "Publishing Flow," 348.

39. Barthes, "Death of the Author," 143.

40. Ibid., 148.

41. Foucault, "What Is an Author?" 144.

42. Ibid., 151.

43. For a close parallel, see Will Brooker on George Lucas's central place within *Star Wars* canon, in *Using the Force*, 101–13.

44. Henry Jenkins, "'Infinite Diversity in Infinite Combinations': Genre and Authorship in *Star Trek*," in John Tulloch and Henry Jenkins, *Science Fiction Audiences: Watching Doctor Who and Star Trek* (New York: Routledge, 1995), 188.

45. Horkheimer and Adorno, *Dialectic of Enlightenment*, 120, 122.

46. Barthes, "Death of the Author," 145.

47. Francesca Coppa, "Writing Bodies in Space: Media Fan Fiction as Theatrical Performance," in *Fan Fiction and Fan Communities in the Age of the Internet:*

New Essays, ed. Karen Hellekson and Kristina Busse (Jefferson, NC: McFarland, 2006), 243.

48. Jurij Lotman, *The Structure of the Artistic Text*, trans. Gail Lenhoff and Ronald Vroon (Ann Arbor: University of Michigan Press, 1977), 288.

49. Patrick Lee, "Joss Whedon Gets Big, Bad and Grown Up with *Angel*," *Science Fiction Weekly* 128 (1999), archived at http://www.scifi.com/sfw/issue128/interview.html.

50. Rachael Thomas, "An Interview with Michael Emerson," *About.com*, http://tvdramas.about.com/od/lost/a/mikeemersonint.htm.

51. Kurt Lancaster, *Interacting with* Babylon 5: *Fan Performances in a Media Universe* (Austin: University of Texas Press, 2001), 20.

52. Jeff Jensen, "'Heroes' Creator Apologizes to Fans," *Entertainment Weekly*, November 7, 2007, archived at http://www.ew.com/ew/article/0,,20158840,00.html.

53. See Sharon Ross, *Beyond the Box: Television and the Internet* (Malden, MA: Blackwell, 2008), 248–49.

54. Ibid.

55. Tasha Robinson, "Interview: Joss Whedon," *The Onion AV Club*, September 5, 2001, archived at http://www.avclub.com/content/node/24238.

56. Barthes, "From Work to Text," 163.

57. Robinson, "Interview: Joss Whedon."

58. Quoted in Kerry Segrave, *Foreign Films in America* (Jefferson, NC: McFarland, 2004), 179.

CHAPTER 4

1. Jenny, "The Strategy of Form," 44.

2. Iampolski, *Memory of Tiresias*, 246.

3. Volosinov, *Marxism and the Philosophy of Language*, 68.

4. Bennett, *Formalism and Marxism*, 59.

5. Nick Couldry, *Inside Culture: Re-Imagining the Method of Cultural Studies* (Thousand Oaks, CA: Sage, 2000), 69.

6. Bertha Chin and Jonathan Gray, "'One Ring to Rule Them All': Pre-Viewers and Pre-Texts of the *Lord of the Rings* Films," *Intensities* 2 (2001), archived at http://intensities.org/Issues/Intensities_Two.htm.

7. Espen J. Aarseth, "Nonlinearity and Literary Theory," in *Hyper/Text/Theory*, ed. George Landow (Baltimore: Johns Hopkins University Press, 1994), 59.

8. Bennett and Woollacott, *Bond and Beyond*, 38.

9. Ibid., 56.

10. Barker and Brooks, *Knowing Audiences*, 60; see also Will Brooker's pre-release examination of *Attack of the Clones* in *Using the Force*, epilogue.

11. Due to the relaxed nature of discussion board and online spelling and grammar, I have chosen not to litter comments with "[*sic*]" but rather flag here that many postings contain such errors.

12. Barker and Brooks, *Knowing Audiences*.

13. J. R. R. Tolkien, *The Two Towers* (London: Unwin, 1985), 403.

14. John Fiske, "Moments of Television: Neither the Text Nor the Audience," in *Remote Control: Television, Audiences, and Cultural Power*, ed. Ellen Seiter et al. (London: Routledge, 1989), 66.

15. Tony Bennett, "Holy Shifting Signifiers: Foreword," in *The Many Lives of the Batman: Critical Approaches to a Superhero and His Media*, ed. Roberta E. Pearson and William Uricchio (London: British Film Institute, 1991), ix.

16. Indeed, one must drop to the fifteenth place on the all-time worldwide box office list (as of early 2009) before reaching a film—*Finding Nemo* (2003)—that is neither a sequel, an adaptation, or a retelling of a known story (if we count *Titanic* as the latter).

17. Barker et al., *The Crash Controversy*; see chapter 1 above.

18. Kristeva, *Desire in Language*, 65.

19. See Will Brooker, *Batman Unmasked: Analyzing a Cultural Icon* (New York: Continuum, 2001); Pearson and Uricchio, eds., *The Many Lives of the Batman*.

20. This notion of a "return" could rightfully be criticized, since Batman has only rarely been dark and sinister in his comic book life. But the *myth* of the Dark Knight's authenticity continues, as evident in the title of Miller's graphic novel—*Batman: The Return of the Dark Knight*—and as marshaled once more during promotions for *Batman Begins*.

21. P. David Marshall, *Celebrity and Power: Fame in Contemporary Culture* (Minneapolis: University of Minnesota Press, 1997).

22. See also Gray, *Watching with The Simpsons*, chap. 3.

23. Henry Jenkins, *Fans, Bloggers, and Gamers: Media Consumers in a Digital Age* (New York: New York University Press, 2006), 118.

24. Pierre Lévy, *Collective Intelligence: Mankind's Emerging World in Cyberspace*, trans. Robert Bononno (New York: Perseus, 2000).

25. Jenkins, *Fans, Bloggers, and Gamers*, 139.

26. Virginia Nightingale, *Studying Audiences: The Shock of the Real* (New York: Routledge, 1996), 107.

27. Harold Bloom, *The Anxiety of Influence: A Theory of Poetry* (London: Oxford University Press, 1973).

28. See particularly Riffaterre, "Compulsory Reader Response," and "Interpretation and Undecidabilty."

CHAPTER 5

1. See in particular Karen Hellekson and Kristina Busse, eds., *Fan Fiction and Fan Communities in the Age of the Internet: New Essays* (Jefferson, NC: McFarland, 2006); and Henry Jenkins, *Textual Poachers: Television Fans and Participating Culture* (New York: Routledge, 1992).

2. Jenkins, *Textual Poachers*, 27, 33.

3. Hills, *Fan Cultures*, 35.

4. Karen Hellekson and Kristina Busse, "Introduction: Work in Progress," in *Fan Fiction and Fan Communities*, 7.

5. Louisa Ellen Stein, "'This Dratted Thing': Fannish Storytelling through New Media," in ibid., 248.

6. See Michel de Certeau, *The Practice of Everyday Life*, trans. Steven F. Rendall (Berkeley: University of California Press, 1984).

7. Constance Penley, *NASA/TREK: Popular Science and Sex in America* (London: Verso, 1997), 3.

8. Jenkins, *Textual Poachers*, 156.

9. H. J. Jackson, *Marginalia: Readers Writing in Books* (New Haven, CT: Yale University Press, 2001), 87.

10. For full survey, see Jonathan Gray and Jason Mittell, "Speculation on Spoilers: Lost Fandom, Narrative Consumption, and Rethinking Textuality," *Particip@tions: Journal of Audience and Reception Studies* 4.1, archived at http://www.participations.org/Volume%204/Issue%201/4_01_graymittell.htm.

11. Jenkins, *Convergence Culture*, 25.

12. Martin Barker, *From Antz to Titanic: Reinventing Film Analysis* (London: Pluto, 2000); Barker and Brooks, *Knowing Audiences*.

13. Laura Carroll, "Cruel Spoiler, the Embosom'd Foe," *The Valve: A Literary Organ* 9 October (2005), archived at http://www.thevalve.org/go/valve/article/cruel_spoiler_that_embosomd_foe.

14. Kompare, *Rerun Nation*.

15. Klinger, *Beyond the Multiplex*.

16. Jason Mittell, "Narrative Complexity in Contemporary American Television," *The Velvet Light Trap* 58 (2006): 29–40.

17. See Ross, *Beyond the Box*, 173.

18. See Brooker, "Television out of Time."

19. For an overview of vids, and for some historical context, see Francesca Coppa, "Women, Star Trek, and the Early Development of Fannish Vidding," *Transformative Works and Culture* 1 (2008), archived at http://journal.transformativeworks.org/index.php/twc/article/view/44/64.

20. Kristina Busse, "Vidding Intro Via Imeem," *Ephemeral Traces*, June 28, 2007, archived at http://kbusse.wordpress.com/2007/06/28/vidding-intro-via-imeem/.

21. See http://obsessive24.livejournal.com/203863.html.

22. Coppa, "Writing Bodies," 236.

23. Ibid., 242.

24. See, for instance, *Mr. Skin, Mr. Skin's Skintastic Video Guide: The 501 Greatest Movies for Sex and Nudity on DVD* (Chicago: SK, 2007); Steve Stewart, ed., *Full Frontal: Male Nudity Video Guide* (Laguna Beach, CA: Companion, 1998).

25. See Geoffrey Baym, "Stephen Colbert's Parody of the Postmodern," in *Satire TV: Politics and Comedy in the Post-Network Era,* ed. Jonathan Gray, Jeffrey P. Jones, and Ethan Thompson (New York: New York University Press, 2009).

26. See Jeff Jensen, "Spoiler Nation: Secrets about Movie/TV Secrets Revealed!" *Entertainment Weekly* (2007), archived at http://www.ew.com/ew/article/0,,20203864,00.html.

27. See "Rowling Rails against Spoilers," BBC News, July 19, 2007, archived at http://news.bbc.co.uk/2/hi/entertainment/6905873.stm.

28. See Rebecca Tushnet, "Copyright Law, Fan Practices, and the Rights of the Author," in *Fandom: Communities and Identities in a Mediated World,* ed. Jonathan Gray, Cornel Sandvoss, and C. Lee Harrington (New York: New York University Press, 2007), 60–71.

29. See Jenkins, *Convergence Culture.*

30. See John Borland, "'Star Wars' and the Fracas over Fan Films," *CNet News,* May 2, 2005, archived at http://news.cnet.com/Star-Wars-and-the-fracas-over-fan-films/2008–1008_3-5690595.html. On *Star Wars* fan film more generally, see Brooker, *Using the Force.*

31. Jenkins, *Convergence Culture,* 138.

32. Lotz, *Television Will Be Revolutionized,* 109.

33. Klinger, *Beyond the Multiplex,* 35.

34. Jonathan Gray, "The Reviews Are In: TV Critics and the (Pre)Creation of Meaning," in *Flow TV: Essays on a Convergent Medium,* ed. Michael Kackman et al. (New York: Routledge, 2009).

35. Matthew Gilbert, "Hard-Hitting 'Lights' Gives 110 Percent," *Boston Globe,* October 3, 2006, archived at http://www.boston.com/ae/tv/articles/2006/10/03/hard_hitting_lights_gives_110_percent/.

36. Tim Goodman, "'Friday Night Lights' Defies Expectations and Has Something to Offer All Comers," *San Francisco Chronicle,* October 2, 2006, archived at http://www.sfgate.com/cgi-bin/article.cgi?f=/c/a/2006/10/02/DDGPOLFJMH1.DTL&type=tvradio.

37. Rob Owen, "'Friday Night Lights' Isn't Just about the Gridiron," *Pittsburgh Post-Gazette* October 1, 2006, archived at http://www.post-gazette.com/pg/06274/726170-237.stm.

38. Diane Werts, "Where High School Football Is Life," *Newsday,* October 3, 2006, archived at http://www.newsday.com/entertainment/tv/ny-ette-l49150300ct03,0,3498786.story?coll=ny-television-headlines.

39. Tom Shales, "'Friday Night' Kicks Off with a Great Formation," *Washington Post,* October 3, 2006, archived at http://www.washingtonpost.com/wp-dyn/content/article/2006/10/02/AR2006100201439.html.

40. Doug Elfman, "NBC's Shining 'Lights,'" *Chicago Sun-Times,* October 3, 2006, archived at http://www.suntimes.com/entertainment/elfman/80613,CST-FTR-elf03.article.

41. Gilbert, "Hard-Hitting 'Lights' Gives 110 Percent."

42. Werts, "Where High School Football Is Life."

43. Hal Boedeker, "Show Scores with Brawn and Brains," *Orlando Sentinel,* October 1, 2006, archived at http://www.orlandosentinel.com/entertainment/tv/orl-lights06oct01,0,4196845.story?coll=orl-caltvtop.

44. Melanie McFarland, "On TV: It Doesn't Get Much Better than 'Friday Night Lights' and 'Nine,'" *Seattle Post-Intelligence,* October 3, 2006, archived at http://seattlepi.nwsource.com/tv/287262_tv03.html.

45. Alessandra Stanley, "On the Field and Off, Losing Isn't an Option," *New York Times,* October 3, 2006, archived at http://www.nytimes.com/2006/10/03/arts/television/03heff.html?ex=1160798400&en=de71fb8a98f52f97&ei=5070.

46. Troy Patterson, "Touchdown TV," *Slate,* October 10, 2006, archived at http://www.slate.com/id/2151266/.

47. Elfman, "NBC's Shining 'Lights.'"

48. Gilbert, "Hard-Hitting'Lights' Gives 110 Percent"; Brian Lowry, "Friday Night Lights," October 1, 2006, archived at http://www.variety.com/review/VE1117 931742?categoryId=32&cs=1.

49. Johnson, *Heartland TV,* 5.

50. Alan Sepinwall, "Bright 'Lights' Has Game," *New Jersey Star-Ledger,* October 3, 2006, archived at http://www.nj.com/columns/ledger/sepinwall/index.ssf?/base/columns-0/115985153292400.xml&coll=1.

51. Mittell, *Genre and Television,* chap. 6.

CHAPTER 6

1. John Fiske, *Understanding Popular Culture* (London: Unwin Hyman, 1989), 124.

2. Stephen Sansweet, *Star Wars: From Concept to Screen to Collectible* (San Francisco: Chronicle, 1992), 14.

3. See Avi Dan Santo, "Transmedia Brand Licensing Prior to Conglomeration: George Trendle and the Lone Ranger and Green Hornet Brands, 1933–1966" (Ph.D. dissertation, University of Texas at Austin, 2006), archived at http://catalog.lib.utexas.edu/search?/asanto%2C+avi/asanto+avi/1%2C2%2C2%2CB/frameset&FF=asanto+avi+dan+1974&1%2C1%2C/indexsort=-.

4. Sansweet, *Star Wars,* 71.

5. Stephen Kline, "Limits to the Imagination: Marketing and Children's Culture," in *Cultural Politics in Contemporary America,* ed. Ian Angus and Sut Jhally

(New York: Routledge, 1989), 299–316; Thomas Englehardt, "The Strawberry Shortcake Strategy," in *Watching Television*, ed. Todd Gitlin (New York: Pantheon, 1986), 68–110.

6. Ellen Seiter, *Sold Separately: Children and Parents in Consumer Culture* (New Brunswick, NJ: Rutgers University Press, 1993), 168.

7. Ibid., 191, 190; see also Erik Erikson, *Childhood and Society* (New York: Norton, 1950).

8. Dan Fleming, *Powerplay: Toys as Popular Culture* (Manchester: Manchester University Press, 1996), 11.

9. Ibid., 15.

10. Ibid., 96, 102.

11. Ibid., 99.

12. Bob Rehak, comment at *The Extratextuals*, http://www.extratextual.tv/2008/05/john-williams-is-my-religion/.

13. Hills, *Fan Cultures*, 137.

14. Fleming, *Powerplay*, 107.

15. Sansweet, *Star Wars*, 87.

16. Hills, *Fan Cultures*.

17. Brooker, *Using the Force*, xii.

18. A later toy moved to shut down some of these meanings by giving Hammerhead a gender and a name, Momaw Nadon, and by labeling him as a gardener. Nevertheless, by this point, undoubtedly many toy owners had invented their own canon regarding Hammerhead.

19. See, for instance, Camille Bacon-Smith, *Enterprising Women: Television Fandom and the Creation of Popular Myth* (Philadelphia: University of Pennsylvania Press, 1992); Jenkins, *Textual Poachers*; Penley, *NASA/TREK*; Brooker, *Using the Force*.

20. Brooker, *Using the Force*.

21. See John Tulloch and Manuel Alvarado, *Doctor Who: The Unfolding Text?* (New York: St. Martin's Press, 1983); Hills, *Fan Cultures*.

22. See Bacon-Smith, *Enterprising Women*; Jenkins, *Textual Poachers*; Penley, *NASA/TREK*.

23. Hills, *Fan Cultures*.

24. Cornel Sandvoss, *Fans: The Mirror of Consumption* (New York: Polity, 2005), 90.

25. Brooker, *Using the Force*, 223.

26. Hills, *Fan Cultures*, 22.

27. Sansweet, *Star Wars*, 57.

28. As Will Brooker points out, this is not to say that the films do not also have a vibrant female fan community; this community, however, remains largely subcultural and out of the public eye. See *Using the Force*, 223.

29. See Barker and Brooks, *Knowing Audiences*.

30. Simon Egenfeldt-Nielson, Jonas Heide Smith, and Susana Pajares Tosca, *Understanding Computer Games: The Essential Introduction* (New York: Routledge, 2008), 13.

31. Ibid., 161.

32. Garry Crawford and Jason Rutter, "Playing the Game: Performance in Digital Gaming Audiences," in *Fandom: Communities and Identities in a Mediated World*, ed. Jonathan Gray, Cornel Sandvoss, and C. Lee Harrington (New York: New York University Press, 2007), 272.

33. Thompson, *The Frodo Franchise*, 228.

34. Tanya Krzywinska, "Hands-On Horror," in *ScreenPlay: Cinema/Videogames/Interfaces*, ed. Geoff King and Tanya Krzywinska (New York: Wallflower, 2002), 216

35. Ibid.

36. Ibid.

37. Ibid.

38. Geoff King and Tanya Krzywinska, "Introduction," in ibid., 14.

39. Wee Liang Tong and Marcus Cheng Chye Tan, "Vision and Virtuality: The Construction of Narrative Space in Film and Computer Games," in ibid., 108.

40. Ibid., 109; see also Stephen Heath, "Narrative Space," *Screen* 17.3 (1976): 68–112.

41. Linda Hutcheon, *A Theory of Adaptation* (New York: Routledge, 2006), xiii.

42. Ibid., 22.

43. Ibid., 4.

44. See Jenkins, *Convergence Culture*, 161–66.

45. For more on MMORPGs, see the special issue on *World of Warcraft* (2004–) edited by Tanya Krzywinska and Henry Lowood for *Games and Culture* 1 (2006).

46. Jenkins, *Convergence Culture*, 104, 98, 121.

47. Thompson, *The Frodo Franchise*, 252.

48. Jenkins, *Convergence Culture*, 104.

49. Lancaster, *Interacting with* Babylon 5; Richard Schechner, *Performance Theory* (New York: Routledge, 1988).

50. Lancaster, *Interacting with* Babylon 5, 43; Daniel Mackay, *The Fantasy Role-Playing Game: A New Performing Art* (Jefferson, NC: McFarland, 2001).

51. See Mia Consalvo, *Cheating: Gaining Advantage in Videogames* (Cambridge, MA: MIT Press, 2007).

52. See Stein, "'This Dratted Thing'"; Robert Jones, "From Shooting Monsters to Shooting Movies: Machinima and the Transformative Play of Video Game Fan Culture," in *Fan Fiction and Fan Communities in the Age of the Internet: New Essays*, ed. Karen Hellekson and Kristina Busse (Jefferson, NC: McFarland, 2006), 261–80; Leo Berkeley, "Situating Machinima in the New Mediascape," *Australian Journal of Emerging Technologies and Society* 4.2 (2006): 65–80.

53. The original *Sims*, in particular, allowed one to upload a photo that the computer would use to create a look-a-like character, greatly facilitating film- or television-based machinima.

54. Jones, "From Shooting Monsters to Shooting Movies," 277.

55. See Stein, "'This Dratted Thing.'"

56. Ibid., 254.

57. Jenkins, *Convergence Culture*, 123–28.

58. See http://www.whathappenedinpiedmont.com.

59. Stuart Hall, "On Postmodernism and Articulation," *Journal of Communication Inquiry* 10.2 (1986): 52.

60. Will Brooker, "Everywhere and Nowhere: Vancouver, Fan Pilgrimage and the Urban Imaginary," *International Journal of Cultural Studies* 10.4 (2007): 423–44.

CONCLUSION

1. Henrik Örnebring, "Alternate Reality Gaming and Convergence Culture: The Case of *Alias*," *International Journal of Cultural Studies* 10.4 (2007): 449, 450.

2. Thompson, *The Frodo Franchise*.

3. See Jonathan Gray, *Television Entertainment* (New York: Routledge, 2008), chap. 3.

4. For more on Marvel and transmediated storytelling, see Derek Johnson, "Will the Real Wolverine Please Stand Up? Marvel's Mutation from Monthlies to Movies," in *Film and Comic Books*, ed. Ian Gordon, Mark Jancovich, and Matthew P. McAllister (Oxford: University of Mississippi Press, 2007), 64–85; Derek Johnson, "A Knight of the Realm vs. The Master of Magnetism: Sexuality, Stardom, and Character Branding," *Popular Communication: The International Journal of Media and Culture* 6.4 (November 2008).

5. See http://www.icetruck.tv.

6. Thompson, *The Frodo Franchise*, 235.

7. Ibid., 251.

8. Ibid., 208–9, 213.

9. Ivan Askwith with Henry Jenkins, Joshua Green, and Tim Crosby, "Deconstructing 'The Lost Experience': In-Depth Analysis of an ARG," A Convergence Culture Consortium White Paper (2007).

10. Thompson, *Frodo Franchise*; Henry Jenkins, *Confessions of an Aca-Fan: The Official Weblog of Henry Jenkins*, http://www.henryjenkins.org; Santo, "Transmedia Brand Licensing."

11. Kevin Jackson, *Invisible Forms: A Guide to Literary Curiosities* (New York: Thomas Dunne, 1999), xvi–xvii.

Index

About the Author

JONATHAN GRAY is Associate Professor of Media and Cultural Studies at University of Wisconsin, Madison. He is author of *Television Entertainment* and *Watching with The Simpsons: Television, Parody, and Intertextuality*, and co-editor of *Battleground: The Media* and *Fandom: Identities and Communities in a Mediated World* and *Satire TV: Politics and Comedy in the Post-Network Era*, both available from NYU Press.